Jurisculture
Volume 3

CHINA

Gray L. Dorsey

Transaction Publishers
New Brunswick (U.S.A.) London (U.K.)

Library of Congress Catalog Number: 88-4752
ISBN: 1-56000-090-2
Printed in the United States of America

Library of Congress Cataloging-in-Publication Data
(Revised for volume 3)
  Dorsey, Gray L.
  Jurisculture
    Includes bibliographical references and indexes.
  Contents: v. 1. Greece and Rome — v. 2. India — v. 3. China.
  1. Sociological jurisprudence.   2. Law—History.   3. Social change.
I. Title.
K370.D67   1989   340'.115   88-4752
  ISBN 0-88738-237-1 (v. 1)
  ISBN 1-56000-090-2 (v. 3)

For
Sarah Elizabeth and *Daniel Gray*

Contents

Preface

It is the human condition that we live in the world as we understand it to be, not as it is in fact. We sort the raw data of sensed experience into categories of meaning. We establish a spectrum of regard for things in accordance with categories of value. We formulate intentions in accordance with categories of purpose. Human beings are not able to survive and flourish by individual efforts. We have to cooperate. In order to cooperate we must share meanings, values, purposes. This common consciousness provides an understanding of ourselves, the world, and what is most worth having. Cooperation involves the organization and regulation of society, understood as sets of auxiliary and complementary activities that are performed by some but benefit all.

The assignment of sets of persons to perform the auxiliary and complementary activities is the organization of society. Inducing the performance of assigned activities and preventing the performance of obstructive or destructive activities is the regulation of society. Human agency in the organization of society may be masked by a common belief that the social order was the work of a god, immemorial custom, or nature. The persons who will then be deemed best able to make important decisions for the common good will be those with access to the god, knowledge of immemorial custom, or knowledge of nature. Therefore, social and political authority will be distributed in accordance with assumed competence to know.

From within a successful society the view of human nature, the world, the good, and the way of knowing of that society's common consciousness appears to be *the* truth about these matters. There is the risk, therefore, that in attempting to understand another people, society, or civilization, we will distort by "reading in" something familiar, instead of seeing what is really there. Jurisculture seeks to avoid this error by focusing attention upon the shared meanings, values, purposes, and modes of cooperation of the other people, society, or civilization. Whether it is successful can now be judged by comparing the first three volumes of this series, *Jurisculture: Greece and Rome*, *Jurisculture: India*, and *Jurisculture: China*. A correct understanding of another society helps us to know our own, by showing us what we are not.

The newest and most widely used system of romanizing Chinese words is called Pinyin. That system is used, for the most part, in the text. However, names very well known in the Wade-Giles form have not been put into Pinyin. Also, names of persons known to me in Taiwan and referred to in the Acknowledgments are given in Wade-Giles, which is still in use there.

Acknowledgments

For whatever understanding of the Chinese I have acquired I owe a debt of gratitude to many persons over a long period of time. At Yale Law School, in the late 1940s, F. S. C. Northrop taught me to understand a people in terms of their own fundamental beliefs. Then I discovered the best account in any Western language of Chinese fundamental beliefs— Marcel Granet's *La Pensée Chinoise*. In reliance upon Northrop and Granet, I undertook a visiting professorship at Taiwan National University, in 1952–53, under the aegis of the Committee for Free Asia, which soon became the Asia Foundation. The professorship was, nominally, in constitutional law. Under the circumstances, I understood it to be an opportunity to contribute to a reconsideration of the intellectual foundations of an effective and authentic modern Chinese society.

In 1952 the Communists were in complete control of the mainland and were reorganizing Chinese society there in accordance with Mao Zedong's view of communism. With the fall of the mainland in 1949, Chiang Kai-shek, leader of the Nationalist party, founded by Sun Yatsen, had come to Taiwan with the remnants of an army and all the officials and scholars who could not stomach communism and were able to get out. In addition, many intellectuals had come over to Taiwan shortly after it was returned to China in 1945, in order to revive Chinese education. The intellectual community in Taiwan, thus comprised, was traumatized and divided. Some wanted to rely more completely on Western science; some wanted to return to Confucianism.

For two millennia prior to 1919, Confucianism had been the unquestioned intellectual foundation of Chinese society. But China had been reeling from the shock of Western incursions since it lost the Opium War to Great Britain in 1842. In the nineteenth century it tried unsuccessfully to remedy its weakness by acquiring Western instruments of force, such as gunboats. At the turn of the century, it turned to institutional reforms, first within the empire and then, in 1912, discarding the empire for the Western political institution, a republic. The country quickly fell under the control of regional warlords and was even more vulnerable to foreign penetration. In 1919, a group of scholars at Beijing University, the center of China's intellectual life, started the May Fourth Movement, which rejected Confucianism and called for reorganization of Chinese society on the basis of modern science.

However, members of the May Fourth Movement were divided on whether to adopt the science of the Western democracies or the science of the revolutionary new regime in the Soviet Union. Philosophy professor Hu Shih and others, under the influence of visiting professors John Dewey and Bertrand Russell, advocated empiricism and pragmatic social science. Chen Duxiu, dean of the college of literature, and Li Dazhao, university librarian, preferred dialectical materialism. A student assistant in the library, Mao Zedong, went along with Chen and Li. Mao, and others, provided the intellectual foundation for a Communist modern Chinese society. The empiricism and pragmatism of the non-Communist Chinese scholars did not lend itself to the sort of utopian ideology that might inspire, guide, and provide the basis for internal discipline of a revolutionary cadre party. Although Chiang Kai-shek, in the civil war, had relied primarily upon the Nationalist party, which had adopted democratic centralism during the period of Soviet tutelage in the early 1920s, and upon the graduates of Whampoa Military Academy, of which he was the first Commandant, he was still Confucian enough to blame the non-Communist Chinese intellectuals for not winning the students (always a key group in China) to his cause. Chiang Monlin told me that Chiang Kai-shek blamed him, as the Chancellor of Beijing University, for the fall of the mainland.

It was, in short, an apt moment in history for a reconsideration of the intellectual foundations of Chinese society. Taiwan was a perfect place to pause and take thought about future directions. Under Japanese occupation from 1895 to 1945 Chinese society in Taiwan had remained as it was fifty years earlier. However, there was psychological resistance to such a reconsideration. Having found peaceful repose, it was not easy for those intellectuals who had come from the mainland to reconsider events that were too often tragic. It is, therefore, a source of wonder to me that my family and I were received with such uniform kindness and easy friendship in that academic year of 1952–53 in Taiwan. I was a brash, young professor with an embryonic theory of social analysis (jurisculture), great empathy and admiration for Chinese culture, but too little real knowledge to fully realize the presumptuousness of attempting to initiate, with my students, a reconsideration of the intellectual foundations of Chinese society.

This volume, which does not attempt a reconsideration of Chinese society in the modern world, but does attempt to understand, in some depth, Chinese society as it was before the upheavals of this century, is an apology and an expression of gratitude to all those people who received us so kindly and treated us so much like family in Taiwan in 1952–53. First and foremost there was Herbert H. P. Ma, who made my work possible and our family's stay in Taiwan memorable. He is now Grand Justice Ma. Wang Shih-hsien and Chang Fo-chuan were frequent companions and good friends. Lexington E. C. and Josephine Hung were more like cousins than neighbors. President Chien Shih-liang, Dean Sah Mong-wu, and Chairman Li Hsiang-lin, my superiors at Taiwan National University, were always supportive. Chiang Monlin and his wife, Lucy, and Hu Shih, were always cordial. Han Li-wu, Ma Shou-hua, and Ran Inting taught us to appreciate Chinese painting and calligraphy. Fang Thomé shared his knowledge of Chinese philosophy. Perhaps the meaning of life in a Chinese intellectual community was most intense on occasions of a chat with neighbor Li Chi during an after-dinner walk through the neighborhood. Tung Tso-pin, on the occasion of the Moon Festival in the fall of 1952, presented us with a scroll on which he had written a poem in the calligraphy of the oracle bones discovered at Anyang, which he and Li Chi were then studying. Neighbor Sheng Cheng had on his shelves rolls of unmounted paintings by his former Beijing neighbor Chi Pei-tze (the most famous modern Chinese painter). He would spread them out on the tatami floor mats to show them and remained completely calm as his children hopscotched around them. Many other neighbors and university colleagues were unfailingly kind.

With respect to the present volume, I am indebted to a number of persons: for library service, Margaret McDermott and Milla Chatman; for research assistance, Constance R. Brown, Lisa Haag, and Debbie Pfeifer; for checking the accuracy of my discussion of plant domestication, Clifford M. Hardin; for reading parts or all of the manuscript, noting errors, lack of clarity, and other shortcomings, and providing encouragement, K. C. Chang, Nelson I. Wu, Frances H. Foster, and my research assistants; for word processor and secretarial services, Portia Hall, Joyce Rucinsky, and Mary Ellen Powers.

PART I

The Ancient Period
(From Earliest Times to the
Birth of Confucius)

1

The Setting

The Aryan-speaking people who developed the culture of ancient Greece migrated from the north into a 25,000 square-mile peninsula. They conquered and expelled the earlier inhabitants, and took over land that was already in cultivation, reorganizing their cooperative activities to get the benefits of fixed agriculture after a seminomadic existence.[1] The Aryan-speaking people who developed the culture of traditional India migrated from the northwest into a subcontinent of 1.6 million square miles and, as in Greece, took over land that was already in cultivation. They did not completely displace the earlier inhabitants, but integrated them into subordinate positions in a society organized and controlled by the conquerors. Gradually they moved east through the basins of the Indus and Ganges rivers and then south into the triangular plateau of South India.[2]

The people who developed the culture of China did not identify themselves by migration from some other place. They had lived in the area since at least 5,000 B.C.E. (before the common era).[3] They were from a single mongoloid branch, physically indistinguishable from modern Chinese,[4] and they were isolated from the centers of early Western and early Indian civilizations by great distances and formidable geographic and climatic barriers. They identified themselves by developing a distinctive civilization. Passage of goods and persons between China and the Mediterranean world across 5,000 miles of deserts, high plains, windswept steppes, and the massive mountain chains of central Asia was not established on a regular basis until about 100 B.C.E.[5] Regular passage by sea from South China to India and thence to the Mediterranean was established somewhat later.[6]

China is bounded on the West by the Pamir mountains, which run north from the Himalayas and the Hindu Kush. From this central Asian massif four great mountain chains run eastward. From south to north, these are

3

the Himalayas, the Kunlun, the Tianshan, and the Altai. South of the Himalayas is the Indian subcontinent. North of the Altai are the arctic wastes of Siberia. Between the Himalayas and the Kunlun is Tibet, with some of the highest mountains in the world and plains of 10,000 feet and higher. Between the Kunlun and the Tianshan is the highland Tarim basin, which consists mostly of the Takla Makan desert. Between the Tianshan and the Altai is Dzungaria, which until the Christian era was the homeland of a fierce nomad confederacy that periodically threatened the emerging Chinese civilization. Greater China includes the area from the Himalayas to the Altai and extends eastward to the Sea of Japan, the Yellow Sea, and the East China Sea, bending south beyond the east end of the Himalayas to the South China Sea and the northern borders of Vietnam, Laos, and Burma.[7]

Two great rivers carry water from the snows of Tibet all the way across China to the eastern seas. The Yellow River runs northeast out of Tibet through Gansu and then makes a great loop north around the Ordos Plateau. Its southern return, during much of which it forms the border between Shanxi and Shaanxi provinces, is blocked by the Qinling mountains, which are the dividing line between north and south China. Augmented by tributaries, the Yellow River then turns eastward and soon issues out of the highlands into the huge north China plain. The plain was built up over the centuries by alluvial deposits of the yellowish loess silt that gives the river its name. The silt was deposited throughout the plain because of the absence of rock formations that would provide a natural channel for the river. As the bed of the river silted up dikes had to be built to contain it. When the silting continued the dikes were raised until they reached as high as forty feet and the river was running twenty feet above the surrounding plain. Any breach in the earthen dikes resulted in the flooding of thousands of square miles, after which the river often settled into a new channel. Historically it has wandered back and forth from north to south of the Shandong promontory.[8]

The Yangzi (Yangtze) River begins in north central Tibet and runs south for several hundred miles. In southeastern Tibet and southwestern China, steep mountain ridges and precipitous valleys run north and south. Parallel to each other and only a few miles apart, in this area, the Salween, Mekong, and Yangzi rivers carry the snowmelt out of Tibet. The Salween continues south through Yunnan province (China) and Burma and reaches the sea to the west of the Malay peninsula. The Mekong wanders southeast, running through Yunnan province and northern Laos, marking the border between Thailand and Laos for about five hundred miles, and continuing down through Vietnam to the South China Sea. The Yangzi's southern progress is blocked about a hundred miles into Yunnan province. It turns back north for seventy miles, then south again for two hundred miles, where it finds an outlet to the northeast. From this point it traverses the highland basin of Sichuan province, before turning east for a thousand-mile journey to the East China Sea at Shanghai. For the most part it runs through mountain gorges and other rock formations that provide a permanent channel and keep it narrow and deep. Large steamers can ascend more than six hundred miles and smaller vessels another thousand miles. Rains of up to sixty inches a year in a catchment basin twice the size of that of the Yellow River augment the flow out of Tibet and may raise the level of the Yangzi forty or fifty feet in flood, despite an extensive system of lakes that serve as storage basins. Along the Yangzi, dike building has not been as prodigious a task and flood damage has not been as frequent or as massive as along the Yellow River.[9]

From Yunnan province a chain of mountains runs southwest to northeast forming, through part of its length, the southern flank of the Sichuan plateau. South of this chain is the West River (Xi) system, which drains into the South China Sea at Guangzhou (Canton). The most southerly arable land is in this watershed. Another chain of mountains begins to the east of the West River watershed and runs northeast almost to Shanghai. The eastern slopes of these mountains drain through a series of coastal valleys into the East and South China seas. These valleys provide the arable land to be found in southeastern China.[10]

The distinctive Chinese civilization was based on agriculture, development of which is, necessarily, responsive to topography, climate, soil, and natural vegetation. North China and South China are distinctly different with respect to these factors. Climate is decisively affected by differential heating of the dry, high heartland of Asia and of the oceans to the east and south of China. During the winter, central Asia is dominated by cold air masses that cause high-pressure systems, while the warm waters of the oceans create low-pressure systems. In summer, the land of central Asia is hot. Therefore, cold, dry winds flow east and south in the winter and warm, moist winds blow north and west in summer. This monsoon system is damped by the Qinling mountains. The result is that north China has a dry, cold, and long winter, and a short, hot summer with light rainfall, and south China has mild, short winters, and up to nine months of warm, moist climate. Natural vegetation, in Neolithic times, was heavy forests in the southeast, shading into mixed forest/grasslands, and finally to arid deserts in the northwest.[11]

For a people wanting to end its dependence upon grassland nomadism, north China offered life opportunities in its fertile soil, and made life precarious by the harshness of its climate and the undependability of its water. The loess soil was loose and easy to work with primitive tools and it was fertile because the light rainfall did not leach out the minerals. Plants grown in the short, hot summer season had to sustain life through the long, severe winter. The staple foods domesticated in north China were dry-field crops: two kinds of millet, wheat, barley, and soybeans. The latter provided an extremely valuable combination of protein and oil, and fixed nitrogen in the soil, thus making crop rotation advantageous. The important trees were those that produced products that could be stored for consumption during the long intervals between harvests. These included the chestnut and the hazelnut, and trees whose fruit remained nutritious when dried, such as jujube (Chinese date), peach, apricot, and persimmon. The important vegetables domesticated in north China were Chinese cabbage, radishes, onions, scallions, turnips, chive, mallow, and melon. Some plants were grown for condiments and some for dyes. Hemp was grown for rough textiles, rope, and food. Fiber for smooth textiles was produced by cultivating mulberry trees and tending silkworms. Domestication of the lacquer tree provided a varnish of the highest quality. Domesticated animals were pigs and poultry for food, and oxen, donkeys, and horses for work and transport. Rivers that silted up, shifted their channels, and (for those not carrying snowmelt out of Tibet) dried up periodically, could not be depended upon for travel and transport, both of which were, accordingly, slow and laborious. Still, constantly renewed deposits of fertile soil over broad areas offered recurring opportunities for agriculture after floods and famine.[12]

South China's topography is mostly mountain ridges and narrow valleys. In neolithic times these were covered by dense forests, which provided security and sustenance for food gatherers but little opportunity for the initiation of dry-field agriculture. However, the middle and lower reaches of the Yangzi valley and the lower delta basin are covered by a continuous series of large and small lakes connected by rivers and interspersed with flood plains, forming a temperate zone freshwater environmental system unique in the world. In this area, wetland agriculture was developed. The heavy rainfall, up to sixty inches a year, tended to leach the soil, but minerals were restored by the practice of fertilizing with night soil. As lower slopes were cleared of trees a mixed agriculture of wet fields and dry fields was developed. The forest soil was not as rich as the alluvial loess of north China, but with ample rain, and a long growing season, two and even three crops a year could be grown. Rice was the staple cereal. Other wetland crops cultivated for food were the lotus, grown for both seed and root, arrowhead, water chestnut, water spinach, water dropwort, and cattail. As the slopes above wetlands were cleared, dry-field tubers, such as Chinese yams, and legumes, including mung and other beans, were grown. Farther up the slopes, tea was cultivated. The use of tea leaves for beverage originated in south China. Trees cultivated in south China were those that produced fruit for immediate consumption, such as the loquat, kumquat, tangerine, and orange. Rush, ramie, and kudzu were grown for fiber. Bamboo was cultivated for its stalks and its sprouts. Gourds were used as vegetable and for containers. The work animal was the water buffalo. Travel and transport were mostly by water. Drought was not a problem and floods were not as frequent or as devastating as in North China.[13]

Notes

1. Gray L. Dorsey, *Jurisculture: Greece and Rome* (New Brunswick, N.J.: Transaction Publishers, 1989), pp. 7–8.
2. Gray L. Dorsey, *Jurisculture: India* (New Brunswick, N.J.: Transaction Publishers, 1990), p. 1.
3. John K. Fairbank, Edwin O. Reischauer, and Albert M. Craig, *East Asia: Tradition and Transformation* (Boston, Mass.: Houghton Mifflin, 1973), pp. 17–32; W. W. Howells, "Origins of the Chinese People: Interpretation of the Recent Evidence," in David N. Keightley, ed., *The Origins of Chinese Civilization* (Berkley, Calif.: University of California Press, 1983), p. 315.
4. Howells, "Origins of the Chinese People," pp. 315–16.
5. Melville Bell Grosvenor, *National Geographic Atlas of the World* (Washington, D.C.: National Geographic Society, 1963), pp. 108–9; Geoffrey Barraclough, ed., *The Times Atlas of World History* (London: Times Books Limited, 1978), pp. 70–71.
6. Barraclough, *Times Atlas*, pp. 70–71.
7. Ibid., pp. 94–95, 230, 108–9, 232–33; Grosvenor, *National Geographic Atlas*, pp. 120–21.
8. Rand McNally, *The New International Atlas* (Chicago: Rand McNally, 1980), pp. 98–99, 102–3; Charles O. Hucker, *China's Imperial Past* (Stanford, Calif.: Stanford University Press, 1975), pp. 3–5; Fairbank, Reischauer, and Craig, *East Asia*, pp. 9–10.

9. Grosvenor, *National Geographic Atlas*, pp. 117, 120-21; Rand McNally, *New International Atlas*, pp. 102-3, 110-11; Fairbank, Reischauer, and Craig, *East Asia*, pp. 9-10.
10. Rand McNally, *New International Atlas*, pp. 100-3.
11. Hui-lin Li, "The Domestication of Plants in China: Ecogeographical Considerations," in Keightley, *Origins of Chinese Civilization*, pp. 22-23.
12. Ibid., pp. 29-37; Barraclough, *Times Atlas*, pp. 62-63; Hucker, *China's Imperial Past*, pp. 3-5; Fairbank, Reischauer, and Craig, *East Asia*, pp. 11-12.
13. Li, "Domestication," pp. 38-51.

2

The Ideas

Chinese civilization was developed to exploit the opportunities of agriculture under the ecological conditions summarized in the previous chapter. Tradition dates the beginning of this process about 2700 B.C.E., under the reign of the Yellow Emperor. The earliest known contemporary written records, however, begin at least a thousand years later. Furthermore, the fundamental ideas and thought processes that shaped Chinese civilization in its ancient period were masked by the ascription of significant contributions to ancient heroes and sages. The Three Sovereigns, Five Emperors, and Three Sages were credited with domesticating plants and animals; organizing the family; inventing writing, ceramics, the calendar, the plough, the rake, wooden houses, silk cloth, boats, carts, and the bow and arrow; establishing government; bringing peace and tranquillity; organizing flood control; and bringing less advanced peoples into Chinese civilization.[1]

Throughout most of Chinese history these ancient heroes and sages were regarded as historical personages. But in the early part of this century, under the influence of Western empiricism, the mythical nature of Chinese culture heroes was recognized. At the same time, doubt was cast upon the authenticity of all books and records prior to the first millennium B.C.E. All texts concerning ancient China, except for the *Yi Jing* (or *Book of Changes*), were ordered destroyed by Qin Shihuangdi, who unified all of China in 221 B.C.E. The Qin dynasty lasted only until 206 B.C.E. Under the succeeding Han dynasty the accounts of ancient China in what were called the "later records" were recovered from hiding or recreated from memory. Furthermore, these "later records" were, for the most part, not contemporary but had been written down from about 600 B.C.E. and hence were subject to the suspicion that they were colored by the influence of one or another of the great philosophers of the period. In fact, the most important of these works are called the Confucian classics. However, contemporary textual data uncovered by archeological work in this century, particularly the study of the inscriptions on bones and shells used for divination, have sufficiently confirmed the traditional texts so that it is now generally believed that the Confucian classics and related texts contain much reliable information about ancient China.[2]

The Confucian classics include the *Yi Jing* (or *Book of Changes*), the *Book of Poetry*, the *Book of History*, the *Spring and Autumn Annals* and its commentaries (*Zhuan*, especially the *Zuo Zhuan*), and the *Three Books of Rituals* (*Yi Li*, *Li Ji*, and *Zhou Li*). These books were studied by Confucius and the other philosophers of the golden age of Chinese thought (550–221 B.C.E.), which coincided with the seminal ages of Western and Indian civilization. By relying on the Confucian classics and books that have relied upon them, such as the second century B.C.E. *Historical Records* of Sima Qian and his father,[3] it is possible to discern some of the fundamental ideas and thought processes of the ancient Chinese.

Historical ancient China is the period of the Three Dynasties—Xia (2200–1750), Shang, sometimes called Yin (1750–1100), and Zhou (1100–256). The dates are, of course, before the common era, and, except for the end of the Zhou dynasty, are not firmly established.[4] A great many of the ox shoulder blades and tortoise plastrons used for pyromantic divination during the Shang dynasty have been found and studied. These indicate that, like the Greeks[5] and the Indo-Aryans,[6] the Chinese, in Shang times, attributed the animation and order of the observed world to a supernatural, omnipotent source. This deity, called Di, which is usually translated as Lord on High, was believed to control all events, and therefore could grant or withhold bountiful harvests and victory in battle. The Shang kings used the popular belief in Di to legitimate their rule and psychologically strengthen their political power. It was asserted that the king's ancestors were able to intercede with Di, and that the king could communicate with his ancestors through divination and influence them through prayer and sacrifice.[7]

The Chinese, however, never developed an anthropomorphic monotheism, or a priesthood, or a corporate (or congregational) church. Aside from the Lord on High, religion in China, at least until the advent of Buddhism and religious Daoism (Taoism), consisted of worshiping ancestors and the forces of nature.[8] Perhaps the early development in China of reliance upon the natural, rather than the supernatural, owed something to the fact that the Chinese were still engaged in plant domestication at the time they were developing the concepts and modes of thought of Chinese civilization. Fossil evidence and references in divination inscriptions indicate that the period of domestication extended from around 5,000 B.C.E. for millets to around 1,000 B.C.E. for soybeans, much later than plant domestication in the Near East and in India.[9] The activities involved in plant domestication would focus attention upon natural processes. These activities include: identifying wild plants with food potential; selecting a site with the right sun, soil, and water; selecting seeds from wild plants that have the most desirable characteristics; determining the time to plant; preparing the ground, planting, and covering the seeds; culling seedlings that do not exhibit the desired characteristics; protecting the growing plants from rats, birds, and other predators; harvesting; selecting the best plants for next season's seed; storing seed under conditions that will keep it in good condition.[10]

Of course, it is impossible to know why certain ideas were prevalent at a given time or place, or among a certain people. However, if the attempt is made to put one's self into the situation of those persons who lived in north China in the third and second millennia before the common era, it is possible to see the relevance to plant domestication of some of the central ideas of Chinese civilization, which were first recorded in the Confucian classics and were subjected to systematic consideration in the golden age of Chinese philosophy. Indeed, the experience leads one to think that distinctively Chinese conceptions of continuity, contingency, prescriptive name, space/time continuum, the "way" (dao), change, life force (yin/yang), harmony, and unity received their first, inchoate form in the endeavor to understand and successfully conduct plant domestication.

Continuity

Plant breeding, whether primitive or sophisticated, depends upon characteristics in the cultigen appearing in subsequent generations. If this did not occur to a significant extent the enterprise would be in vain. Last century we learned the Mendelian laws of genetics. Lately, we have learned that genetic information chemically encoded in genes linearly linked in chromosomes account for the characteristics of a plant, such as height of stem or rate of growth, and that this information is transmitted through sex cells to succeeding generations. But continuity from cultigen to ultimate cultivar was plain before genetics and molecular biology explicated it, and must have been assumed by those of every early civilization who undertook domestication of wild plants.

Contingency

Plant breeding, however, would not be necessary, or possible, if there were perfect and complete continuity between plant generations. Breeding in desirable characteristics is, necessarily, breeding out undesirable characteristics, such as weak stalks, small seeds, or disease susceptibility. We now know that each plant cell contains two genes (alleles) for each characteristic, and that one is dominant and the other recessive. If, for stem height, the dominant allele is tall and the recessive allele is short, a plant that has one tall gene and one short gene will be tall, as will, of course, a plant with two tall genes. Only a plant with two short genes will be short. (Not all gene-pairs work on this either/or principle, but most do.) The sex cells of plants, however, receive only one from each pair of genes, so that the ova of a tall plant may contain the short gene, and if it is pollinated by a male cell that also contains the short gene, the resulting seed from a tall plant will produce a short plant. Further, the two linear chains of genes in a chromosome can break and rejoin in a different order, and segments of genes can break free of both chains and each rejoin the other chain. Also, genetic changes can occur for reasons as yet unknown (mutations). Therefore, modern science not only confirms observed continuity it also confirms observed contingency, and it reconciles the two by showing that invariant continuity is in the genes and contingency is in the organism.

Prescriptive Name; Space/Time Continuum

Plant domestication requires careful attention to location and sequence. Where was the cultigen of this plant found to flourish—in full sun, full shade, or mixed sun and shade? in a well-drained field or a flooded field? on a slope or a flat terrace? open to the wind or sheltered? When did the earth thaw and loosen, so that seeds could germinate? When did weeds or a superabundance of seedlings begin to choke off growth? When did the plants mature? When did they drop their seeds? The purpose of such observations, obviously, is not just to determine facts about the cultigen, but to guide development of the cultivar, the variation of the original wild plant that has the most desirable characteristics and the fewest undesirable ones. The result, therefore, is not descriptive (indicating where and when events of plant life occurred), but prescriptive (indicating where and when events should occur if that plant is to realize its highest potential). This suggests an idea of name as an indication of what an entity should become, instead of a designation of an entity as presently, or previously observed. Similarly, space and time can be seen as prescriptive. Prescriptive locations and prescriptive sequences of plant events (and human events with respect to plants, and indeed all human events) can be seen as constituting a space/time continuum, which is nothing but the sites where and the occasions when events should occur.[11]

The "Way" (Dao)

If name indicates what an entity should become, and space/time are the sites where and the occasions when events should occur that will result in the entity becoming what its name indicates, then the agenda of events necessary to that end is the "way" (dao) of that entity. Each time the entity follows its dao its name is "rectified." Each time it fails to follow its dao it falls short of being what its name signifies. An individual millet plant with small, bitter seeds resulting from fertilization by cells from an inferior strain is something less than the cultivar whose name is millet. The actuality (*shi*) is not in accordance with the name (*ming*). The theory of correspondence of names and actualities became an important doctrine of many Chinese philosophies.[12]

Every individual plant, animal, reptile, insect, fish, bird, and human being has its dao. A mountain has its dao, as does a valley, a lake, a river, the sun, the moon, the planets, wind, rain, thunder, lightning, spring, summer, autumn, and winter. These myriad daos were, inevitably, interrelated. In north China when the sun had moved far enough north to heat the lands of Central Asia, the winds shifted from the west to the east, bringing in warm, moist air from the oceans. "The east wind dispels the cold, the hibernating insects and reptiles begin to stir, the fish rise up under the ice where the otter catches them to eat, and the wild geese fly north in season."[13] Thunder streams out of the earth arousing creativity after winter stillness and signaling the receptivity of the earth to tillage. Farmers go into the fields with their digging sticks to plant the new crops, and germination and sprouting begin. The mulberry trees put out new leaves that women pick and feed to the silkworms.[14]

Change

An organic entity cannot be adequately understood in terms of fixed attributes of form and substance because these change in each stage of its life cycle from the concentration and quiescence of the seed to the full foliation and fruition of the mature plant and back to seed. The ancient Chinese, accordingly, paid close attention to recurrent changes. They observed the characteristics of form and substance of each plant in each transformation. This gave them foreknowledge of what would occur if continuity held and enabled them to spot in its incipiency any regressive characteristic that contingency might allow. Knowledge of its recurrent changes, however, was not sufficient to understand an organic entity. The name of an entity indicated the characteristics of form and substance it *should* have. An individual plant that had some, but not all, of the characteristics of *shu* (millet) was something less than the entity indicated by the name, but it was not a completely different entity, such as *mai* (wheat), or *mi* (rice).[15] Further, it was assumed that actual characteristics (*shi*) could change, or be changed, so that they accorded with the name (*ming*). These progressive changes, which were crucial to plant domestication, required an understanding of influences other than the (continuous or contingent) internal transmission of hereditary information from generation to generation.

A millet seed carried information from the cultigen telling it when to sprout and what kind of characteristics to have. But it could not germinate and sprout until the earth thawed and loosened, and this could not occur in north China until the sun had moved north, the wind had shifted around to the east, water had come down from clouds or from mountains through rivers and irrigation ditches, and the earth had enough nutrients (perhaps fixed by last year's soybean crop) to nourish plant life. This is an empirical paradigm of the associative thinking of China, in which causal influences arose from several interacting sources and flowed through interconnected channels. Needham has suggested the analogy of the endocrine system in the human body in which hormones secreted in several different glands interact to stimulate or inhibit growth or sexual functions.[16] The cause of change is not to be understood as direct, singular impulsion such as one billiard ball hitting another, but rather, in Needham's words:

> Things behaved in particular ways not necessarily because of prior actions or impulsions of other things, but because their position in the ever-moving cyclical universe was such that they were endowed with intrinsic natures which made that behavior inevitable for them. If they did not behave in those particular ways they would lose their relational positions in the whole (which made them what they were), and turn into something other than themselves. They were thus parts in existential dependence upon the whole world-organism. And they reacted upon one another not so much by mechanical impulsion or causation as by a kind of mysterious resonance.[17]

The *Book of Changes* accumulated the wisdom and the superstition regarding changes, recurrent and progressive. For more than three thousand years the people of China have turned to it for every purpose from forecasting future events and seeking good fortune to reaching for the mysteries of the universe. It probably began as a collection of linear signs used in divination, an unbroken line ___ indicating "yes," and a broken line __ __ indicating "no."[18] At some very early, but unknown, date broken and unbroken lines were vertically juxtaposed in eight sets of three, as follows:

Qian	Kun	Zhen	Kan	Gen	Sun	Li	Dui

These were said to represent the principles of change, namely, the Creative *Qian*, the Receptive *Kun*, the Arousing *Zhen*, the Abysmal *Kan*, Keeping Still *Gen*, the Gentle *Sun*, the Clinging *Li*, and the Joyous *Dui*.[19]

The principles of change were associated with images, attributes, family relationships, orients, and seasons. According to the tradition attributed to Fuxi, a legendary figure, the Creative is associated with heaven, strong, father, south, and summer. The Receptive is associated with earth, devotion/yielding, mother, north, and winter. The Arousing is associated with thunder, inciting movement, first son, northeast, and early spring. The Abysmal is associated with running water, danger, second son, west, and autumn. Keeping Still is associated with mountain, resting, third son, northwest, and late autumn. The Gentle is associated with wind, penetration, first daughter, southwest, and late summer. The Clinging is associated with fire, light-giving, second daughter, east, and spring. The Joyous is associated with lake, joy, third daughter, southeast, and late spring.[20] At a very early date sixty-four sets of two vertically juxtaposed trigrams were formed and these sixty-four hexagrams were supposed to represent all the processes of nature. As one of the lines of a hexagram moved to a different position a new hexagram was created, and this represented the way the organic entities of the universe interpenetrated each other, stimulating each to be fully itself through the resonance of association—as a tone sounded on a horn causes the spontaneous vibration of a stringed instrument.[21]

The Life Force (Yin/Yang)

Every thing, every organic entity, had its dao, its set of recurrent and progressive changes that would bring it to full realization of its nature, as indicated by its prescriptive name. And every organic entity was subject to resonant stimulation from other entities whose changes were closely associated through juxtaposition in time or space. But something within each entity responded to the resonance. A life force quickened the seed in response to the spring flow of water and the nutrients in the soil, and pushed the sprout up through the ground where it could begin to draw strength from the warm sun. But at some point growth, foliation, and fruition ended and, as we would say, the plant began to die. Consistent with the idea of recurrent change, however, the Chinese did not conceive of this event as death, but as a different direction of the life force—toward fulfillment, withdrawal, concentration, as life is stored in the seed ready for regeneration of the plant in the next season. Instead of a life force and a death force the Chinese developed the idea of a duality of forces that were not in opposition to each other, but performed different functions, succeeding each other as appropriate to the situation in space/time and the dao of the particular entity.[22] The regulator of the alternating dominance of the two aspects of the life force was also dao.

The idea of a dual life force had many, many applications. One of the earliest, and most significant, was to the broken and unbroken lines of the trigrams and hexagrams. Broken lines were said to be yielding, unbroken ones firm. Yielding and firm were associated, respectively, with dark and light, and night and day. Later yin and yang were adopted. The trigram of three unbroken lines, Creativity, and the hexagram composed of two of these trigrams, were associated with heaven, superiority, movement. In the *Book of Changes* every hexagram is followed by a "judgment," which is a short explanation of the hexagram. These judgments were attributed to King Wen, founding sage of the Zhou dynasty. King Wen's son, the Duke of Zhou, who extended the Zhou realm, is credited with adding explanations of each line of the hexagrams, called "appended judgments." Later scholars, including Confucius, added further commentaries, which are referred to as the "Ten Wings." Images and attributes are also indicated in the *Book of Changes*.[23]

The complementary duality of yin/yang can be seen in the passages of the *Book of Changes* on the hexagrams *Qian*, composed of six unbroken lines, and *Kun*, composed of six broken lines. The attribute of *Qian*, the Creative, is said to be strength. The judgment is:

> The Creative works sublime success,
> Furthering through perseverance.

Commentaries include:

> Great indeed is the sublimity of the Creative, to which all beings owe their beginning and which permeates all heaven.
> The clouds pass and the rain does its work, and all individual beings flow into their forms.
> The way of the Creative works through change and transformation, so that each thing receives its true nature and destiny and comes into permanent accord with the Great Harmony: this is what furthers and perseveres.

The attribute of *Kun*, the Receptive, is said to be yielding. The judgment is:

> The Receptive brings about sublime success,
> Furthering through the perseverance of a mare.
> If the superior man undertakes something and tries to lead
> [at this time or circumstance],
> He goes astray;
> But if he follows, he finds guidance.

Commentaries on the judgment include:

> Perfect indeed is the sublimity of the Receptive.
> All beings owe their birth to it, because it receives the heav-
> enly with devotion. [The Receptive takes the seed of the
> heavenly into itself and gives to beings their bodily form.]
> The Receptive in its riches carries all things.
> Its nature is in harmony with the boundless.
> A mare belongs to the creatures of the earth [whereas the
> dragon, associated with the Creative, flies through the heav-
> ens]; she roams the earth without bound. Yielding, devoted,
> furthering through perseverance: thus the superior man has
> a direction for his way of life.
> The good fortune of rest and perseverance depends upon
> our being in accord with the boundless nature of the earth.[24]

Underlying the duality of the two primal forces was a unity of the energy of life. Broken and unbroken lines displaced each other in the hexagrams. "[T]he firm is transformed, melts as it were, and becomes yielding; the yielding changes, coalesces, as it were, and becomes firm."[25] In this way the hexagrams change one into another, and each responds to a particular concatenation of heredity, time, place, and circumstance in the life of an individual entity and also indicates whether a yin or yang expression of its life force will enable the entity to do or be what it should at that moment, in order to follow its dao.

Harmony and Unity

There is nothing in the above conceptions to suggest bringing order out of chaos, or struggling to overcome and subdue the forces of nature. All of these conceptions are attuned to unity and harmony.[26] All organic entities are subsystems within the world organism, and when every entity follows its dao the harmony of health, vigor, and exuberance reverberates throughout the whole universe. The harmony that is prefigured in this formative period of Chinese thought, and which permeated that thought in all systematic developments and permutations, is not a harmony of mathematical and geometric proportion, such as Plato gave to Western thought,[27] nor a harmony of release from all sensed experience into unity with universal, undifferentiated spirit, as in the orthodox philosophies of India.[28] It is a harmony that is immanent in the life experience of every human being and every other organic entity: everything joyfully partic-ipates in the universal flow of life. As a modern author puts it:

For several thousands of years, we Chinese have been thinking . . . in terms of comprehensive harmony which permeates anything and everything. It sounds like an eternal symphony swaying and swinging all the sky, all the earth, all the air, all the water, merging all forms of existence in one supreme bliss of unity.[29]

Notes

1. Charles O. Hucker, *China's Imperial Past* (Stanford, Calif.: Stanford University Press, 1975), pp. 3-5; K. C. Chang, *Art, Myth, and Ritual: The Path to Political Authority in Ancient China* (Cambridge, Mass.: Harvard University Press, 1983), pp. 1-2; K. C. Wu, *The Chinese Heritage* (New York: Crown Publishers, 1982), pp. 21-101.

2. Chang, *Art, Myth, and Ritual*, pp. 1-5. See also Cho-yun Hsu, *Ancient China in Transition* (Stanford, Calif.: Stanford University Press, 1965), appendix, "Authenticity and Dating of Pre-Ch'in [Qin] Texts," pp. 183-92.

3. Hucker, *China's Imperial Past*, pp. 223-26.

4. Chang, *Art, Myth, and Ritual*, pp. 1-2.

5. Gray L. Dorsey, *Jurisculture: Greece and Rome* (New Brunswick, N.J.: Transaction Publishers, 1989), pp. 7-12.

6. Gray L. Dorsey, *Jurisculture: India* (New Brunswick, N.J.: Transaction Publishers, 1990), pp. 1-3.

7. David N. Keightley, "The Religious Commitment: Shang Theology and the Genesis of Chinese Political Culture," in *History of Religions*, vol. 17, (February-May 1978), pp. 211, 212-13.

8. Marcel Granet stated this position summarily in *Fêtes et Chanson Anciennes de la Chine* (Paris: Éditions Ernest Leroux, 1919), pp. 1-2, and expounded it fully in *The Religion of the Chinese People*, trans., Maurice Freedman (Oxford: Basil Blackwell, 1975), pp. 37-119.

9. Te-Tzu Chang, "The Origins and Early Cultures of the Cereal Grains and Food Legumes," in David N. Keightley, ed., *The Origins of Chinese Civilization* (Berkeley, Calif.: University of California Press, 1983), pp. 66-67, 80-81; K. C. Chang, *Early Chinese Civilization: Anthropological Perspectives* (Cambridge, Mass.: Harvard University Press, 1976), pp. 1-16.

10. Wayne H. Fogg, "Swidden Cultivation of Foxtail Millet by Taiwan Aborigines: A Cultural Analogue of the Domestication of *Setaria italica* in China," in Keightley, *Origins of Chinese Civilization*, pp. 95-115.

11. Marcel Granet, *La Pensée Chinoise* (Paris: Éditions Albin Michel, 1950), pp. 86-114.

12. Wing-tsit Chan, *A Source Book in Chinese Philosophy* (Princeton, N.J.: Princeton University Press, 1963), p. 257.

13. Wm. Theodore de Bary, Wing-tsit Chan, and Burton Watson, *Sources of Chinese Tradition*, vol. 1 (New York: Columbia University Press, 1960), p. 208. The quotation is from a *Qin* dynasty (221-206 B.C.E.) work.

14. Hellmut Wilhelm, ed., Richard Wilhelm and Cary F. Baynes, trans., *The I Ching, or Book of Changes*, 3rd. ed. (Princeton, N.J.: Princeton University Press, 1967), p. 270; Marcel Granet, Kathleen E. Innes, trans., *Chinese Civilization* (New York: Meridian Books, 1958), pp. 139-51.

15. Te-Tzu Chang, "The Origins and Early Cultures of the Cereal Grains and Food Legumes," pp. 65, 73.

16. Joseph Needham, *Science and Civilisation in China*, vol. 2 (Cambridge: Cambridge University Press, 1956) p. 289.
17. Ibid., p. 281.
18. Wilhelm and Baynes, *The I Ching*, p. xlix.
19. Ibid., pp. l-li.
20. Ibid., pp. l-li, 266; Wu, *The Chinese Heritage*, p. 26.
21. Needham, *Science and Civilisation in China*, vol. 2, pp. 304-5; Wilhelm and Baynes, *The I Ching*, p. 263.
22. Wilhelm and Baynes, *The I Ching*, pp. 281-82; Needham, *Science and Civilisation in China*, vol. 2, p. 277.
23. Needham, *Science and Civilisation in China*, vol. 2, pp. 304-07; Chang, *Art, Myth, and Ritual*, p. 2; Wilhelm and Baynes, *The I Ching*, p. liii; Hucker, *China's Imperial Past*, pp. 31-32.
24. Wilhelm and Baynes, *The I Ching*, pp. 369-88.
25. Ibid., pp. 283-84.
26. Needham, *Science and Civilisation in China*, vol. 2, p. 277.
27. Dorsey, *Greece and Rome*, pp. 33-51.
28. Dorsey, *India*, pp. 37-52.
29. Thomé H. Fang, *The Chinese View of Life* (Hong Kong: The Union Press, 1957), p. 18.

3

The Need for a Common Consciousness

In Chinese thought, human nature was never opposed to the rest of nature; it was always a part of it. Like all organic entities, human beings participated in a natural world of continuity, contingency, prescriptive name, space/time continuum, dao, change, yin/yang life force, harmony, and unity. But, of course, this was nature as understood by human beings, not nature as it was in fact. For instance, millet, which was so important that the legendary ancestor of the Zhou dynasty was given the name "Lord Millet,"[1] was the product of human intervention in natural processes. The pattern of the natural process of evolution is to produce a proliferation of species with varying characteristics, which then survive and multiply or die out depending upon the success of each in exploiting the life opportunities of various habitats and environments.[2] The cultivar, millet, began as a human idea, came to be desired, and was pursued by purposeful actions of selection and cultivation.

Building an agricultural civilization required more than developing techniques of beneficial intervention in natural processes of plant evolution. It also required organization of society. The same piece of ground could not be worked to two different purposes at the same time; dwellings had to be built and maintained; roads had to be laid out; clothing had to be made; the young had to be produced and reared; all had to be protected from wild animals, ruthless neighbors, and foreign invaders; dikes, dams, canals, and irrigation ditches had to be built and maintained. All of these activities, by many individuals, had to be organized and regulated.

Society builds on evolution. Evolution is the story of increasingly complex organization of organisms—from one-cell organisms floating in a warm, protein-rich saline solution and able to take nourishment by chemical processes and reproduce by mitosis, which appeared several thousand million years ago, to human beings with incredible complexity of organization and great plasticity of behavior, who appeared a very few million years ago. Increased complexity of organization enables organisms to exploit more effectively the life opportunities of various habitats and environments of the earth. Society extends organization to the relations between organisms. Sets of individuals perform activities that are auxiliary and complementary. Each of the activities is performed by some of the members but benefits all members, thus increasing the effectiveness of the social group above the result attainable by independent efforts.

Nonhuman societies (insect and animal) are organized and regulated by natural processes. Among the social insects, sets of individuals are specialized to activities by morphology (development of structures) and by stimulation or inhibition of behavior. Instances of structural specialization are the immense ovaries of queen honey bees, the poison-equipped squirt-gun heads of soldier termites, and the trail-marking pheromone glands of worker ants. Worker honey bees are behaviorally specialized to different tasks at successive stages of life. For the first three days they loiter, groom themselves, and are fed; from the third to the twelfth day they nurse immature bees in the hive; from the twelfth to the eighteenth day they produce wax for the comb; from the nineteenth to the twenty-first day they guard the entrance of the hive, and then they spend the rest of their lives gathering water, pollen, and nectar.

There are no human beings structurally or behaviorally specialized to specific foods, habitats, or activities; none provided with fangs and claws to serve an appetite for meat; none with a ruminant's set of stomachs for grazing quickly in dangerous places and digesting slowly in safe places; none with lungs, mouth, and stomach suitable for living on plankton strained from sea water as do the baleen whales; none with winged, miniaturized bodies for catching insects in flight; none equipped with pouches to carry food to other members of the social unit; none compelled by stimuli beyond their control to sweep the village street during the twenty-first through the twenty-fifth years of their lives. Evolution gave human beings a greatly enlarged brain and generalized structure.

The human condition is a mixed blessing. Generalized structure enables human beings to perform a great variety of activities, thus making possible great complexity of social organization and increasing the power of human societies to exploit the life opportunities of the earth. But without specialized weapons or means of escape, human beings *must* form societies; they cannot survive by individual efforts. And, not being naturally directed to sets of auxiliary and complementary activities, they must direct themselves by cultural means, using their superior brains. Human beings participate in nature consciously. They have to learn about various environments and successful responses to each, and how to accumulate such information and transmit it to others, including succeeding generations; they have to choose life opportunities and decide what sets of activities will be needed to attain them; then they have to see to it that sets of individuals perform each of the needed activities and do not perform destructive or obstructive activities.

However, cultural processes do not operate with the necessity of natural processes. Plant cells, and social insects, can perform only limited, specific activities. They do what they are structured and stimulated to do; they cannot do what they are not structured and stimulated to do. What is beneficial and what is harmful is never in dispute; it is naturally determined. The beneficial is done; the harmful is not done. Organizing society by cultural processes is fraught with difficulties because every potential member has the necessary equipment—a brain— and human brains are not set automatically to the same wave length. Therefore, human beings can disagree about the world and themselves, they can desire different things and when they desire the same things they can disagree about effective means to attain them; they can refuse to do what others think they should, and do things others think they should not. In short, human beings can disagree about every aspect of knowing, desiring, and acting. That they are ever able to overcome this recipe for misunderstanding, conflict, and chaos and form a society is owing to the fact that they build a common consciousness.

A common consciousness is composed of beliefs. The product of an individual consciousness is an idea. Ideas can be doubted, argued with. When an idea has seeped into the consciousness of many persons so pervasively that, for them, it has become reality itself, which must be reckoned with, like it or not, it has become a belief.[3] A human society is able to achieve, by a common consciousness, some of the reliability and effectiveness that natural systems achieve by necessity because members learn to understand in accordance with shared meanings, desire in accordance with shared values, intend in accordance with shared purposes, and guide and limit actions in accordance with shared principles and rules.

Notes

1. Te-Tzu Chang, "The Origins and Early Cultures of the Cereal Grains and Food
   Legumes," in David N. Keightley, ed., *The Origins of Chinese Civilization* (Berke-
   ley, Calif.: University of California Press, 1983), p. 70; K. C. Chang, *Art, Myth, and
   Ritual: The Path to Political Authority in Ancient China* (Cambridge, Mass.:
   Harvard University Press, 1983), p. 12.
2. See Julian Huxley, *Evolution, The Modern Synthesis* (New York and London:
   Harper & Brothers, 1943), and Jacques Monod, *Chance and Necessity*, trans. A.
   Wainhouse (New York: Knopf, 1971).
3. José Ortega y Gasset, *Concord and Liberty*, trans. Helen Weyl (New York: W. W.
   Norton, 1946), pp. 17–21.

4

The Complementary Roles of Myth and Science

Organizing a society was an integral part of developing Chinese civilization. The ideas of continuity, contingency, prescriptive name, space/time continuum, dao, change, yin/yang life force, harmony, and unity became unquestionable truths for those who, by believing, began the process of creating a Chinese people, consciousness, society, civilization. However, truth plays a subtly different role with respect to human social systems than it does with respect to biological, or physical, systems. A biological, or physical, system—or a nonhuman social system—is created by natural processes, and has an existence independent of human thought and action. Discovering the truth about such a system enables human beings to anticipate events and, perhaps, to use the system to human benefit. Newtonian physics makes space explorations possible, but human beings had nothing to do with the creation of the planetary system. Discovering the secrets of bee society facilitated production of honey, but bee society was created by morphological and behavioral specialization. A human social system is *created by human beings* in accordance with a set of ideas about the world and themselves that they *believe* to be true.

Beliefs unify thought into a common consciousness and action into cooperation. An appeal to the truth of the beliefs reinforces the common consciousness, dissolves doubts, removes inhibitions, stimulates and channels aspirations and energy, inspires hope, provides the basis for development of character and conscience, and justifies discipline and punishment—all of which encourages performance of duties, compliance with required restraints, and peaceful resolution of conflicts of interest. All of these psychological building blocks of a human society flow from *belief* that a set of ideas is true, not from the objective truth of

25

the ideas. A human social system does not have an independent existence, which is discovered by human thought; it is the product of human thought and action. It is created on the basis of a set of *assumed* truths, and is what it is regardless of whether the assumptions could be shown to be objectively true, or false. In the last century of the Roman republic, Greek philosophical ideas that the world is rationally ordered, human beings have reason and can know that order, and ought to live accordingly, became beliefs.[1] At about the same time, the Hindu ideas that all things and creatures are but temporary differentiations of universal spirit, which is pure existence, consciousness, and bliss, and human beings ought to withdraw form the world of time and order into eternal union with spirit, became beliefs.[2] These two sets of assumed truths had profound effects upon the organization of society in Western and Indian civilizations, respectively. Yet neither could be shown to be objectively true, or false.

The Chinese set of assumed truths, like the Western and Indian, could not be shown to be objectively true or false, but this only enhanced its psychological power to unify thought and action. The unquestionable truth is more reassuring than the proven truth. Faith is stronger than rational conviction. Myth does not try to convince. It invites faith and offers "the peace that passes all understanding." Therefore, the search for objective facts about ancient China is somewhat beside the mark. Accurate empirical facts tell us who did what and when, but for the *why* we need to get inside the emerging consciousness so that we can understand the evolving Chinese society. This is why Marcel Granet, a sociological analyst of myths, produced what Needham calls the best book in any Western language on the world outlook of the ancient Chinese, namely, *La Pensée Chinoise*.[3] That the history of ancient China remained mythological until the beginning of this century,[4] was a strength rather than a weakness.

On the other hand, Chinese society did not defeat its enemies, feed its members, control rivers, clear forests, cultivate mountains, build cities and the Great Wall, multiply its population, and increase the area of its control merely by the power of its myths. The effectiveness that made possible these accomplishments was due not only to myth-generated vigor and cohesion, but also to military, political, and agricultural organization, technology, planning, and strategy. These factors depend upon the cognitive, not the psychological, function of truth. They depend upon discovery of natural processes and beneficial use of, or intervention in, those processes. The Chinese had more and better food, more and healthier children, better shelter and clothing than neighboring grazing-culture peoples because of success in plant domestication and cultivation. By discovering bronze technology the Chinese acquired war chariots and better weapons. The Chinese learned how to embody meanings in written symbols, which was advantageous in accumulating, preserving, and transmitting knowledge accurately, and they had the only written language in east Asia for centuries.

From the discussion, above, of the steps involved in plant domestication and the organic concepts that were so appropriate for that process, it should be clear that even in the ancient period the Chinese were developing an impressive protoscience consisting of empirical observations, manual operations, experiments, and accurate records. This aspect of Chinese thought developed so successfully that China was far ahead of Europe in science and technology until the birth of modern Western science in the seventeenth century.[5] In his *Novum Organum*, published in 1620, Francis Bacon wrote of the (Chinese) discoveries of printing, gunpowder, and the magnet:

> [T]hese three have changed the whole face and state of things throughout the world, the first in literature, the second in warfare, and the third in navigation; whence have followed innumerable changes; insomuch that no empire, no sect, no star, seems to have exerted greater power and influence in human affairs than these mechanical discoveries.[6]

The differing roles of truth, the psychological and the cognitive, are the substrata of two fundamental tendencies in Chinese thought—toward myth, and toward science. With respect to myth and science, as with respect to many other aspects of Chinese thought, the seemingly contradictory should be understood as complementary.

Notes

1. Gray L. Dorsey, *Jurisculture: Greece and Rome* (New Brunswick, N.J.: Transaction Publishers, 1989), pp. 33–51.
2. Gray L. Dorsey, *Jurisculture: India* (New Brunswick, N.J.: Transaction Publishers, 1990), pp. 58–64.
3. Joseph Needham, *Science and Civilisation in China*, vol. 2 (Cambridge: Cambridge University Press, 1956), pp. 216–17.
4. See text, above, at chap. 2, note 2.
5. See the multivolume work of Needham, *Science and Civilisation in China*, which has reached sixteen volumes and is not yet completed.

6. Quoted in Needham, *Science and Civilisations in China*, vol. 2, p. 19. Bacon probably did not know that these were Chinese inventions.

5

Organizing Chinese Society

Western and Westernized scholars discuss the process of organizing
society in ancient China under headings that include the family, ancestor
worship, the countryside, villages, towns, states, government, and feudalism. However, to separate out sets of events and discuss them under
these headings is to approach the Chinese process from the perspective
of Western analytical consciousness. From the perspective of the beliefs
that were shaping the Chinese consciousness, organizing society was a
process of the human organic entity finding its role in the world organism.
An attempt is made, herein, to see formation of society in ancient China
from the Chinese perspective, with its blend of myth and observational-
experimental science.

Society as an Organic Entity

Other organic entities, such as plants, were identified by changing
characteristics of form and substance. Human beings, who participate
consciously in the world organism, were additionally identified by
changing characteristics of attitude and action. Chinese society comprised all those individuals who were engaged in the exploitation of
agricultural life opportunities in accordance with the emerging Chinese
consciousness. Prescriptive name was involved in this identification. To
fall short, in any respect, of what "Chinese" was coming to mean was to
be something less than human. Here is the root of that conceit, so
persistent in Chinese history, that only the Chinese were fully human; all
others, who had human form and substance but not human (Chinese)
consciousness and cooperation, were barbarians.

The human society, like other organic entities, had to move through
recurrent changes and progressive changes from cultigen to cultivar; but
this passage had to be accomplished by building common consciousness

and cooperative action. What we can discern of this process, in the earliest period, is to be found in the myths of the culture heroes, the Three Sovereigns, the Five Emperors, and the Three Sages. They were celebrated for making larger-than-life contributions to Chinese culture and society. According to one version, Fuxi, the first of the Three Sovereigns, whose reign supposedly began in 2852 B.C.E., domesticated animals, organized family life, and invented the eight trigrams. The second, Suiren, invented fire, and the third, Shennong, invented the plow and the hoe, introduced settled agriculture, and organized the first markets.[1] According to another version, Youchao, who taught the people how to build wooden houses, was the first of the Three Sovereigns.[2]

In the analogy to plant domestication, these are the cultigens of the Chinese people. However, it was not genetic information that was passed on, but cultural information. The culture heroes symbolize significant developments in learning about the various environments and making successful responses to each, accumulating such information and transmitting it to others, including succeeding generations, choosing life opportunities and deciding what sets of activities will be needed to attain them, organizing sets of individuals to perform each of the needed activities, and assuring the performance of needed activities and the nonperformance of obstructive or destructive activities.[3] Here is an account, from the third century B.C.E. of the contributions of Youchao and Suiren:

> In the ancient times there were fewer people and more animals. The people were victimized by beasts and reptiles. Then there came a sage who taught them how to build nests with wood in order to avoid harm; and the people were happy. So they made him their ruler and called him Youchao, "Have Nest."

> However, the people continued to eat fruits, berries, fish, clams, which were raw, fetid, malodorous, and causing so much injury to the digestive organs that they were ill most of the time. So there came another sage who taught them how to obtain fire by drilling wood and then cure the food of its stench and decay. And the people were happy and made him their ruler and called him Suiren, "Fire Maker."[4]

The way in which myths encapsulated experience gained by observation and experiment is shown in an account, of about the same time, of the contribution of Shennong:

> In ancient times the people ate and drank whatever and wherever they could, gathering fruits and berries from trees and plants and feeding on beasts and reptiles. And they were most of the time afflicted with disease, poison, and injuries. Then came

Shennong, who taught the people to plant and cultivate the five cereals, to observe the differences of soil, to take note of what grains are suited to what kind of land, dry or wet, rich or poor, high or low. He himself tasted hundreds of plants as well as spring waters, both sweet and bitter, so that the people might know what to avoid. Once in this experiment, in a single day, he took poison seventy times.[5]

The greatest of the culture heroes was the first of the Five Emperors, the Yellow Emperor. Legend associates with his name the invention of surnames, the calendar, silk cloth, boats, the bow and arrow, ceramics, writing, and the keeping of historical records.[6] The fact that there were many different groups of people trying to organize effective societies and competing to exploit the resources of north China and the Yangzi basin is acknowledged in the account of another accomplishment of the Yellow Emperor. According to the *Historical Records*, a work of Sima Qian in the second century B.C.E., the Yellow Emperor unified many of the groups by military force:

Wherever under heaven there were people who disobeyed him, he would go after them; but as soon as they were pacified, he would leave them. He crossed mountains and opened roads, never stopping anywhere to rest for long. On the east he went as far as the ocean and ascended the venerable Taishan. On the west he went as far as the Kongtong mountains and ascended the Rooster-Head Peak. On the south he went as far as the Yangtze [Yangzi] and ascended the Bear and Xiang ranges. On the north he chased away the Hunzhou barbarians and convoked a meeting of the lords and princes at Mount Fu.[7]

Writing and Reality

It is easy to see that inventions attributed to the Three Sovereigns would give a social group great advantages over competing groups. Domestication of plants and animals, wooden houses, fire, the plow and hoe, settled agriculture, and markets would provide safe shelter, more and better food, less disease, and the increased efficiency of trading surplus goods. With the Five Emperors, however, there seems to have been a marked increase in the pace of social organization. The bow and arrow, attributed to the Yellow Emperor, would give a great advantage in battle, because the Chinese compound bow of wood, bone, and horn, was very powerful.[8] Writing, also attributed to the first of the Five Emperors, would enable the nascent Chinese social group to accumulate and preserve information more effectively, and to communicate at a distance more precisely and dependably, greatly facilitating the supervision of increasing numbers of persons engaged in complex activities. The written language that evolved reflected, as was to be expected, a basic characteristic of the emerging Chinese consciousness, and had a profound influence upon Chinese culture and civilization.

Human consciousness is first aware of the world of sensed experience. If this is assumed to be the real world, it is very difficult to understand how and why things happen, and to use this understanding to human advantage, because it is necessary to accumulate information in terms of a very great number of specific and concrete events that are related to each other only by whether they occurred at the same time and the same place. The ancient Greeks avoided the problem by ascribing the causes of events to the gods, thus reducing the human task to consulting or propitiating the gods. Later, the Greek natural philosophers said that the real is not particular, concrete, and known by the senses, but general, abstract, and known by pure reason.[9] Very early, the Indians also looked to gods who controlled events. Later, they said that the real is not sensed experience, but undifferentiated spirit, union with which can be won by withdrawing from experience into being.[10]

The Chinese, as late as the Shang dynasty (1750–1100 B.C.E.), worshiped the Lord on High, who was believed to control events.[11] But when they gave up this belief in the supernatural they did not seek to withdraw into being, and they did not seek to understand the natural world in terms of general concepts related by pure logic, which gave rise to (or were abstracted from) the myriad phenomena of the sensed world. They stayed with the particular, concrete, and empirical and looked for relations of association, instead of deduction.[12] The written language developed by the Chinese was admirably suited to knowing and understanding such a world.

The *Book of Changes* says that people used knotted cords to record events and keep accounts until an associate of the Yellow Emperor invented written records.[13] It is generally accepted that the knotted cord device used by the ancient Chinese was the quipu, which is used to the present day in Peru,[14] and which consists of a cord to which strings are attached at intervals. Knots are then tied in the strings to record facts about crops, livestock, land, and human events. The Spanish were amazed at how the Inca state used the quipu to control trade, without losing "count of a single hen or load of firewood."[15] A string could carry all information about one subject matter, such as sheep, goats, wheat, millet, or the cultivation of a piece of land. Knots could indicate quantities by size or multiples, and time by the length of intervals between knots. Location in space might be indicated by the spacing of subject-matter strings on the cord, or possibly by interconnecting the cords and strings of more than one quipu, thus forming a net, which would be well suited to represent visually and tactilely the relation of events in time and space, and would prefigure the organic view of the universe, with its reticular pattern of causation.[16]

The Chinese written language substitutes monosyllabic words for quipu knots, each referring directly to a particular, concrete aspect of the sensed world, or to an idea arising from the juxtaposition in time or space of two or more such phenomena. Many Chinese words are stylized pictures of the empirical referent, such as man, woman, child, sun, moon, and tree. These are pictographs. Other written words convey an idea by reference to general experience. These ideographs include a vertical line rising from a horizontal line to indicate up, and a vertical line descending from a horizontal line to indicate down. Compound ideographs depend upon general experience with respect to the association of the phenomena indicated by the pictographic components. For example, a pig under a roof indicates home; a woman under a roof, contentment; a woman and a child, good; the sun and moon, brightness; a closed eye above a bench, a sleeping person—when a hand holding a stick is added, the suggested meaning of the sleeping person being beaten indicates a nightmare. Some ideas are conveyed by two graphs in succession, such as going, in which the first graph shows a man standing at a place and the second graph shows the man moving away from the represented place. Most written Chinese words are logographs that have a significant component and a phonetic component. The signific indicates an area of meaning, the phonetic indicates a sound. For instance the signific might be the pictograph for trees, and the phonetic would indicate something about trees. A series of such logographs would correspond precisely with the knots in a quipu string for managing an orchard. Phonetic components would indicate aspects of the activity, such as peach, apricot, persimmon, chestnut, or hazelnut trees; or parts of trees, such as trunk, branch, leaf; or aspects of cultivation, such as planting, grafting, or pruning. There are hundreds of logographs for words associated with trees and wood.[17]

The origin of writing is alternatively attributed to Fuxi and the Yellow Emperor, which would place it ten or more centuries before the Shang dynasty.[18] Tung Tso-pin found that 3,000 graphs were used in Shang oracle bone inscriptions, which date from 1384 to 1111 B.C.E. When Xu Shen compiled the first Chinese dictionary, in the second century, C.E., he listed 9,353 graphs. Modern Chinese dictionaries list more than 40,000 graphs, and recognition of at least 5,000 is necessary for conventional literacy. Multigraph combinations in common use add thousands more items to the normal reader's vocabulary.[19]

It appears that from the beginning of their written language the Chinese were seeking to know and cope with the world of sensed experience, with all its multiform particularity. They might pray or sacrifice to gods, spirits, or ancestors to help out, but from earliest times they apparently were also looking for order and meaning in the events of sensed experience. They did not simplify the accumulation of that experience by subsuming common aspects of many particular phenomena into abstract general categories, and they did not reduce the thousands of nametags for specific phenomena into words composed from the few elements of an alphabet. One thing they did do was to group all words with the same signific together in their dictionaries, ordering them under the classifying signific in accordance with the number of strokes of the brush needed to complete the graph. Since most Chinese words are logographs this achieved at least "some order in what is otherwise an ocean of unique symbols."[20]

Trigrams, Hexagrams, and Social Innovation

If Chinese written language served to identify all of the specific, particular aspects of sensed reality, another distinctively Chinese invention provided a method for accumulating and transmitting information about the interrelationships of phenomena and for learning how to use such information to advantage. This invention was the numerology of the eight trigrams and the sixty-four hexagrams. This numerology, like the monosyllabic written language, persisted from earliest myth to the present day. It reputedly began with the invention of the eight trigrams. The Great Commentary in the *Book of Changes* says:

> When in early antiquity Fu Xi [Fuxi] ruled the world, he looked upward and contemplated the images in the heavens; he looked downward and contemplated the patterns on earth. He contemplated the markings of birds and beasts and the adaptations to the regions. He proceeded directly from himself and indirectly from objects. Thus he invented the eight trigrams in order to enter into connection with the virtues of the light of the gods and to regulate the conditions of all beings.[21]

The eight trigrams represented the principles of change, that is, the Creative, the Receptive, the Arousing, the Abysmal, Keeping Still, Gentle, Clinging, and Joyous. These were very early further differentiated into the sixty-four hexagrams, which, therefore, represented all kinds of changes of every organic entity, that is, all the natural phenomena in the universe.[22] The *Book of Changes* encapsulated all this information by using numerical symbols. Each symbol referred to a set of concrete phenomena associated by juxtaposition in time and space—that is they were related sequentially and geometrically. Each set of changes in its sequential/geometric matrix could be followed from incipiency to full development, and it could then be determined by practical judgment whether the result was good or bad. A person who was faced with an unfamiliar situation and forced to make a choice about courses of action would be helped by being able to see in the *Book of Changes* how a proposed course of action could be expected to turn out. But such a person would not know which hexagram to consult. This problem was solved by the manipulation of yarrow stalks.

Forty-nine yarrow stalks were divided at random into two heaps and stalks were withdrawn from each heap by fours until four or less remained. This was done twice more, with the remaining stalks. This yielded three numbers. The actual numbers were given symbolic numerical values of either two or three in accordance with an arcane formula. The three numbers, thus obtained, added up to six, seven, eight, or nine. By convention nine was the old yang number, a firm (unbroken) line that moved; eight was the young yin number, a yielding (broken) line that was at rest; seven was the young yang number, a firm line that was at rest; and six was the old yin number, a yielding line that moved. When the above procedure had been followed six times the resulting six numbers designated the six lines of the hexagram that was to be consulted for oracular purposes. If none of the lines of the hexagram was moving, only the image and judgment of the hexagram as a whole was consulted. If one of the lines was moving, the commentary on that line was also consulted. The line was then permitted to move, that is, to change from yielding to firm, or vice versa, thus creating a new hexagram, and then the new hexagram as a whole was consulted.[23]

Those who take modern Western science for granted tend to denigrate the *Book of Changes* as a book of magic. But Needham points out that magic involves a technique, as do medicine and chemistry. Magic is an "art of doing things," instead of appealing to omnipotent gods to do things. And, Needham says, "At that ancient stage of thought, how could they know what would conduce to the success of technique and what would not?" What makes magic the precursor of science is the search for correlations. In the case of the Chinese the correlations were intuitive, not rational.[24] But this was perfectly appropriate for a sensed reality. The important thing about the search for meaningful correlations was to obtain help for progressive changes in human society. Remember that the Chinese viewed entities not as material objects with fixed attributes, but as processes of recurrent and progressive change.[25]

In the case of nonhuman organic entities, the activities of recurrent change were determined by the inner (genetic) nature of the entity; progressive changes—to move the entity toward the potentiality indicated by its prescriptive name—were determined by evolutionary events or by human interventions such as plant breeding and cultivation. In the case of human society, activities of both recurrent and progressive change had to be determined by conscious processes. The activities of recurrent change would be easy—simply refer to records and organize planting, harvesting, road work, canal work, maintenance of dwellings, protection against attack, in the same ways as the previous year. But, in order to build a new society and a new civilization, the Chinese needed progressive changes, new techniques and technologies, new sets of activities, and new modes of cooperation. These could not be initiated until they were "thought of."

The numerology of the trigrams and hexagrams was, no doubt, often used to deceive and defraud, but it was also capable of suggesting new initiatives. The randomness of the process was a strength, rather than a weakness. Recent neurological research, using a computer-graphics program based on nonlinear equations, has discovered that some brain wave activity which in an encephalogram appears to be chaotic, is actually random scanning for a new solution to a problem. This random scanning prevents the brain from prematurely locking on to a less than optimal solution.[26] The hexagrams of the *Book of Changes* suggested observed phenomena, such as the sky, the earth, sun, moon, water, and mountains; attitudes, such as receptivity, joy, modesty, enthusiasm, and innocence; general actions, such as peace, conflict, dispersion, and oppression; and processes, such as decrease, increase, revolution, and development.[27] In short, the *Book of Changes*, by means of numerical symbols, accumulated sets of changes of organic entities, natural and human, in their full sequential/geometrical context. Oracular appeal to this fund of existential experience could suggest ways to avoid undesirable results of recurrent changes and could suggest progressive changes that might have desirable results. Of course, the numerology could only suggest changes. Whether suggested changes were desirable or undesirable had to be determined on the basis of general experience.

The Calendar and Reality

The main task of building a society is organization—determining who will perform what activities, where, and when. From the perspective of the emerging Chinese consciousness, the calendar performed this ordering function. The myths indicate that aspects of calendar making included a chronology, observations of astronomical events, ordering of all activities, and governmental supervision.

The ganzhi (stem-branch) chronology employed a denary and a duo-denary series, called the "ten heavenly stems" and the "twelve earthly branches." The construction of the chronology was begun by combining the first stem and the first branch. Subsequent days were designated by combining the next stem and the next branch (starting through each series again as necessary) until the combination of the last stem and the last branch was reached. This produced a sixty-day cycle that was not dependent upon phases of the moon or north-south movements of the sun, and that could be repeated indefinitely. Tradition attributes the ganzhi chronology to Danao, an advisor to the Yellow Emperor. No one knows when, in fact, it was devised, but it was mentioned in the Shang oracle bone inscriptions, which date from 1384 to 1111 B.C.E. At a later date the ten stems and twelve branches were given names that could be easily remembered. The ten stems were named for the five elements, wood, fire, earth, metal, and water, which were doubled by distinguishing between hard and soft wood, sun and kitchen fire, mountain and sand earth, rough and refined metal, and sea and rain water. The twelve branches were named for animals, the rat, ox, tiger, hare, dragon, serpent, horse, sheep, monkey, cock, dog, and pig. The first day of a sequence was a hard wood-rat day, and the last was rain water-pig day.[28]

The Yellow Emperor also reputedly initiated the study of astronomical events and the correlation of them with governmental supervision of human activities. He is said to have named offices after clouds. The Yellow Emperor's son, Shao Hao, who succeeded him, changed from clouds to birds. Birds and the activities for which they were responsible included: Phoenix, the calendar in general; Swallow, the equinoxes; Shrike, the solstices; Green and Red, "opening" and "closing" (presumably of the growing season). Five Pigeons were responsible for peace keeping, education, war, public works, and justice (punishment). Nine Jays supervised measurements, implement making, and agriculture in the nine regions of the empire.[29]

Shao Hao failed to put down an uprising by tribes in the south, who had signalled their rebellion by refusing to follow his calendar. He was considered weak and ineffective and was not included as one of the Five Emperors. He was succeeded by his nephew, Zhuan Xu, who restored peace in the south and improved the accuracy of his predecessors' calendars by stationing observers at the southern and northern limits of the empire to record equinoxes and solstices. Zhuan Xu, the second of the Five Emperors, was succeeded by Shao Hao's grandson, Ku, who reigned during a long period of peace, for which he was given the credit and counted as the third of the Five Emperors. After a short reign by Ku's son Zhi, another son, Yao, succeeded, and his accomplishments earned him the position of the fourth of the Five Emperors.[30]

Yao is said to have stationed observers at the four cardinal points with instructions, respectively, to: "[R]eceive as a guest the rising sun, in order to regulate the labours of the east (the spring) . . . to regulate the works of the south and pay respectful attention to the (summer) solstice . . . to bid farewell respectfully to the setting sun, in order to regulate the western (autumnal) accomplishment . . . [and] to supervise the works of the north."[31] Soon after Yao ascended the throne he was so successful that all the people became prosperous and amply nourished, and harmony was established in the nine branches of the family, the hundred surnames, and the myriad nations.[32]

Modern scholarship confirms the accuracy of the astronomical observations on which early Chinese calendars were based and the correlation of astronomical events with the events in the life of an agricultural society in north China. Tung Tso-pin found that the calendars of the Xia, Shang, and Zhou dynasties calculated the solar year at 365 1/4 days, and reconciled it with the lunar month by inserting seven intercalary months in nineteen years. This accuracy was achieved 1,000 years before the

Babylonians and 1,300 years before the Romans. The ancient Chinese calendar divided the year into twenty-four sections, instead of the four seasons. Each two sections constituted an "astronomical month," each of which had a beginning point and a middle point. The solstices and equinoxes were the beginning points of the first of the three astronomical months in each season. The other beginning and middle points were named for aspects of agricultural life or for natural phenomena. Each of the twenty-four sections was further divided into three subsections. The resulting seventy-two subsections, according to Tung, "provide a very detailed description of the weather, the animal and vegetable life, the phases of an agricultural society in the Hwang Ho [Yellow River] valley throughout a whole solar year."[33]

Note that the ancient Chinese calendar is said to provide an accurate *description* of life in an agricultural society in north China. But in the myths the calendar is clearly *prescriptive*. Tribes signal their rebellion against a ruler by refusing to follow his calendar. Officials use the calendar to supervise all sorts of activities. A calendar can fail, or be successful—bringing peace and prosperity. How could the ancient calendar, which seems to the modern observer to *describe*, have functioned to *prescribe*? To answer this we need to look again at the Chinese view of reality.

Their written language indicates that the Chinese took the sensed world to be the real world.[34] But this did not mean that every sensed phenomenon was real. Name was prescriptive. It indicated the characteristics an individual plant *should* have. An individual that had some, but not all, of the characteristics of millet was something less than millet. Full reality was indicated by prescriptive name. Therefore sensed phenomena that were not in accordance with the prescribed order were actual, but not real, and progressive changes were needed to bring them to reality. Similarly, space and time were prescriptive, consisting of the sites where and the occasions when an entity should follow the changes of form and substance indicated in its dao, thus becoming correctly ordered and constituting a part of reality. All parts of reality were interrelated, or interpenetrating, evoking each other by resonance when they were equivalent (in the same sector of space/time) or by sequential rhythm when they were opposed (as in yin and yang). The whole of reality was a unity, an organism, in which all parts functioned harmoniously. Therefore, to the extent that the Chinese were rationalistic, reality was the totality of *correctly ordered* sensed phenomena.[35]

In such a reality the calendar charted the role of humanity as an organic entity within the organic universe; it was the dao of human (Chinese) society. It contained the agendas for every activity of every human individual throughout the whole year, coordinated all human agendas, and correlated them with the agendas of all nonhuman entities. It was able to do this, even though the Chinese written language preserved the uniqueness and particularity of sensed phenomena, by using numerical symbols, each of which stood for a batch of concrete phenomena associated by their situation in the space/time continuum.

For instance, "*Ren*, in the denary series, suggested to Sima Qian the idea of burden, and recalls the 10,000 species of beings at the moment when they are borne and nourished in the bottom of the world. The *Chou wen*, on the other hand, identifies in *ren* the figure of a woman, who carries her burden, who nourishes an embryo."[36] *Ren* also indicated full north and the winter solstice. *Chen*, in the duodenary series, denoted the shaking and stirring that produces thunder, also the stirring of the woman at the moment of fecundation. It also indicated east-southeast and the third month of spring. The numerical symbols were arranged geometrically to represent distribution of the concrete phenomena in space. The ten heavenly stems were placed in pairs in the form of a cross to represent the four orients and the center of the earth. (Heavenly numbers in earthly configuration signified the interdependence of heaven and earth.) The twelve earthly branches were arranged in a circle, the shape of heaven. Circle and cross were superimposed.

Where numbers in the two series coincided it signified that the batches of phenomena they referred to were equivalent rather than opposed. For instance *zu*, in the duodenary series, "enclosed" *ren* and *gui*, in the denary series. *Ren* signified gestation, and *gui* signified the water from the four orients that penetrated into the womb of the earth, which opened to it toward the north pole. *Gui* also designated the fecund humours that permit women to conceive and to nourish their embryos. The times propitious for conception were mid-winter and midnight, and full north was the favorable orient. The wife's pallet and the seeds for spring planting were also kept in the dark in the north part of the house. The rebirth of yang, the active aspect of universal life force, was signified by *su*, which was equivalent (in the same sector of space/time) with *ren*, which indicated full north and winter solstice, and which was said to "preside" at the birth of yang.[37]

Similar reasoning served to distribute all of the activities of all entities in the universe to prescribed sectors of space/ time. Therefore, the calendar was the dao for all entities, not just human society. And the calendar was prescriptive, the supreme law, because there was contingency throughout the whole of nature, not just in human affairs. Space was composed of events that were scheduled for those sites. Time was composed of events that were scheduled for those occasions. Where the geometrical and rhythmical order of the Chinese calendar was not followed space/time were weak and empty and would support only imperfect beings.[38] The real was the totality of all the unique, particular, sensed phenomena ordered in accordance with the calendar.

The prescriptive ordering of human events presented a special problem. It was relatively easy to prescribe what a plant *should* do, when, and where, because what it *could* do was so closely determined by observable form and substance. But what human beings could do depended not upon observable form and substance but upon development of common consciousness and cooperative action. We have discussed aspects of the emerging Chinese common consciousness. What we are now concerned with is the projection of that consciousness into cooperative action, as the human organic entity found its role in the Chinese organic universe by becoming a social organism. Determining the sets of activities to be performed, and sets of individuals to perform them, required the creation of social names.

Human individuals were not limited to one set of activities, for which they had been prepared by structure and behavioral control, like plants. Because of the great plasticity of human thought and action, human individuals could function in many sets. A social name did not indicate a fixed set of individuals. It indicated the state of mind and the actions prescribed for any individual who, at a given time and place, was included in a set. And social conventions, which were sometimes based on gender or age, determined which individuals were included in each set.

The most inclusive set of individuals was humanity, which consisted of those having human form and substance who utilized the inventions of the Chinese culture heroes—wooden houses, fire, settled agriculture, the bow and arrow, hoe, plow, boats, Chinese written language, the trigrams and hexagrams, and the calendar. The next most inclusive sets consisted of individuals who, at a time or place, or with respect to certain other individuals, were under the influence of yin or yang. In the countryside the men and women composed complementary groups that divided between themselves the various jobs and the times and places for doing them. Each had a formula of life, and at rhythmic intervals these intersected and men and women joined in celebrations of union and interaction. According to Granet, in his study of the *Book of Poetry*, in the spring and again in the fall, the opposing choirs of men and women joined in jousts preceding hierogamies, at which they chanted various natural signs of the changing universe that furnished material for the calendar.[39] This sounds too precious to be credible except as myth. But that the ancient calendars reflected the order of life of rural China is beyond doubt,[40] and it cannot be denied that chants of opposing choirs celebrating union after separation were collected in the *Book of Poetry*.

Social names indicated relationships, which carried reciprocal obligations of attitude and action. These names greatly increased in number as society became more complex and more thoroughly delineated. Perhaps at one time family names and generational names sufficed to organize daily life. All who shared genealogical ties through male lineage and who shared an obligation to till and defend a piece of territory bore the same name. Within generations authority was said to reside in the eldest and most respected father or mother, rather than the particular biological parent.[41] Later, as intrafamily obligations were more fully delineated, more names were needed, and the *Er Ya*, the oldest Chinese dictionary, dating from the second century C.E., lists more than one hundred names for family relations, most of which have no English equivalent.[42] For society as a whole, there developed five binomes that designated the master relationships of Chinese society. These were sovereign-family head, parent-offspring, husband-wife, elder-younger, and friend-friend. In the Canon of Yao, the first document in the *Book of History*, the prescribed sets of attitudes and actions for each of these relationships were called the Five Codes.[43]

Notes

1. Charles O. Hucker, *China's Imperial Past* (Stanford, Calif.: Stanford University Press, 1975), pp. 22-24; K. C. Chang, *Art, Myth, and Ritual: The Path to Political Authority in Ancient China* (Cambridge, Mass.: Harvard University Press, 1983),

p. 2; K. C. Wu, *The Chinese Heritage* (New York: Crown Publishers, 1982), pp. 51-52.

2. Wu, *The Chinese Heritage*, p. 50.
3. See above, chap. 4.
4. Quoted in Wu, *The Chinese Heritage*, p. 51.
5. Ibid., p. 54.
6. Hucker, *China's Imperial Past*, p. 22; Wu, *The Chinese Heritage*, pp. 21-44, 55-60.
7. Quoted in Wu, *The Chinese Heritage*, p. 58.
8. Hucker, *China's Imperial Past*, p. 28.
9. Gray L. Dorsey, *Jurisculture: Greece and Rome* (New Brunswick, N.J.: Transaction Publishers, 1989), pp. 7-12, 22-29.
10. Gray L. Dorsey, *Jurisculture: India* (New Brunswick, N.J.: Transaction Publishers, 1990), pp. 1-3, 58-64.
11. See text above at chap. 2, note 7; Wm. Theodore de Bary, Wing-tsit Chan, and Burton Watson, *Sources of Chinese Tradition*, vol. 1 (New York: Columbia University Press, 1960), pp. 5-6.
12. Joseph Needham, *Science and Civilisation in China*, vol. 3 (Cambridge: Cambridge University Press, 1959), pp. 150-51.
13. Hellmut Wilhelm, ed., Richard Wilhelm and Cary F. Baynes, trans., *The I-Ching, or Book of Changes*, 3rd ed. (Princeton, N.J.: Princeton University Press, 1967), p. 335; Needham, *Science and Civilisation in China*, vol. 2, p. 327.
14. Needham, *Science and Civilisation in China*, vol. 3, p. 69.
15. John B. Carlson, "America's Ancient Skywatchers," *National Geographic*, March 1990, pp. 76, 91.
16. See above, at chap. 2, note 17; Needham, *Science and Civilisation in China*, vol. 3, p. 556, note d.
17. John K. Fairbank, Edwin O. Reischauer, and Albert M. Craig, *East Asia: Tradition and Transformation* (Boston, Mass.: Houghton Mifflin, 1973), pp. 22-25; Hucker, *China's Imperial Past*, pp. 8-9; A scroll by Tung Tso-pin of a moon festival poem written in Shang oracle bone characters presented to the author by Tung in 1953.
18. Wu, *The Chinese Heritage*, p. 26.
19. Ibid., p. 31; Hucker, *China's Imperial Past*, pp. 7-8.
20. Fairbank, Reischauer, and Craig, *East Asia*, pp. 22-25; Hucker, *China's Imperial Past*, pp. 8-9.
21. Wilhelm and Baynes, *The I Ching*, pp. 328-29.
22. See the section, "Change," chap. 2. Also Wilhelm and Baynes, *The I Ching*, p. 320.
23. Wilhelm and Baynes, *The I Ching*, pp. 721-23.
24. Needham, *Science and Civilisation*, vol. 2, pp. 280-81.
25. See the section, "Change," chap. 2.
26. Kathleen McAuliffe, "Get Smart: Controlling Chaos," *Omni Magazine*, February 1990, pp. 43ff.
27. Wilhelm and Baynes, *The I Ching*, see hexagrams 1, 2, 5, 6, 11, 15, 16, 24, 25, 33, 41, 42, 47, 49, 53, 58, and 59.
28. Tung Tso-pin, "The Chinese and the World's Calendars," in *A Symposium on the World Calendar* (Taipei, Taiwan: Chinese Association for the United Nations, 1951), pp. 3, 22; Needham, *Science and Civilisation in China*, vol. 3, pp. 396-98; Wu, *The Chinese Heritage*, pp. 26, 31-35.

29. Wu, *The Chinese Heritage*, p. 60. Wu relies, for this account, on a work by the Duke of Zhou, who consolidated the Zhou dynasty (1100–256 B.C.E.). Wu's view that these legends record actual historical events several centuries before the Xia Dynasty is not generally accepted, and is not espoused herein. However, Wu provides detailed accounts in English of the feats attributed to the culture heroes, and these can show the Chinese consciousness in its later developed form, with an inference that at an earlier period it was moving in that direction.
30. Wu, *The Chinese Heritage*, pp. 63–64.
31. Needham, *Science and Civilisation in China*, vol. 3, pp. 186–88.
32. de Bary, Chan, and Watson, *Sources of Chinese Tradition*, vol. 1, p. 8; Hucker, *China's Imperial Past*, p. 23; Wu, *The Chinese Heritage*, pp. 65–69.
33. Tung, "The Chinese and the World's Calendars," pp. 4–12, 21; Needham, *Science and Civilisation in China*, vol. 3, pp. 402–5.
34. Carson Chang, formerly a professor of philosophy at the University of Jena, in a letter to the author dated 29 January 1956 (and in the author's possession), expressed the view that the Chinese adhered to the reality of the sensed world into the present century.
35. Marcel Granet, *La Pensée Chinoise* (Paris: Éditions Albin Michel, 1950), pp. 147–48.
36. Ibid., p. 152.
37. Ibid., pp. 152–53.
38. Ibid., pp. 92–107.
39. Granet, *Fêtes et Chansons Anciennes de la Chine* (Paris: Éditions Ernest Leroux, 1919), pp. 232–49.
40. Granet, *Pensée*, pp. 139–40.
41. Marcel Granet, Kathleen E. Innes, trans., *Chinese Civilization* (New York: Meridian Books, 1958), pp. 312–30.
42. Fung Yu-lan, "The Philosophy at the Basis of Traditional Chinese Society," in F. S. C. Northrop, ed., *Ideological Differences and World Order* (New Haven, Conn.: Yale University Press, 1949), pp. 18, 25.
43. Ibid., p. 25; Wu, *The Chinese Heritage*, p. 75.

6

Governing Chinese Society

Rulers and Reality

From earliest times, with remarkable consistency, the implication for political authority of the Chinese view of reality seems to have been unitary and universal. This differs radically from the Greek and Indian cultures. In early Greece the belief that the gods caused events to happen, together with the belief that some men possessed some of the efficacious power of the gods and could pass it to the eldest son, gave rise to the implication that political authority resided in these several eponymous heroes and succeeding patersfamilias. Replication of this family authority structure in city-states made it impossible to establish one political order throughout all of Greece.[1] In late Republican Rome it came to be believed that the universe is rationally ordered and that all human beings have reason and can know that order. The implication of equal competence to make important decisions was implemented by creation of a universal private law, but it had no impact whatever upon the structure of political authority.[2] In India, where governing, which consisted principally of punishing justly, was the duty of a caste, there was no implication of political authority. Every member of the kingly caste had the obligation to get as much political power as he could, retain and increase it as he might, and use it to punish as he should.[3]

There is no hint in Chinese myth or history of multiple political authority, or (except for the Legalists) of reliance upon pure power rather than political authority. In the tradition, the Three Sovereigns, Five Emperors, and the Three Sages, and their successors, each exercised political authority—all there was or could be, and wherever there was any. Where they did not rule, space and time were too culturally anemic to support human (Chinese) activities. According to the emerging view of reality, there was one universal organism, every subsystem of which was interconnected and had to function harmoniously within the whole. Ergo, there could be only one order of human comportments, which was embodied in the calendar. Therefore, the primary function of governing was to promulgate the calendar. Where would-be rulers issued competing calendars, only one could be based on political authority. The competition between would-be rulers, therefore, proceeded in terms of credibility of the competing claims of authority.

One basis of authority was clan allegiance, evoked by totemic symbols.[4] A more important basis was merit—some great service for the good of the people.[5] Merit as a basis of authority is clearly indicated in the myths of the culture heroes, who were said to have taught the people how to build wooden houses, or make fire, as a result of which the grateful people made the benefactor their ruler.[6] The clan allegiance and merit bases of authority were merged by the claim of every clan head to have descended from one of the mythical culture heroes. Another important basis of political authority was effectiveness. The Yellow Emperor, who went everywhere under heaven to compel people to obey him, was proclaimed the first and greatest of the Five Emperors. His son, Shao Hao, who failed to compel southern tribes to follow his calendar, was considered a failure. The fourth and fifth of the Five Emperors, Yao and Shun, when selecting their successors, passed over their own sons, who were considered ineffective, in favor of persons who had demonstrated their ability to deal with the problems of the empire. Shun selected Yu, who reputedly had controlled a great flood. Yu founded the Xia dynasty. Yao, Shun, and Yu are known as the Three Sages.

In historical ancient China, clan allegiance, merit, and effectiveness were all merged in the idea of access to ancient wisdom as the basis of political authority. Kings had claimed access to the wisdom of their mythological ancestors, and had reinforced clan allegiance with shamanistic ceremonies to solicit the assistance of ancestral ghosts and spirits, who supposedly possessed some of that wisdom.[7] But some time, perhaps in the Xia dynasty, the idea formed of a complete body of wisdom for dealing with every problem on earth. Where was this wisdom to be found? If it were within the realm of earth all affairs would already be correctly ordered, and there would be nothing for a ruler to do. Therefore, it was said that the complete body of wisdom was in heaven.[8] The Shang dynasty rulers sought access to this wisdom through worship of the Lord on High, who was deemed to be the God of heaven.[9] But by the time of the Zhou dynasty heaven had become impersonal—more the wisdom itself, rather than a god who dispensed it. There was a Zhou-era myth that at one time the wisdom of heaven was available to everybody, but through the intermingling of people and spirits, during the degenerate time of Shao Hao, everything became disordered and so Zhuan Xu had ordered the connection between heaven and earth to be cut.[10] Communication was reestablished by the One Man, through whom the order embodied in the wisdom of heaven would flow into all earthly things, natural and human. It was said that the person who came to be recognized as the One Man was chosen by heaven and had received heaven's mandate. From the time of the Zhou until the end of the empire in 1912, the authority of the ruler was justified by his possession of the mandate of heaven.[11] Zhou and Han texts established a tradition that the founder of the Shang dynasty had been chosen by heaven to overthrow the Xia, and that Shun and Yu had been selected by heaven.[12]

The Chinese word that is translated as "mandate" carries a meaning of command and also of giving,[13] indicating that the One Man had the obligation as well as the right to cause the order of heaven to flow into everything on earth—including, but not limited to, human affairs. The appearance of the ruler at the appropriate station in the ceremonial Ming Tang (House of the Calendar), in accordance with the astronomical signs of heaven supposedly enabled the order of heaven to flow into things of the earth so that plants could sprout and grow in season, and rivers would not burst out of their banks but bring needed water to the fields. A natural disaster, such as a flood, indicated that the ruler was not performing his function as the channel between heaven and earth.[14] The ability of the ruler to perform this function was his "virtue." When disorder occurred it was said to show that the ruler's virtue was weak. His virtue was strong when the flow of order was unimpeded. Because this indicated that the channel between heaven and earth was open and clear, and because heaven was associated with light, the successful ruler was said to possess "clear," or "brilliant" virtue. The famous Duke of Zhou was said to possess brilliant virtue.[15] The Confucian classic *The Great Learning* teaches how the ancients manifested clear virtue.[16]

Manifesting clear virtue, to the Western ear, sounds passive and impractical. In fact, it was active and practical. To manifest clear virtue the One Man—the ruler—had to do nothing less than organize and regulate society. He had to designate what sets of persons would perform what activities, where and when; instruct them, specifically and in detail, what each was to do, see that they knew how to do it, instill the habit of compliance; prevent them from obstructing the cooperative activities by wrong attitudes or actions; and do anything else necessary to accomplish these ends. To achieve this, he had to have complete control over the land available for the cooperative activities, and over all persons who could either help or obstruct. Control over people included the right to kill. According to a document in the *Book of History*, Tang, founder of the Shang dynasty, told the people that heaven had charged him to kill the Xia king, Jie, because he had impeded the work of the people by injurious and uncaring government, causing the people to become slack and disaffected. He also told the people that he would greatly benefit them if they obeyed him, but if they disobeyed, "I will kill you and your wife and children; there will be nobody who will be pardoned."[17]

Sets of persons to perform designated activities were determined in a way entirely consistent with the Chinese view of reality. The closest, most continuous, most cooperative relations between persons in the sensed world are those of the family. Where polygamy prevailed, blood relationship was counted through the male. This connection was identified, reinforced, and preserved very early in China by the giving of family names, an invention attributed to the Yellow Emperor.[18] As lineages branched off they were reminded of their common heritage and their continuing obligations of support by clan names and ancestral worship conducted at the level of the ruling clan, thus providing continuity of identity and cooperation much to their advantage over neighboring peoples who did not have clan names.[19]

At one time lineages and clans lived in independent villages in north China.[20] However, by the time of the Three Dynasties (Xia, Shang, and Zhou) villages were clustered under the control of a lord, or prince, whose seat was a walled town. Towns, in turn, were subordinate units within the state, or *guo*, which was ruled by the king from his royal capital.[21] The change had been gradual. Organization of activities had become more complex within villages and had been extended to the relations between villages, thus increasing the productivity of agriculture, animal husbandry, and pottery making, and adding new manual arts.[22] The resulting surplus of wealth, people, skills, and energies, enabled the politically ambitious to gather together specialists in the techniques and technologies of emerging Chinese civilization, especially writing, thus enabling would-be rulers to earn, by effective administration, the political authority that they claimed.[23]

When a *guo*'s surplus of wealth, skills, and population permitted, the king sent out complete sets of lineages and specialists to establish new villages, towns, and subordinate states. A sixth century B.C.E. entry in the *Zuo Zhuan* describes the dispatch of such expeditionary forces early in the Zhou dynasty. "King Cheng completed the establishment of the new dynasty, and chose and appointed [the princes of] intelligent virtue, to act as bulwarks and screens to Zhou." A son of the famous Duke of Zhou was to rule over the territory of Lu. He was given a grand chariot, a grand flag, the *huang*-stone of the sovereigns of Xia, a great bow, together with priests, superintendents of the ancestral temple, diviners, historiographers, all the appendages of state, the tablets of historical records, the various officers and the ordinary instruments of their offices, and the "old capital of Shao Gao was assigned as the center of his State." The heads of six clans of the people of Yin "were ordered to lead the chiefs of their kindred, to collect their branches, remoter as well as the near, to conduct the multitude of their connexions, and repair with them to Zhou," to receive the instructions and laws of the Duke of Zhou, and then to perform duty in Lu. Kang Shu was given symbols of authority and seven clans of the people of Yin and was sent to a territory that had included a part of Yuyan, in order "that he might discharge his duty to the king, and a portion of the lands belonging to the eastern capital of Xiang-tu, that he might be able to better attend at the king's journeys to the east." Tang Shu was ordered to territory around the old capital of the Xia dynasty, and was assigned "nine clans of the surname Huai, and five presidents over the different departments of office."[24]

By such a process the king distributed sets of individuals under command and control of persons beholden to him to territories of the kingdom. The lords or princes were given titles that have been translated as duke, marquis, earl, viscount, and baron, which came to indicate a hierarchy of rank and had significance in terms of access to the king and size of territory.[25] The resulting social and political system has been called feudalism. It has been frequently said that all land and people in the kingdom were owned by the king. This assertion rests principally on a Zhou-era poem in the *Book of Poetry*:

> Everywhere under vast Heaven
> There is no land that is not the king's.
> To the borders of those lands
> There are none who are not the king's servants.[26]

Maspero, however, held the opinion that only political authority, not a property right, was indicated.[27] This view accords with the literal meaning of the Chinese term that is translated "feudalism," namely, *fengjian*. *Feng* means to put borders to a piece of land, and *jian* means to establish rulership over the land.[28] Maspero's view is also consistent with the view traced herein that the organization of society in ancient China was a process of molding all human beings into a social organism. All human beings had to work and live harmoniously with each other. This entailed a disposition of individuals so that everywhere needed activities were performed, and nowhere were there competing sets of individuals seeking to work and live on the same piece of land at the same time. Ownership is not a necessary inference from the authority of the king to make such a distribution.

The ruler was symbolically the One Man, the clear channel through which the correct order of events flowed from heaven into the earth. The ruler was functionally the politically ambitious person who was able to gather around him the most specialists in nascent Chinese culture, who were scientists in the sense of seeking out the order of the sensed world, who were ethicists in the sense of determining the implications of that understanding for regulating human activities, and who were also administrators with responsibility for planning and supervising activities. Whoever got the most wealth, the most experts in Chinese culture, and did the people the most good was accorded political authority. It is in this sense that the legendary Yao, the fourth of the Five Emperors, was said, early in his reign, to have established harmony and prosperity among the nine branches of the family, the hundred surnames, and the myriad nations.[29] In the Chinese feudal system, the king's benevolent influence and his effective administration organized and regulated all human activities in the kingdom, beginning with the royal lineage, going next to the closely related lineages (nine branches of the family), then to all the lineages and clans that were fully integrated into Chinese civilization (the hundred surnames), and then to barbarians who remained peaceful and paid tribute (the myriad nations).

If the paradigm of political authority in ancient China was always unitary and universal, the Xia, Shang, and Zhou states fell short. They were the most prominent, but by no means the only states. However, the trend was toward the paradigm. According to one account, there were 10,000 *guo* at the beginning of the Xia dynasty (2200 B.C.E.), more than 3,000 at the beginning of the Shang dynasty (1750 B.C.E.), and 1,800 at the beginning of the Zhou dynasty (1100 B.C.E.). "At the beginning of the Eastern Zhou (771 B.C.E.), 1,200 *guo* were left, and at the end of the Spring-and-Autumn period (481 B.C.E.) that number decreased to just over a hundred, of which only fourteen were considered major states."[30] In 221 B.C.E., Qin Shihuangdi brought all the Chinese people and territory into a single empire.[31]

Obedience

We have discussed the Chinese view of reality: how it could be known, who could know it, how knowledge of that reality was used to build a common consciousness, and how sets of individuals were designated and assigned to perform sets of activities in specified places in order to translate common consciousness into the cooperative activities of Chinese society. We have not yet discussed whether and why individuals did what they were assigned to do and refrained from doing other things that would be obstructive or destructive. These matters of compliance and restraint were functions of the individual, hierarchy, ancestors and other spirits, ritual, and punishment.

The Individual

Individual plants sometimes failed to do what was expected of them. Because plant activities are controlled by natural processes, such a failure must have been due to a fault in the nature of the individual plant, or to some influence that prevented the individual from fulfilling its nature. Plants were identified by changing characteristics of form and substance. This identification was prescriptive. As discussed in chapter 2, to be a millet plant was to manifest the characteristics indicated by the name. To fall short of those characteristics was to be something less than millet, but not something other than millet, such as rice, or wheat. The dao of millet would tell an individual plant to develop the characteristics indicated by the prescriptive name, millet. But any given plant might have something less than millet dao, either because the seed plant's dao was deficient or because of contingency in the transmission of what we now know to be genetic information. Whether its dao was full or deficient an individual plant needed energy to convert genetic information into form and substance. This physical energy was the yin/yang of the plant. A plant's dao and yin/yang constituted its intrinsic physical nature, which guided and animated its responses to the influences of sun, soil, water, wind, and cultivation, as indicated by Needham when he said, "Things behaved in particular ways . . . [because] they were endowed with intrinsic natures which made that behavior inevitable for them."[32] Plants were obedient by nature, to the extent of that nature.

The individual person, of course, had an intrinsic physical nature, which guided and animated characteristics of form and substance. But the problems of human obedience arose with respect to prescribed characteristics of attitude and action, which were controlled by cultural processes. The cooperative activities of human society were organized through development of a Chinese consciousness that enabled individuals to understand in accordance with shared meanings, desire in accordance with shared values, intend in accordance with shared purposes, and guide and limit attitudes and actions in accordance with shared principles and rules. This common consciousness had to be implanted in every individual in each generation, by precept and example. Further, each individual was particularly situated in society, and the particular consciousness appropriate to that situation also had to be implanted in each person. By absorbing and accepting the common consciousness and the particular consciousness the individual internalized a social dao.

Names were prescriptive with respect to the social characteristics of attitudes and action, as well as with respect to the physical characteristics of form and substance. To be Ma was to manifest the changing attitudes and actions indicated by that family name. To fall short of those characteristics was to be something less than Ma, but not something other than Ma, such as Jiang or Wang. The social dao of Ma would tell the individual to manifest the Ma characteristics, but the individual might have less than Ma dao, either because the parents' dao was deficient or because of contingency in the cultural transmission of social dao.

Whatever the social dao of an individual person, he or she needed motivational energy to execute the prescribed attitudes and actions. This motivational energy—which would be called "will" in Western thought—was the social yin/yang of human beings. The social yin/yang grew out of commitment to live by the imbued consciousness, and was nourished by ritual. A person's social dao and social yin/yang constituted his or her intrinsic social nature, which guided and animated responses to all life situations. To the extent of their intrinsic social natures, people responded with expected attitudes and actions without the need for outside inducement or constraint. They were obedient by social nature, to the extent of that nature.

Hierarchy

If an individual millet plant, because of faulty dao, failed to develop some of the characteristics of form and substance prescribed by its name, little could be done about it. A plant's intrinsic physical nature was almost exclusively the determinant of its behavior. No adjoining plant could correct another's behavior, and none had authority to do so. There was no head plant in a millet field. Only a supramillet organism, the farmer, could intervene, and he could do little to correct the behavior of that plant. To some extent he might improve stem strength or seed formation by cultivation, but for the most part his corrective measures would affect only the next generation. The faulty plant would have to be culled, or used for some purpose for which its development was sufficient.

An individual person's intrinsic social nature was by no means the exclusive determinant of that person's behavior. Because social dao and yin/yang were the products of the conscious processes of culture, persons could interact with respect to them. The nature of this interaction was determined by the hierarchical organization of Chinese society. Within the household, older brother had authority over younger, and husband over wife. The head of the household was subject to the head of the lineage, who was subject to the head of the clan. The ruler of the village was subject to the ruler of the town, who was subject to the ruler of the *guo*, who was subject to the ruler of the kingdom, who was answerable to heaven.

Individual persons were not discrete entities who had autonomous control over their attitudes and actions. An individual person was "individual" by being a particular perceived actualization of a prescriptive entity, and by the degree to which he or she possessed the dao and yin/yang indicated by the name of the prescriptive entity. The head of a Ma household could be expected to know, better than any other household member, what attitudes and actions Ma dao required in a given situation, and could be expected to have stronger motivation to see that those requirements were met. If a son's social dao was deficient, it was the job of the father to show him what attitudes and actions were called for. If the son knew what he should do but lacked the motivation to do it, the father could provide further motivation by persuasion, reward, or sanction. Similarly, the head of the lineage and the head of the clan were charged with seeing that all of the dao-prescribed attitudes and actions of all members of the Ma family were executed where and when they should be.

The family, which was the earliest form of social organization in ancient China, was well suited to largely self-sufficient farming communities. Within these communities the family responded to social situations with expected attitudes and actions to the extent that the head of the family correctly understood the family dao and commanded sufficient motivational energy to cause the members of the family to follow it. The help that ancestral members of the family provided in understanding and executing the social obligations of the family will be discussed below. Kinship was ostensibly the basis of social organization at the village, town, *guo*, and kingdom levels until the end of the Western Zhou period.[33] But, increasingly, economic and political organizations were formed. The heads of these organizations had the difficult task of inculcating members of the group with the intrinsic social nature of the guild, or town, or country without the close association of child rearing in which family dao was implanted. The use of ritual was common to these other groups as well as the family, as will be discussed below.

Ancestors and Other Spirits

To understand the nature of ancestors, it is necessary to begin with the nature of living persons. As discussed above, the person was thought to consist of external characteristics of form and substance, and of attitude and action, and internal characteristics of guidance (dao) and animation (yin/yang). In this view of human nature there was no persistent soul, possessed of reason, or created by an omnipotent God. Indeed, there was no creator God in Chinese thought.[34] The changing external characteristics could be sensed. The internal causes of those changes could not be sensed directly, but it was a central theme of the *Book of Changes* that the acute observer could detect impending changes. The observable clue of impending change in form and substance might be the first stage of desiccation, a leaf becoming limp or changing color slightly. A change of attitude and action might be preceded by a slight change of facial expression, or by increased tension in the body. From such observed events an inference could be drawn that something in the plant or person was providing guidance and animation for the changes.

The inner characteristics of the person, like the outer characteristics, were part of that totality of correctly ordered sensed phenomena that constituted reality, according to the rationalistic view. Nevertheless, the inner characteristics were different from the outer. They were not palpable. They were numinous. Naturally, it was the numinous characteristics that were thought to survive the death of the body. But there were two sets of numinous characteristics, which provided guidance and animation, respectively, for the physical person and for the social person.[35] The rich and varied history of Chinese ancestor worship contains elements that respond to both of these components.

Belief in the survival of the spirit of the physical body is very ancient. Granet saw it as influential in the beginning of social hierarchy, as the overlord of the newly established town drew into himself the power of the Holy Place of each village by "eating his fief." By consuming the essence of all of the products of his domain he strengthened his own essence so that it could live on after his death and continue to exercise a beneficial influence over physical events. The spirits of ordinary people, who ate only the products of their own farm, did not survive.[36]

A number of aspects of ancestor worship seem to be particularly responsive to the idea of the survival of the spirit of the physical body. Some of the food and drink at every meal was set aside for the ancestors. It was believed that they needed these comestibles to sustain them.[37] Every clan claimed as an ancestor a mythical culture hero, who had invented some especially useful control over physical events, such as farming, fire, wooden houses.[38] Particularly in the Shang period, ancestors were thought to be influential with respect to human and agricultural fertility, health, hunting, and war.[39] Further, for a long time, only royal and noble families conducted ancestor worship.[40] This would seem to be linked with the idea that a person's physical spirit could survive only if that person had eaten the products of a wide domain. Certainly, ancestor worship was important, in Shang times, in justifying and reinforcing political authority.[41]

The Ma family, like millet, was a physical organism, each generation of which manifested the changing characteristics of form and substance from birth to death of the body appropriate for any member of the Ma family. The guidance and animation that constituted the intrinsic physical nature of the Ma family was passed from one generation to the next. Because that transmission was degraded by contingency, the particular physical characteristics of any given member of the Ma family was distinct. The physical spirit of a female ancestor who had been especially fertile might be thought to have the power to influence fertility in the present generation. The physical spirit of a male ancestor who was an especially productive farmer might be thought to have the power to aid the present generation of farmers. Similarly, other spirits were thought to have control over other physical events. The ancestral tablet of a renowned warrior was always carried on a military expedition.[42]

The family was also a social organism. In the very early time of independent villages, it was the family that organized and supervised all the activities of agriculture, sericulture, and the manual arts, especially the making of pottery and implements, the building of houses, stables, arsenals, roads, dikes, canals, ancestral temples, peace keeping, and defense. Assignment of specific individuals to specific activities in accordance with the family hierarchy determined the social obligations of every member of the social unit. The assignment of sets of persons to certain activities was continued by custom and usage, and eventually became a set of rules that the head of clan or lineage had the authority to enforce and the duty to supervise.[43] Ancestors were an integral part of the social family, as well as the physical family. Not only did the ancestors participate in the formulation of the rules of society, but also they were important in the continuing administration of those rules. The ancestral temple was the first building to be constructed in a new town.[44] It was the center for all social activities because everything had to be done with ritual. At the level of the *guo*, or the kingdom, diplomacy was conducted in the ancestral temple, officials were invested and feudal lords enfiefed there. Military expeditions departed from the ancestral temple, and reported there upon their return.[45]

The good will and assistance of the ancestors were invoked for every activity and enterprise of the social family. The ritual of the sacrifices was conducted in accordance with the family hierarchy, each member being called upon to perform some act to manifest the proper awe and respect. Conversely, the moral authority of the ancestors was established by the appeal to them as arbiters of right and wrong actions.[46] The moral authority of the ancestors was further enhanced by the selection of the ancestors to be included in the sacrificial canon. Sacrifices were offered to an ancestor who had given good laws, or who had adopted wise policies that successfully overcame great calamities or warded off impending disasters, or who had shown great diligence in performance of duties.[47] On the other hand, persons who had made no contribution to the welfare of the family, including those who had never married and those who died before the age of twelve, were not even remembered by a spirit tablet in the ancestral temple.[48]

From earliest times it was believed that ancestral spirits were dangerous. If they were not pleased with their living descendants they could mete out severe punishment, including sickness, death, famine, and defeat in battle.[49] This was consistent with the physical spirit component of ancestor worship. The head of the clan had authority to enforce clan rules by punishments including mutilation and death.[50] It was a logical step to assume similar authority in ancestors who were believed to be able to control physical events for good or ill.

During the time of the Western Zhou, the emphasis of ancestor worship shifted away from control of physical events to the moral and ethical.[51] At some unknown time, ancestral temples began to include, along with the spirit tablets, information about the accomplishments and honors of ancestors. When the clans met in their ancestral temples in spring and fall, members were surrounded by reminders of the illustrious deeds of their ancestors and what was expected of them. The sacrificial rituals would be carried out in great detail, with every member kowtowing in order of seniority, participating in the reiteration of the moral and ethical standards and aspirations of the family and renewing in his own heart the filial piety that was the life force of the family.[52] Whether ancestors were viewed as spirits living in the heavens,[53] or as the numinous essence of the family immanent in the sensed world, it was certainly the case that ancestral spirits maintained "an organic relationship with their living descendants."[54]

The individual person was also subject to influences from beyond the organic family. These included not only interactions by marriage, or political and economic association with members of other families, but also interactions with all the organic phenomena of nature. The earth, the sun, wind, water, and other natural phenomena had intrinsic natures of dao and yin/yang that gave rise to their sensed manifestations. Since continuity and contingency were believed to be inherent in the whole universe, the intrinsic nature of earth—or sun, wind, or water—might be deficient at any particular time or place, so that the sun might burn the crops instead of strengthen them, the earth might not yield the needed nutrients, wind might destroy, and water might flood a river basin instead of flowing in appointed channels in suitable amounts.

When natural phenomena were disordered the purposes of human society could not be accomplished. Therefore, it was wise to assume an attitude of respect and deference to the natural spirits as well as ancestral spirits. Emperor Yao, who instructed his astronomical observers to "receive as a guest the rising sun" and to "bid farewell respectfully to the setting sun," was able to establish harmony and prosperity.[55] As the *Book of Changes* so poetically indicates, the subtle hints of impending changes had to be understood if desired consequences were to be attained and unwanted consequences avoided. To move with the ever-changing flux of the universe, and to encourage natural entities to act in accordance with their true natures, it was advisable to address the natural spirits with the same mixture of fealty and fear that characterized the worship of ancestral spirits. In the early period of independent villages these natural spirits were worshiped at the Holy Place, which was believed to control human and agricultural fertility and human solidarity.[56] In later times, every town, *guo*, and kingdom had an altar where the spirits of land and grain were worshiped. This worship was so important that when territory was conquered its land and grain altar was destroyed.[57] The king worshiped his ancestors, the spirits of land and grain in the territory directly ruled by him, and, on behalf of the whole kingdom, the spirit of the whole organic universe, represented as the Lord on High, or from the time of Zhou, as heaven.[58]

Ritual

Ritual evoked and sustained the motivational energy of Chinese society. The dao of a social organism, such as a family, prescribed what should be done, when, and under what conditions. But knowing what should be done was not enough. Motivational energy to manifest the attitudes and perform the acts was also needed. This energy began in emotions, but not every emotion was constructive. Jealousy, selfishness, pride, and greed, which would be destructive of the desired cooperation, had to be rejected. Emotions such as joy or sorrow, which would be constructive in some situations but not others, had to be limited to the appropriate situations. Fleeting emotions had to be sustained, and reinforcing emotions had to be simultaneously evoked. It was the task of ritual to turn spontaneous emotions into constructive attitudes.

In the very ancient Chinese villages the joy felt in the spring as life was being renewed, and the sadness felt in the fall as a cycle of life was ending, and the camaraderie felt in the year-end games and drinking bouts, were fused by rituals at the village Holy Place into a sensed solidarity that provided the motivational energy for the yin activities of the women of the village as they made silk, wove cloth, and tended the houses on the shady slopes, and for the yang activities of the men as they planted, cultivated, and harvested the crops in the sunny fields. Indeed the sensed solidarity sustained even time and space by causing events to occur where and when they should. (Time and space were composed of concrete groupings of events that were correctly ordered geometrically and rhythmically.) As memory of the experienced solidarity faded, the motivation declined. Things did not get done, time became weak, space diluted, and the sensed solidarity had to be rekindled by another periodic ritual.[59] In this case the motivating attitude emerged in custom and usage over a long period of time in which few changes occurred in the organization of society.

After Chinese society became hierarchical the heads of social units began to draw into their service increasing numbers of culture experts. New techniques and technologies required social changes. Consolidation of small units into larger units also led to social changes. The head of a clan wanted the rules of his lineage to apply to all. The new feudal lord wanted his clan rules to apply throughout his territory. The king wanted to establish the order of events throughout his kingdom. In this situation, ritual was not merely rededication of the same people to the same ways of working together. Instead, new people had to be motivated to cooperate, and people who had worked together in familiar ways had to be motivated to work together in new ways. Ritual could no longer be left

to evolve in custom and usage. A conscious process of building spontaneous emotions into constructive attitudes had to be devised.

Those with governing authority were in a position to lead in the
development of ritual because there was no priesthood. During the Shang
and early Zhou periods shamanism was important.[60] The shaman was
believed to be able to move back and forth from the realm of the living
to the realm of the gods and spirits, perhaps aided by the winged animals
depicted on sacrificial vessels.[61] However, the king was always the chief
shaman, although professional men and women shamans assisted him.[62]
And the purpose of approaching the gods and ancestral spirits, at least in
the Zhou period, was not to persuade the gods to control events in ways
beneficial to the supplicant, but to gain access to the wisdom of heaven,
which would enable the king to correctly order events on earth.[63]

First of all, the king, territorial lord, or clan patriarch, employed ritual
to express his own inner feelings. The *Li Ji*, one of the three classics on
ritual, says:

> [Rituals] . . . are not a thing coming to a man from without; it issues from within him,
> and has its birth in his heart. When the heart is deeply moved, expression is given to
> it by ceremonies; and hence, only men of ability and virtues can give complete
> exhibition to the idea of [rituals].[64]

If the king sincerely felt reverence, awe, and submission, his spirit was
ready to serve as the clear channel between heaven and earth. Manifesting those feelings would signal that readiness to all the spirits whose
interpenetrating influences affected events in the ever-changing organic
universe. At the same time the king's manifested feelings would evoke
responsive feelings in those who participated in the rituals. The royal
princes, great officers, and ordinary officers, the lords and their great and
ordinary officers, and the clan patriarchs would, in turn, conduct rituals,
thus carrying the regulation of attitudes down to every person.

Following is an example of the molding of feelings into the attitude
of reverence in the ritual of sacrifice to an ancestor:

> What the sacrifice of a filial son should be can be known. While he is standing (waiting
> for the service to commence), he should be reverent, with his body somewhat bent;
> while he is engaged in carrying forward the service, he should be reverent, with an
> expression of pleasure; when he is presenting offerings, he should be reverent, with
> an expression of desire. He should then retire and stand, as if he were about to receive
> orders; when he has removed the offerings and (finally) retires, the expression of
> reverent gravity should continue to be worn on his face. Such is the sacrifice of the
> filial son.

To stand without any inclination of the body would show insensibility; to carry the service forward without an expression of pleasure would show indifference; to present the offerings without an expression of desire (that they may be enjoyed) would show a want of love; to retire and stand without seeming to expect to receive orders would show pride; to retire and stand, after the removal of the offerings, without an expression of reverent gravity would show a forgetfulness of the parent to whom he owes his being. A sacrifice so conducted would be wanting in its proper characteristics.[65]

Through the leadership of those in authority in the feudal society of the Western Zhou dynasty, an exhaustive and detailed body of rituals was developed covering every activity of every person in Chinese society. Perhaps inevitably, the ritual evocation of correct attitude merged with the substance of the duty, so that *li* came to mean not only the ritual but the right action that was sought to be induced by the ritual. *Li*, in this meaning of propriety, was to play an extremely important part in later Chinese thought. In the *Li Ji*, a collection of Confucian treatises including the extremely influential *Great Learning* and *Doctrine of the Mean*, *li* refers to principles by which to regulate one's life.[66]

The Chinese person was guided and motivated to obedient performance of duty first by his or her own intrinsic nature, second by supervision of superiors in the living family, third by ancestral spirits, and fourth by the spirits of all the other organic entities in the universe. Pervasive ritual constantly reminded everyone of the attitude that would induce obedience. If, despite all these influences, a person still failed to obey, punishment was the final resort.

Punishment

At a later period, Chinese philosophers would dispute whether human beings were born with feelings of greed, envy, and hate and were, therefore, evil by nature, or were born with feelings of commiseration, shame, and reverence and were good by nature.[67] In the period with which we are presently concerned, we have only the emerging ideas of organic entities, prescriptive names, and the transmission of social natures to the next generation by cultural means, subject to contingency as well as continuity. In light of these aspects of the Chinese common consciousness, proper behavior, in every situation, was defined for the paradigm individual of the social entity (family, clan, town, *guo*, kingdom) and implanted in each generation by education and ritual. Therefore, if the individual, in a given situation, did not do what he or she should, the fault lay with those charged with instructing and inspiring that individual.

Disorder in the kingdom indicated that the king was not doing his job as the clear channel between heaven and earth.[68] And if, instead of correcting his own deficiencies, he punished the people, this was oppression that warranted overthrow and the transfer of the mandate of heaven to the founder of a new dynasty.[69] This was said to be the nature of the transition from the Hsia to the Shang, and from the Shang to the Zhou.[70] No wonder that tradition ascribed the origin of punishments to a barbarian tribe, the Miao, of whom it was said: "The Miao people made no use of spiritual cultivation, but controlled by means of punishments (*hsing*), creating five oppressive punishments, which they called law (*fa*)."[71] These punishments, which were tattooing the face (or branding the forehead), amputation of the nose, amputation of one or both feet, castration, or death (by public decapitation), were used by all three pre-imperial dynasties.[72] But scholars agree that the use of punishments was a symptom of social disorder, rather than a means of keeping or restoring order.[73]

These harsh, public, corporal punishments were unlikely to have much effect in correcting the behavior of the individuals who were punished. But they did eliminate, or exclude, those individuals from positions where they could harm family, or state, by destructive or obstructive actions. Like individual plants that did not exhibit the characteristics of millet, punished persons were effectively culled from the current crop of civilized human beings so they could not deleteriously affect others in their own generation or the next. Sometimes, a whole clan was exterminated, but this may have been as much to obviate revenge by a powerful unit in feudal society as to reach all those deemed to be likely to engage in destructive or obstructive activities.[74]

Notes

1. Gray L. Dorsey, *Jurisculture: Greece and Rome* (New Brunswick, N.J.: Transaction Publishers, 1989), pp. 7–12.
2. Ibid., pp. 64–71.
3. Gray L. Dorsey, *Jurisculture: India* (New Brunswick, N.J.: Transaction Publishers, 1990), pp. 95–101.
4. Li Chi, *The Beginning of Chinese Civilization* (Seattle and London: University of Washington Press, 1957), p. 20.

5. K. C. Chang, *Art, Myth, and Ritual: The Path to Political Authority* (Cambridge, Mass.: Harvard University Press, 1983), pp. 9–12, 33–34.
6. See text above at chap. 5, note 4.
7. Chang, *Art, Myth, and Ritual*, pp. 9, 44–55.
8. Ibid., p. 45.
9. David N. Keightley, "The Religious Commitment: Shang Theology and the Genesis of Chinese Political Culture," *History of Religions*, vol. 17, (February-May 1978), pp. 212–13.
10. Chang, *Art, Myth, and Ritual*, pp. 44–45.
11. Herrlee G. Creel, *The Origins of Statecraft in China*, vol. 1 (Chicago and London: University of Chicago Press, 1970), pp. 44–45; Wm. Theodore de Bary, Wing-tsit Chan, and Burton Watson, *Sources of Chinese Tradition*, vol. 1 (New York: Columbia University Press, 1960), pp. 5–6.
12. Chang, *Art, Myth, and Ritual*, p. 34; de Bary, Chan, and Watson, *Sources of Chinese Tradition*, pp. 176–77.
13. Donald J. Munro, *The Concept of Man in Early China* (Stanford, Calif.: Stanford University Press, 1969), p. 85.
14. Joseph Needham, *Science and Civilisation in China*, vol. 2 (Cambridge: Cambridge University Press, 1956), p. 287; Marcel Granet, *La Pensée Chinoise* (Paris: Éditions Albin Michel, 1950), pp. 102–3; Nelson I. Wu, *Chinese and Indian Architecture* (New York: George Brazilier, 1963), pp. 41, 46, and plates 129, 130.
15. Chang, *Art, Myth, and Ritual*, pp. 16–17, note 12.
16. Wing-tsit Chan, *A Source Book in Chinese Philosophy* (Princeton, N.J.: Princeton University Press, 1963), p. 88.
17. Chang, *Art, Myth, and Ritual*, p. 34.
18. Charles O. Hucker, *China's Imperial Past* (Stanford, Calif.: Stanford University Press, 1975), p. 22.
19. John K. Fairbank, Edwin O. Reischauer, and Albert M. Craig, *East Asia: Tradition and Transformation* (Boston, Mass.: Houghton Mifflin, 1973), p. 157.
20. K. C. Chang, *Early Chinese Civilization: Anthropological Perspectives* (Cambridge, Mass.: Harvard University Press, 1976), pp. 27–28, 36–37, 40–41.
21. Chang, *Art, Myth, and Ritual*, pp. 17–20.
22. Chang, *Early Chinese Civilization*, pp. 27–41.
23. Chang, *Art, Myth, and Ritual*, pp. 81–106, 124.
24. Ibid., pp. 16–17, note 12.
25. Creel, *The Origins of Statecraft*, pp. 32–34, 324–28; Derk Bodde, *Essays on Chinese Civilization* (Princeton, N.J.: Princeton University Press, 1981), pp. 88–98.
26. Bodde, *Essays on Chinese Civilization*, p. 94.
27. Ibid.
28. Chang, *Art, Myth, and Ritual*, pp. 16–17, note 12.
29. See text above, at chap. 5, note 32.
30. Chang, *Art, Myth, and Ritual*, pp. 26–27.
31. Hucker, *China's Imperial Past*, pp. 41–47.
32. Needham, *Science and Civilisation in China*, vol. 2, p. 289.
33. Chang, *Art, Myth, and Ritual*, pp. 16–20, 26–27.
34. See text above at chap. 5, note 35.
35. Wolfram Eberhard, *A History of China* (Berkeley, Calif.: University of California Press, 1969), p. 32.

36. Marcel Granet, Kathleen Innes, trans., *Chinese Civilization* (New York: Meridian Books, 1958), p. 250 et seq.
37. Herrlee G. Creel, *The Birth of China: A Study of the Formative Period of Chinese Civilization* (New York: John Day, 1937), pp. 335-36.
38. Chang, *Art, Myth, and Ritual*, pp. 9-15.
39. Creel, *The Birth of China*, pp. 170, 180.
40. Ibid., p. 178; Chang, *Art, Myth, and Ritual*, p. 8; Benjamin Schwartz, *The World of Thought in Ancient China* (Cambridge, Mass.: Harvard University Press, 1985), p. 21.
41. Chang, *Art, Myth, and Ritual*, p. 8.
42. Creel, *The Birth of China*, pp. 338-39.
43. Chang, *Art, Myth, and Ritual*, pp. 15-17, 33-41.
44. Ibid., p. 37.
45. Creel, *The Birth of China*, p. 336.
46. C. K. Yang, *Religion in Chinese Society* (Berkeley: University of California Press, 1961), pp. 40-41.
47. Chang, *Art, Myth, and Ritual*, p. 41.
48. Ibid., p. 42.
49. Creel, *The Birth of China*, p. 175.
50. Chang, *Art, Myth, and Ritual*, p. 35.
51. Creel, *The Birth of China*, p. 344.
52. K. C. Wu, *The Chinese Heritage* (New York: Crown Publishers, 1982), pp. 35-37; Yang, *Religion in Chinese Society*, pp. 40-41; Raymond Dawson, *The Chinese Experience* (New York: Charles Scribner's and Sons, 1978), pp. 156-57.
53. Yang, *Religion in Chinese Society*, pp. 31-33.
54. Schwartz, *The World of Thought in Ancient China*, p. 21.
55. Needham, *Science and Civilisation in China*, vol. 3, pp. 186-88.
56. Granet, *Chinese Civilization*, pp. 170-71.
57. Creel, *The Birth of China*, pp. 180-81, 337.
58. Ibid., 337; Schwartz, *The World of Thought in Ancient China*, pp. 21, 35-36; Chang, *Art, Myth, and Ritual*, pp. 45, 47.
59. Granet, *Penseé*, pp. 86-111.
60. Chang, *Art, Myth, and Ritual*, pp. 44-55.
61. Ibid., pp. 56-80.
62. Ibid., p. 45.
63. Chan, *A Source Book in Chinese Philosophy*, pp. 3-4.
64. Chang, *Art, Myth, and Ritual*, p. 41.
65. Ch'u Chai and Winberg Chai, *Li Chi: Book of Rites*, vol. 2 (New Hyde Park, N.Y.: University Books, 1967), p. 215.
66. Fung Yu-lan, *A Short History of Chinese Philosophy* (New York: Macmillan Co., 1958), pp. 43-44.
67. de Bary, Chan and Watson, *Sources of Chinese Tradition*, vol. 1, p. 104; Fung Yu-lan, *A History of Chinese Philosophy*, vol. 1, *The Period of the Philosophers* (Princeton, N.J.: Princeton University Press, 1983), pp. 124-28.
68. Yang, *Religion in Chinese Society*, pp. 128-29; Schwartz, *The World of Thought in Ancient China*, pp. 50-51.
69. Schwartz, *The World of Thought in Ancient China*, pp. 46-47, 50-51; Chang, *Art, Myth, and Ritual*, pp. 34-35.
70. Ibid.

71. Derk Bodde and Clarence Morris, *Law in Imperial China* (Cambridge, Mass.: Harvard University Press, 1967), p. 13.
72. Ibid., p. 76; A. F. P. Hulsewe, *Remnants of Han Law*, vol. 1 (Leiden, Netherlands: E. J. Brill, 1955), pp. 124–28.
73. Creel, *The Origins of Statecraft*, p. 162.
74. Creel, *The Birth of China*, pp. 341, 344, 353–54; Hulsewe, *Remnants of Han Law*, pp. 112–22.

7

Seeds of Change

The Shang kings based their authority upon claimed access to the Lord on High, who could supernaturally cause beneficial or harmful events. The Zhou kings based their authority on the mandate of heaven, which was the embodiment of the natural order of the universe.[1] This transition was the culmination of a rational trend in the development of Chinese consciousness.

That trend had begun with individual perception of particular events— a plant seen, tasted, touched, cultivated. The first step in preserving this perception beyond individual memory was the quipu knot, which merely aided individual memory. Next came the Chinese written word, which preserved a particular sensed experience, retaining it more dependably than the unspecific quipu knot and making it transmissible to others. Next, these individual bits of sensed experience were associated in accordance with nascent conceptions of continuity, contingency, prescriptive name, space/time continuum, dao, change, yin/yang life force, harmony, and unity, thus gradually turning the kaleidoscopic view of reality as an immediate unreconstructed sense experience into an ever-increasing number of clear lenses through which sensed reality was seen in terms of underlying order.

These clear vistas evoked the invention of techniques and technologies, and made possible the organization of human activities that were increasingly effective in exploiting the agricultural resources of the Yellow River basin. The specialists, in searching out the clear understanding of sensed reality (protoscientists) and the implications of that understanding for ordering human activities (protoethicists), gradually increased in number and competence. The politically ambitious gathered increasing numbers of these culture specialists under their control; they supported and encouraged them, and used them in the competition between rulers for control of ever more land and people. The idea emerged of one perfect lens through which the complete order of all reality could be seen with perfect clarity. The mandate of heaven designated the Zhou king as the channel through which the complete and perfect clarity of this heavenly perspective on reality could be suffused into all creatures and events on earth. The virtue of a ruler who could make this happen would, indeed, be clear and brilliant, and all under heaven would do well to obey him.

The Western Zhou kings could not directly carry out the mandate of heaven throughout the empire. The Chinese consciousness was not yet sufficiently explicit to permit the training of a body of professional administrators.[2] In the absence of such a bureaucracy, it was impossible to exercise centralized control throughout the Zhou territory, which was as large as the combined areas of France, Belgium, and the Netherlands.[3] The alternative was feudal states, whose heads owed familial allegiance to the king.[4] Of the seventy-one feudal states in the Western Zhou empire, royal kinsmen ruled fifty-three, and many other rulers were linked to the Zhou clan by repeated intermarriages.[5] Since there were about 1,800 states at the beginning of the Western Zhou period, and about 1,200 when it ended in 771 B.C.E., it is obvious that the Zhou states, although dominant, did not exercise complete control throughout the territory of China.[6]

The Zhou established garrison towns, which contained quarters for artisans and were surrounded by villages for peasant farmers. The Zhou feudal lords and nobles had to gain the submission of the farmers in these villages, govern them, and tax them.[7] Between these garrison towns lived people that were subjugated, but not integrated into the social, economic, and political institutions of Zhou. In the eastern part of the empire these people were agrarian and relatively peaceful. But around Xian, the capital of the Western Zhou, the subjugated population consisted of nomadic Turks and Mongols, and seminomadic Tibetans.[8] The Western Zhou king had sufficient fungible resources from tribute, taxes, and gifts to support fourteen armies, with which he fought uprisings of barbarian tribes, with the help of the armies of feudal states.[9] The king's armies were also used to keep trade and travel safe by establishing guard posts and military patrols on principal roads.[10] The feudal lords had their hands full organizing and supervising the activities of their subjects and pacifying surrounding tribes. They paid less and less attention to central direction although they continued to be dependent upon the king to conduct the worship of heaven.[11] As an entry to the *Zuo Zhuan* for 535 B.C.E. put it:

> [T]he king has the ruler (of each feudal state) as his subject; the rulers have the great prefects as their subjects; the prefects have their officers; the officers have their subalterns; the subalterns have their multitude of petty officers; the petty officers have their assistants; the assistants have their employees; the employees have their menials. For the menials there are helpers, for the horses there are grooms, and for the cattle there are cowherds. And thus there is provision for all things.[12]

Despite its tenuous nature the Western Zhou empire was remarkably stable for most of its existence. After the opening years of the dynasty there was a period of two centuries in which there were no engagements between Chinese armies.[13] As a part of its efforts to governing effectively at a distance and indirectly, the Western Zhou significantly increased the uses of writing, which had the effect of making the Chinese consciousness more explicit. From earliest times the Chinese had kept "lineage tablets" of the great families in the ancestral temples. Also, "tablet records" contained a chronology of a ruler's reign and brief accounts of events in each year.[14] The Zhou kept detailed records of everything. Financial records were extensive. Bestowals of offices or lands to royal retainers were recorded in a "commanding document" that contained a list of the things given to the recipient of favor, including land, persons, regalia, cowrie shells (used as money), ceremonial vessels, horses, and silk. The commanding document also included the charge to the new feudal lord indicating his duties and obligations. A copy was given to the recipient of the grant and a copy was kept in the royal archives. The royal archives also contained documents on the relations between feudal lords, and even some important private persons. The staffs of the Director of Agreements and the Director of Covenants recorded treaties and covenants between feudal lords, and some contracts between private persons. The parties were each given a copy of the document and a copy was retained in the royal archives. When a dispute arose, enforcement was in accordance with the archival copy. Royal officials sometimes served as guarantors of contracts.[15]

In addition to the extensive archival use of writing, the Zhou used written records to improve planning and administration. Creel writes:

> Written instructions and programs were drawn up for many sorts of activity. When the Chou [Zhou] were about to build their new capital near the present site of Loyang, the Duke of Chou [Zhou] gave out written orders to the chiefs of the various groups

of the conquered Shang people, who were to perform the labor. After the death of King Ch'eng [Cheng], a written program was drawn up for the ceremonies of his funeral and the accession of the new King. An army, sent by the King on a distant mission, carried written orders; . . .[16]

The oral instruction was effective only so long as it was accurately remembered. The written instruction retained its clarity as a guide to those with good intentions and as the basis for corrective supervision of those of bad faith. Also, writing carried an aura of useful mystery, especially to common people. The *Book of Poetry* contains a lament by a soldier on a distant mission under written orders: "Do we not long to return? But we are in awe of the writing on those bamboo slips."[17]

The Zhou also increased the use of historical records. The early Zhou kings admonished princes, lords, and great officers to follow the policies and rituals of the Shang that were wise and resulted in harmony and tranquillity.[18] Thus, guidance and motivation in particular cases were generalized into principles of government and attributed to the order of heaven.[19] The Zhou also greatly expanded the written records of their own policies and rituals in order that every action of a ruler could be judged and the good emulated and the bad avoided by subsequent generations.[20] The king was not the only ruler who wished to be remembered and honored. Feudal lords saw to it that detailed annals were kept of their accomplishments. These state chronicles were recorded on bamboo and on bronze vessels. Little of the bamboo has survived, but much of the bronze has been recovered in recent decades.[21]

All of these written records, and especially the state chronicles, provided the subject matter in terms of which good and bad policies could be argued. For the first time culture specialists could begin to function *as* culture specialists. Up to this time culture specialists had not been employed to study and teach. They had been employed as administrators, although it was their knowledge that made them good administrators. Soon there would be a need for a systematic reconsideration of the Chinese consciousness and some culture specialists would metamorphose into scholars, fully occupied in studying and teaching.

In 771 B.C.E. two feudal states and two barbarian tribes defeated King Yu, killed him, and carried off the imperial treasure. Other feudal lords set up a son of Yu as the new king and he moved the seat of administration to a previously unused eastern capital near modern Loyang.[22] This ended the period of the Western Zhou and began the period of the Eastern Zhou, which, in turn, is usually divided into the Spring and Autumn period from 770 to 481, and the Warring States period from 481 to 221 B.C.E.[23] Despite the Western Zhou dependence upon rational understanding instead of divine favor, the qualification for office was birth, not knowledge or ability.[24] The collapse of the Western Zhou marked the failure of this feudal system at the level of the empire. During the Spring and Autumn period the noble families lost control within the states to those who were more able in war, commerce, and administration, setting off both upward and downward social mobility.[25] At the same time the practical arts were flourishing, creating new opportunities for wealth and power for those able to utilize them.[26]

During the Spring and Autumn period, the feudal states, no longer restricted to territory granted them by the king, began to incorporate surrounding tribes, creating something closer to modern territorial states instead of garrison towns. This entailed war against tribes and war with each other.[27] The result was a tremendous consolidation, from 1,200 states at the beginning of the Spring and Autumn period to just over a hundred states, of which only fourteen were considered major states, at the beginning of the Warring States period.[28] During the Warring States period war became more inclusive and intensive. More inclusive because peasants were organized as infantry, whereas battles were formerly fought by the upper classes using bronze chariots. More intensive because of the invention and utilization of the crossbow, iron and steel weapons, and poison gas.[29] Finally, in 221 B.C.E. the king of Qin conquered all other states and proclaimed himself emperor of all of China.

The whole of the Eastern Zhou period was a time of change and crisis. The perfect time for those who could offer solutions to problems. A time when culture specialists who were so inclined could become scholars, occupied full time with studying and teaching. Thus arose a new institution in which students lived with a master and learned from him how to restore harmony and unity in the world.[30] Confucius, who was born in 551 B.C.E., was the first such master.

Notes

1. Herrlee G. Creel, *The Origins of Statecraft in China*, vol. 1 (Chicago: University of Chicago Press, 1970), pp. 83–84.
2. Ibid., pp. 419–23.

3. Ibid., p. 101; Geoffrey Barraclough, ed., *The Times Atlas of World History* (London: Times Books Limited, 1978), p. 62.
4. Creel, *The Origins of Statecraft in China*, p. 423; Cho-yun Hsu, *Ancient China in Transition* (Stanford, Calif.: Stanford University Press, 1965), p. 3.
5. Hsu, *Ancient China in Transition*, p. 53.
6. K. C. Chang, *Art, Myth and Ritual: The Path to Political Authority in Ancient China* (Cambridge, Mass.: Harvard University Press, 1983), pp. 26-29.
7. Wolfram Eberhard, *A History of China* (Berkeley, Calif.: University of California Press, 1969), pp. 32-35.
8. Ibid.
9. Creel, *The Origins of Statecraft in China*, pp. 315, 351.
10. Ibid., pp. 134, 155, 307, 349, 414-16.
11. Eberhard, *A History of China*, p. 35-37.
12. Creel, *The Origins of Statecraft in China*, p. 261.
13. Ibid., pp. 45, 54-55.
14. K. C. Wu, *The Chinese Heritage* (New York: Crown Publishers, 1982), pp. 35-37.
15. Creel, *The Origins of Statecraft in China*, pp. 184-85.
16. Ibid., p. 128.
17. Ibid.
18. James Legge, *The Chinese Classics*, vol. 3, *The Shoo-king* (Hong Kong: n.p., 1865), pp. 381-98, 474-86.
19. Ibid.
20. Herrlee G. Creel, *The Birth of China* (New York: Reynal & Hitchcock, 1937), p. 259.
21. Ibid., pp. 259-67.
22. Creel, *The Origins of Statecraft in China*, pp. 438-39.
23. Arthur Cotterell, *The First Emperor of China* (New York: Holt, Rinehart and Winston, 1981), pp. 84, 101.
24. Hsu, *Ancient China in Transition*, p. 3.
25. Ibid., pp. 86-92.
26. Robert Temple, *The Genius of China: 3000 Years of Science, Discovery and Invention* (New York: Simon & Schuster, 1989), pp. 15-20.
27. Hsu, *Ancient China in Transition*, p. 40.
28. K. C. Chang, *Art, Myth and Ritual*, pp. 26-27.
29. Eberhard, *A History of China*, pp. 51-53; Temple, *The Genius of China*, pp. 42-44, 215-24.
30. Hsu, *Ancient China in Transition*, pp. 100-05.

PART II

The Classical Period
(From the Birth of Confucius to the End of the Han Dynasty)

8

Philosophy and Science

To refer to the reported thoughts of Confucius, or Mo Zi (Mo Tzu), or Lao Zi (Lao Tzu) as "philosophy" is to lead the Western reader to expect systematic arguments. What one finds, however, according to Fung Yu-lan, are aphorisms, apothegms, allusions, and illustrations.[1] These modes of expression are imprecise, suggestive, and evocative—not at all suitable for Western philosophy, which values the precise, articulate, and denotative. Western philosophy and Chinese philosophy differ in modes of expression because they differ in the answers to fundamental questions, and because of the time those answers were reached.

Until the sixth century B.C.E. the Greeks believed that events were caused by gods outside things pushing them about. It was the first of the pre-Socratic philosophers, Thales (c. 580 B.C.E.), who rejected that view with his aphorism, "All things are full of gods," by which he meant that what causes a thing to function in a certain way is within the thing itself.[2] If this is accepted, it becomes necessary to discover the real nature of things, in order to understand why events happen, to anticipate, and possibly to beneficially influence, events. But, if events can be influenced it also becomes necessary to determine the ideal, toward which events should be nudged. And then procedures are needed for correctly applying knowledge of reality so as to influence events in the desired way. Greek philosophy was centrally concerned with the real and the ideal. Satisfactory procedures for influencing physical events were not developed in the West until the birth of modern science in the seventeenth century.

The pre-Socratics started looking for something simple and elemental that combined to form all gross, complex, observed objects. Earth, air, fire, and water were proposed, by one or another pre-Socratic, as the ultimate stuff. Pythagoras, on the other hand, said that ultimate reality is number, not material stuff.[3] Heraclitus said that change is ultimate. Soon, the pre-Socratics began to trust the functioning of their minds more than the testimony of their senses. Parmenides, who was held in awe and reverence by Socrates, sought the basic nature of reality by asking himself, "What does it mean, when I say, 'What is, is'?" Others agreed that truth lay in reason, rather than experience. Thus human reason became the measure of external reality. What was illogical could not exist. Because of this mindset the pre-Socratics had to revise their view of reality when they ran into a logical contradiction.

For instance, Democritus of Abdera suggested that everything is composed of indivisible bits of matter, called atoms. But then it was discovered that in some triangles the lengths of the sides and the hypotenuse cannot all be expressed in whole numbers, no matter what the unit of measure. Accordingly, the Greeks gave up the atomic theory, and it was not taken up again until modern times. However, in the attempt to salvage his cosmology, Democritus said that the incommensurability was not in the real world but only in the sensed world.

Plato firmly fixed in Western thought the distinction between the apparent world, with its images and common sense objects, and the real world, known only by reason, and characterized by a single, noncontradictory, eternal, universal, order. He also made the paradigm definition of the ideal in Western civilization, saying that action in accordance with the order of the rational world is good, thought in accordance with that order is true, and structure in accordance with that order is beautiful. Only the few, whose rational souls had overcome (by years of training in arithmetic, plain and solid geometry, astronomy, and dialectics in Plato's academy) the disordering effects of embodied birth, could know the order of the rational world. Since that order should be reflected in the sensed world, only those few who had achieved clear and pure reason should govern. Ergo, the philosopher-king.[4]

Plato was the high watermark, in the ancient world, of the view that the real is abstract, general, and mathematical, known by pure reason. Aristotle shifted Western thought to classification, studying various life forms and classifying their characteristics. This orientation continued into the Middle Ages. According to Whitehead, "[c]lassification is a halfway house between the immediate concreteness of the individual thing and the complete abstraction of mathematical notions."[5] During the Middle Ages, efforts to cope with the external world were directed by "a metaphysical analysis of the nature of things, which would thereby determine how things acted and functioned."[6] Mathematical notions were again seriously considered in the seventeenth century. This time the relation of mathematical notions to the facts of nature was not speculative, as with Plato, but, rather, followed the procedures of measurement, geometrical relations, and types of order, which resulted in modern science.[7] The necessity of understanding reality in terms of postulated entities with fixed characteristics that functioned in invariant ways seemed to have been irrevocably established. Newton's laws of motion apply to postulated material bodies in absolute, true, mathematical space and time, not to observed objects in relative, apparent, observed space and time.[8] Modern science took over from philosophy and theology all calculations with respect to the external material world. As a result the two dominant themes in modern philosophy, according to Whitehead, have been psychology and epistemology (the mind in itself, and the mind as it relates to the external world).[9]

Whereas the Greeks believed in the divine causation of physical events until the eve of Greek natural philosophy, the Chinese began to move away from supernatural causation as early as 1100 B.C.E.[10] Therefore, they needed to know the real nature of the world, determine the ideal, and develop procedures for anticipating and beneficially influencing events about six hundred years before Chinese philosophy began. These questions were partially answered, in the intervening period, by anonymous persons who were not interested in knowledge for its own sake; they wanted knowledge in order to plan and direct activities. They were farmers and administrators. They did not look for something simple, elemental, and unchanging that gave rise to the changing characteristics of sensed objects. They did not think of entities as discrete objects possessing characteristics of extension, weight, color, and density. They thought of entities as organic processes, moving through sets of observable characteristics.

The same anonymous persons developed the ideal. The farmer's acute and self-interested observation of the changes of form and substance of a plant could lead to a sense of what it could become if all its potentialities were fully developed. Observation of the effects of various types of soil, various amounts of water, sun, wind, of weeding, of culling, of cross-pollination could lead to knowledge of how to move particular plants toward the ideal, as indicated by its prescriptive name. The Chinese understood causation in terms of the symbiotic effects of such associations within a harmonious, organic universe, instead of linear impulsion of one discrete object upon another. The nature of the Chinese written language, the calendar, the use of numerical symbols to refer to sets of sensed phenomena, and the *Book of Changes* with its play of numbers suggesting associations of the phenomena to which they refer, all indicate that for this period reality was believed to consist of the totality of correctly ordered sensed phenomena.[11]

Chinese philosophers inherited the traditional view that the world of sensed experience is the real world. Fung Yu-lan suggested this by his statement that the outlook of Chinese philosophers was that of the farmer. The philosophers' education, he said, "gave them the power to express what an actual farmer felt but was incapable of expressing himself. This expression took the form of Chinese philosophy, literature, and art."[12] Fung also made this suggestion explicit in a response to F. S. C. Northrop. In a major initiative to enhance appreciation of non-Western philosophies, Northrop rejected the Western view that *only* the world known indirectly by reason is real. He said that concepts the complete meaning of which is given by immediate apprehension are just as real as concepts the complete meaning of which is given by the postulates of a logical theory; they are just different kinds of concepts responding to different views of reality.[13] This was the thesis of Northrop's paper in the 1939 East-West Philosophers' Conference, which he further expounded in the widely influential book, *The Meeting of East and West*.[14] In his *Short History of Chinese Philosophy*, written in 1946–47, Fung said that Northrop's distinction between concepts that refer to sensed experience and concepts that refer to postulated, logically related propositions grasps "the fundamental difference between Chinese and Western philosophy."[15]

In light of the tremendous power over physical nature achieved by modern Western science and technology, it might appear that the Chinese view of sensed reality, developed by the ancient culture specialists and accepted by the philosophers, must have resulted in a very low capacity to understand, anticipate, and beneficially influence physical events. Lucien Lévy-Bruhl, one of the founders of anthropology, said that to be without modern Western science was to live in a world of magic and superstition, in which no two things are connected in a way that can be verified or predicted.[16] Nevertheless, the Chinese, relying solely upon sensed experience, developed sufficient control of natural events to enable them to support a population in 400 B.C.E. estimated at 25 million (about one-fourth of the world population at that time), despite the constant wars of the period.[17]

The Greek abstract and mathematical view of reality ultimately led, for instance, to the knowledge that graphite, which is black, soft, and slick, is composed of molecules consisting of flat hexagonal sheets of carbon atoms, and that diamonds, which are white and hard, are composed of molecules consisting of carbon atoms bonded in sets of five in the pyramidal shape of a regular tetrahedron.[18] The Chinese studied softness and hardness, sensed that it was the "way" of some organic entities to be soft and others hard, explored the usefulness of various spatial and temporal juxtapositions of these and other entities, and possibilities of changes from softness to hardness, and vice versa. The associational science, thus developed, was producing powerful technologies and techniques before and during the Chinese age of philosophy, and continued to do so for several hundred years. This body of inventions and discoveries has been ignored by philosophers, including Fung Yu-lan, because it was not philosophy.

Chinese inventions and discoveries and the methods of inquiry that resulted in them are now being brought to light in the monumental, multivolume work of the historian of science, Joseph Needham, and his many Chinese collaborators, and in the brilliant one-volume distillation by Robert Temple.[19] Needham has thoroughly discredited the view epitomized by Lévy-Bruhl, but unfortunately he has himself treated Chinese science as an imperfect version of modern Western science, asking why the Chinese, who invented and discovered so much, did not go on to develop "true" science.[20] The pejorative question is avoided if the distinction accepted by Northrop and Fung with respect to philosophy is also applied to science. The real world for the Chinese continued to be the sensed world; they developed the science of the sensed world. The real world for the West became the postulated world; they developed the science of that world.

Chinese associational science produced useful results much earlier than Western postulational science. The first plastic to be discovered by modern Western chemistry was celluloid, in 1869. The next was Bakelite, in 1907. Today the plastics industry is huge and its products are legion. The first plastic to be discovered by Chinese associational science was lacquer, a natural plastic processed from the sap of a tree, in the thirteenth century B.C.E. Lacquer, applied in thin coats to wood, bamboo, or cloth, is strong and durable, not affected by bacteria, water, acids, or alkalis, and is heat resistant to 400 degrees centigrade. Lacquer utensils were used for cooking and serving food. Carved lacquerware was used for furniture, screens, pillows, boxes, bonnets, shoes, weapon accessories, and coffins.[21]

Chinese agricultural productivity was greatly increased, beginning in the sixth century B.C.E., by row cultivation and intensive hoeing, made possible by the invention of the iron plow and the iron hoe. Seed had been sown broadcast by hand, as it was in Europe until the eighteenth century. Seeds that landed on even ground tended not to germinate, and seeds that landed in hollows, where water collected, tended to grow in clumps too thick for good growth. This was very wasteful; as much as half the crop had to be saved for next year's seed. With the iron plow, the soil was prepared in ridges and furrows, and seeds were planted at regular intervals along the ridges. (Beginning in the second century B.C.E. planting was done by multiple seed drills.) With the iron hoe, weeds were eliminated and soil was heaped up around the plants, thus conserving moisture in arid north China. Prosperous farmers used horse-drawn hoes.[22]

The curved moldboard of the Chinese iron plow reduced friction significantly and curled the soil neatly to one side in a continuous ridge. The efficiency of this moldboard, which was not adopted in Europe, again, until the eighteenth century, enabled the Chinese farmer, with one or two oxen, to plow land that the European farmer could not work with less than six or eight. The invention of cast iron, in the fourth century B.C.E. made farm implements and iron weapons cheaper and more plentiful. Cast iron requires a large supply of oxygen and therefore an efficient blast furnace. The Chinese were able to develop this efficiency by inventing, also in the fourth century B.C.E., the double-acting piston bellows. By means of an ingenious set of chambers, the piston was caused to pump air coming and going. China had good refractory clay for the walls of the blast furnace, and they lowered the temperature needed to melt iron from 1130 to 950 degrees centigrade by the use of up to 6 percent of phosphorus in the iron mixture. Of course they did not know it as the chemical element phosphorus, but by their associational method of investigation they had learned to put in the right amount of "black earth," which, in fact, was iron phosphate. The double-acting piston bellows was never invented or used in the West. Blast furnaces were to be found in the late eighth century in Scandinavia, but cast iron was not widely available in Europe until the late fourteenth century. In the third century B.C.E. the Chinese learned to take the brittleness out of cast iron by holding it at a high temperature for a week or more.[23]

Although the Chinese were not the first to make steel, they were the first to make it from cast iron. Cast iron is about 4.5 percent carbon. Steel is up to 1.8 percent carbon. Wrought iron has only traces of carbon. In the second century B.C.E. the Chinese learned to make steel by heating cast iron and blowing air over it, thus oxidizing, and thereby removing, some of the carbon. Of course, they understood this process not in the chemical terms it has just been stated, but in terms of their associational science. They called cast iron "raw iron," steel "great iron," and wrought iron "ripe iron." They understood that the cast iron was losing something, which they called "vital juices." The Chinese called this method of making steel "the hundred refinings method," because it had to be done over and over, testing the result for hardness or softness, brittleness or elasticity. Steel was used for improved weapons. Wrought iron was used for suspension bridges capable of carrying vehicles, beginning perhaps as early as the first century B.C.E. The first Western suspension bridge capable of carrying vehicles was built over the Merrimac River in Massachusetts in 1809.[24]

The efficiency of transport by horse-drawn carts was significantly increased by the invention of a better harness. Everywhere in the ancient world a harness consisted of a strap around the horse's neck, above the sternum, and a strap around the ribs, behind the front legs. Lines for pulling the load were attached where these two met, at the top of the shoulders. This is called a throat and girth harness. As soon as the horse started to pull the load the strap around its neck began to choke it. Throat and girth harness was used in Europe until the eighth century. It was so inefficient that grain from Italian farms could not be hauled to Rome in sufficient quantities to feed the population, and so grain was brought by ship from Egypt. In the fourth century B.C.E. the Chinese invented the trace harness, which consists of a strap around the sternum running horizontally around the horse's hind quarters and held in place by connecting straps over the back. Load bearing lines are attached half way along the side. The pressure of the load is borne by the breast bone instead of the neck. In the third century B.C.E. the Chinese invented the horse collar, which transmits the load to the horse's frame even more effectively.[25]

The efficiency of separating grain from husks and stalks was greatly increased by the Chinese invention in the second century B.C.E. of the rotary winnowing fan. Prior to that date, and until the eighteenth century in the West, the harvested grain was thrown up in the air by shovels or winnowing baskets so that the wind could blow away the chaff. This was slow, laborious, and depended upon the weather. With the winnowing fan, the unhusked grain was placed in a hopper and fed down into a tunnel through which a continuous stream of air was forced by a rotary fan. Chaff was blown out a vent at the end, grain dropped through a hole in the bottom. This winnowing fan was made possible by placing a handle at right angles to a wheel. By means of the handle the wheel, in this case a rotary fan, could be easily rotated. The Chinese invented the crank handle in the second century B.C.E. They also used it in well-windlasses, querns, mills, and many machines used in making silk.[26]

Perhaps the epitome of utilizing naturally occurring associations was geobotanical prospecting, in which the presence or condition of a certain plant was found to indicate the presence of a certain mineral in the soil beneath. The Chinese were using the technique as early as the fifth century B.C.E. It was a natural development from their highly proficient study of different types of soils and their suitability for different crops.[27] It would be surprising if the Chinese did not use their technique of referring to sets of sensed phenomena by numerical symbols to explore useful associations not occurring naturally.[28] A play of numbers, as in divinatory procedures, would suggest association of the sensed phenomena referred to by the numbers. Trying out the associations could lead to new discoveries. This occurred with respect to gunpowder.

A Chinese text on making gunpowder (probably of the seventh century C.E.) is titled *Explanation of the Inventory of Metals and Minerals According to the Numbers Five and Nine*. Needham says that when the Chinese found some saltpeter (potassium nitrate), they determined its efficacy by burning samples and testing to see whether the resulting flame would liquify the ores of the "Five Metals." By means of an "elaborate doctrine of categories or affinities," which led them to try "all kinds of permutations and combinations," they finally discovered gunpowder by mixing the right strength saltpeter with the correct amounts of sulfur and charcoal.[29]

The difference between Chinese science and modern Western science can be seen by comparing gunpowder with guncotton, which for most uses today has replaced gunpowder because it is much more powerful, controllable, and cleaner-burning. Gunpowder is a mixture of saltpeter (potassium nitrate), sulfur, and charcoal, all of which occur naturally and can be identified by sensed observation. Guncotton is any of a series of chemical compounds, the most explosive of which is $C_{12}H_{14}O_4(NO_3)_6$. Observation, a technique of imagination (manipulating numerical symbols to suggest fruitful associations of phenomena), and practical experiments were sufficient to discover gunpowder. To invent guncotton it was necessary to step outside sensed experience and to postulate theoretical entities and their relations (atoms, molecules, and the periodic table), which might or might not have any practical consequences.

The Greek philosophers began the use of rational theory, which is expressed mathematically. But it was more than 2000 years before this way of knowing began to yield practical consequences. Without the step into rational theory Chinese science was limited. In the fourth or third century B.C.E. a Mohist philosopher said, "The cessation of motion is due to the opposing force. . . . If there is no opposing force . . . the motion will never stop."[30] In 1686 Newton said, "Every body continues in its state of rest or of uniform motion in a right line unless it is compelled to change that state by forces impressed upon it."[31] The Mohist statement was an isolated insight about observed phenomena. Nothing came of it. Newton's statement was the first law in a scientific theory consisting of eight definitions and three laws. Using these definitions, the solar system can be described uniquely and completely by stating the position and motion (mass, direction, and speed) of each body in the system at a given time (T_1). With this set of data and Newton's laws of motion it is possible to precisely predict the state of that system (the position and motion of each body) at any given time (T_2) in the future.[32]

Western theoretical science made it possible, in the twentieth century, to overcome gravity, and to predict accurately the time at which a projectile thrust into orbit around the sun at a given time, speed, and direction will rendezvous with a given planet many months hence. Chinese associational science never achieved that level of power and precision, but it was already yielding astonishing practical results in the sixth century B.C.E. Therefore, by the time the age of philosophy opened with Confucius, who was born in 551 B.C.E., it must have seemed to the

Chinese that their understanding of reality was correct, even though they had not taken the step from the observed physical into the theoretically known metaphysical. Their procedures for applying that understanding to the beneficial control of physical events must also have seemed satisfactory. It was the social world that was seriously disordered. Even in the social world, the ideal of harmony and unity still held its thrall despite all the conflict and division, because every head of a state sought to rule throughout the civilized world.[33] No wonder that Chinese philosophy was predominantly social and ethical, whereas Greek philosophy was predominantly metaphysical.[34]

Notes

1. Fung Yu-lan, *A Short History of Chinese Philosophy* (New York: Macmillan Co., 1958), p. 12.
2. F. S. C. Northrop, *Science and First Principles* (New York: Macmillan, 1931), p. 3.
3. Gray L. Dorsey, *Jurisculture: Greece and Rome* (New Brunswick, N.J.: Transaction Publishers, 1989) pp. 15–16.
4. Ibid., pp. 22–30, 34–35, 37–51, 54–55.
5. Alfred North Whitehead, *Science and the Modern World* (New York: Macmillan Co., 1925), p. 28.
6. Ibid., p. 39.
7. Ibid., p. 28.
8. Sir Isaac Newton, *Newton's Philosophy of Nature* (New York: Hafner Publishing Company, 1953), pp. 12–26.
9. Whitehead, *Science and the Modern World*, p. 146.
10. See above, chap. 7, text at note 1.
11. See above, chap. 2, text at notes 26–29.
12. Fung Yu-lan, *A Short History of Chinese Philosophy*, p. 18.
13. F. S. C. Northrop, "The Complementary Emphases of Eastern Intuitive Philosophy and Western Scientific Philosophy," in C. A. Moore, ed., *Philosophy, East and West* (Princeton, N.J.: Princeton University Press, 1946), p. 187.
14. F. S. C. Northrop, *The Meeting of East and West* (New York: Macmillan Co., 1946).
15. Fung, *A Short History of Chinese Philosophy*, p. 24.
16. Lucien Levy-Bruhl, trans. Lilian A. Clare, *How Natives Think* (New York: A. Knopf, 1926), pp. 105–36.
17. Wolfram Eberhard, *A History of China* (Berkeley, Calif.: University of California Press, 1969), p. 55; McEvedy and R. Jones, *Atlas of World Population History* (Middlesex, U.K.: Penguin, 1978), figure 6.2.
18. Edward Edelson, "Buckyball, the Magic Molecule," in *Popular Science*, August 1991, p. 52.
19. Joseph Needham, *Science and Civilisation in China*, a multivolume work that has reached sixteen volumes and is not yet completed (Cambridge: Cambridge University Press, 1956-present); Robert Temple, *The Genius of China: 3000 Years of Science, Discovery and Invention* (New York: Simon and Schuster, 1989).
20. Needham, *Science and Civilisation in China*, vol. 1, pp. 3–4, 18–19.

21. Temple, *The Genius of China*, pp. 75–77.
22. Ibid., pp. 15–16, 25.
23. Ibid., pp. 16–20, 42–46.
24. Ibid., pp. 49–50, 58–62.
25. Ibid., pp. 20–23.
26. Ibid., pp. 23–25, 46.
27. Ibid., pp. 159–62.
28. Marcel Granet, *La Penseé Chinoise* (Paris: Éditions Albin Michel, 1950), pp. 149–51.
29. Joseph Needham, "The Guns of Khaifeng-fu: China's Development of Man's First Chemical Explosive," *Times Literary Supplement*, 11 January 1980, pp. 39–41.
30. Temple, *The Genius of China*, p. 161.
31. Newton, *Newton's Philosophy of Nature*, p. 25.
32. Ibid., pp. 12–40.
33. Eberhard, *A History of China*, pp. 51–57.
34. Ibid., pp. 44–45.

9

The Schools of Philosophy

The schools of philosophy, which flourished in China in the fifth to the third centuries B.C.E., grew up in response to the need for new ways of thinking about human relations and activities. Previously, those who mastered some part of the emerging Chinese consciousness used that special knowledge to carry out official functions. They were the rulers, ministers, and officials of states and the heads of families and clans. New techniques and technologies of farming, water control, weaving, building, and defense were developed and applied by persons with those practical responsibilities, and this knowledge was passed on by incumbents to their successors. There were no private purveyors or private consumers of education.[1]

The disintegration of the feudal society of the Western Zhou created the need for independent thinking. Traditional ways of doing things no longer worked; someone had to think about what should be done in the new circumstances. Personal dislocations resulted in educated men who no longer held official positions, and were, therefore, free to think independently and to teach others.[2] Some of these ex-officials offered only the special knowledge of their former positions, such as former officials of the Ministry of Soil and Grain, who taught agricultural arts, and former officials of the Ministry of Embassies, who taught diplomacy. Others addressed, from the viewpoint of their specialties, fundamental problems of organizing and governing human activities. These philosophers, of whom Confucius (551–479 B.C.E.) was the first, were generally considered to fall into six categories, which the Chinese called *jia*. This word means family or home, but with respect to sets of related thoughts it is translated "school."[3] It is necessary to understand what each of these schools believed and taught before their influence can be assessed.

The *Ru Jia*

The *Ru* were literati, scholars, who were said by the historian Liu Xin
(c.46 B.C.E.-23 C.E.) to have had their origin in the Ministry of Education.
Confucius was the founder, and predominant figure, in this school, which
is known in the West by his name. Confucianists taught the *Liu Yi* (Six
Classics), consisting of the *Book of Changes*, the *Book of Poetry*, the
Book of History, the *Book of Rituals* (*Li*), the *Book of Music*, and the
Spring and Autumn Annals (the state chronicles of the state of Lu).[4]

According to one tradition, Confucius was the author of all of these
works. This, however, could not be true because, with the exception of
the *Spring and Autumn Annals*, these classics had been the basis of
education for the *junzi* families during the feudal period.[5] However,
teaching and practice had been neglected and corrupted as the ruling and
noble families lost their status and uneducated families took positions of
responsibility. Confucius sought to correct errors and to eliminate dupli-
cations. He searched records all the way back to the Xia dynasty, and
compared the rituals of the Xia, Shang, and Zhou dynasties. He particularly admired Kings Wu and Wen, and the Duke of Zhou, the founders
of the Zhou dynasty. However, he sought not just accuracy, but understanding. He may have written the *Spring and Autumn Annals*, and he
commented on the other classics in the light of the underlying principles
of the Chinese consciousness. His comments and those of his pupils and
successors were later regarded as more important than the original texts.
This was especially true of the *Book of Changes*.[6]

Confucius did not systematically reconsider the fundamental ideas
that had been the basis of the development of Chinese culture in the
ancient period. But he did reaffirm them by teaching attitudes and
conduct based on those ideas. For instance, one of his main teachings
was the rectification of names.[7] This doctrine is inexplicable without a
belief in prescriptive names, contingency, dao (to indicate the direction
of change), and yin/yang life force (to provide the moral motivation for
changes). His philosophy lay in the systematic reconsideration of the
applications of the fundamental ideas—the rules of conduct, the standards, the attitudes, the historical traditions, the ceremonies, the processes of change, and the rhythm of life. In the course of this
reconsideration, he looked for the principles implied by the ideas. Thus,

he was able to approve or criticize a particular application on an objective basis, not just personal preference.

Perhaps even more important than *what* Confucius taught, was *who* he taught. The Western Zhou feudal society was disintegrating. Yet Confucius proposed to restore the harmony and unity of the social order by teaching the culture of that society. This proposal implied either the restoration of those "sons of princes" (*junzi*) who had held positions of power and responsibility by virtue of birth, or the education of those who had replaced, or would replace, them. Confucius chose the second alternative. He would take any student who showed promise and diligence, regardless of birth. This position is both the core of Chinese humanism and the origin of an enduring tradition of Chinese pedagogy. Wing-tsit Chan has described humanism as the "outstanding characteristic" of Chinese philosophy, and has declared that Confucius made it so.[8] By asserting that the order of heaven (the Dao, the essence of all the particular daos) could be *learned*, Confucius was saying that it was not something emanating from a supernatural source, quickening those upon whom it descended, but the sum and synthesis of human efforts to understand and cope. As Chan put it, "believing that man 'can make the Way (Dao) great,' and not that 'the Way can make man great,' he concentrated on man."[9] By teaching whoever had, or hoped to attain, a position of power and responsibility, Confucius was asserting that *anyone could learn* something of the order of heaven and could, therefore, assist in infusing it into events of the earth, thereby discharging the obligations of such a position. This is the seed of the remarkable examination system of Imperial China, which for hundreds of years qualified persons for positions in society and the state. Confucius changed *junzi* from a term of preferred birth to a term of moral superiority.[10]

The view of human nature implicit in Confucius's philosophy was consistent with the ancient Chinese view of an organic universe known by sensed observation plus a minimal use of inference. Confucian humanism meant that social obligations were created by human beings themselves, as they participated consciously in the universe. Recent history showed that disagreements about obligations and delinquencies of performance had become widespread and Chinese society had become factious and dysfunctional. Confucius was asserting that harmony and unity could be restored to the social order by human effort. The Greeks postulated a human faculty, called reason, which was capable of knowing absolute, unchanging, objective, universal truth, and they said that society should be ordered in accordance with the social implications of that truth.[11] Confucius was content to infer similarity of sentiments and feelings. He implicitly assumed that all persons had the same sentiments and would reach the same conclusions about social obligations.

The sentiment that Confucius proposed as the guiding principle for determining social obligations was *ren*, which is translated as "human heartedness," or "humanity." He said that it had a positive and a negative side. The positive side was conscientiousness to, or concern for, others. He is quoted as saying, "The man of *ren* is one who, desiring to sustain himself, sustains others, and desiring to develop himself, develops others. To be able from one's own self to draw a parallel for the treatment of others; that may be called the practice of *ren*." Positively, the practice of *ren* meant, "Do to others what you wish yourself." Negatively, it meant, "Do not do to others what you do not wish yourself."[12] Thus the dao for each person in every life situation was to be determined by the practice of *ren*.

But if the harmony and unity of society were to be restored, the social obligations determined by the practice of *ren* had to be performed. This required mobilization of the motivational energy of social yin/yang. The aspect of human nature that Confucius relied on to stimulate and sustain this motivational energy was the commitment of the superior man to do what was right, rather than what was personally advantageous, or profitable. This seems to be an intention, rather than a sentiment or feeling. Confucius said very little about it. Perhaps he did not need to. His whole life was an expression of it. He was trying to restore order and harmony in a society that continued to tear itself apart, and he could not even find a ruler who would give him an official position. Yet he never despaired. A disciple of his replied to one who mocked Confucius: "The reason why the superior man tries to go into politics, is because he holds this to be right, even though he is well aware that his principle cannot prevail."[13] Confucius said, "The superior man understands righteousness; the inferior man understands profit."[14]

It was not enough to merely perform the correct actions; the correct attitude was even more the mark of a human being. Speaking of the obligation owed to one's parents, Confucius said, "Filial piety nowadays means to be able to support one's parents. But we support even dogs and horses. If there is no feeling of reverence, wherein lies the difference?"[15]

Confucius assumed the continuing validity of the five categories of social relations—ruler-subject, husband-wife, father-son, older brother-younger brother, and friend-friend. The obligation that the love of others, *ren*, required was graded in accordance with these categories, and in accordance with the circumstances. The Chinese understanding of the social world, like the Chinese science of the physical world, was associational, not abstract and deductive. Confucius said, "The relative degree of affection we ought to feel for our relatives and the relative grades in honoring the worthy give rise to the rules of propriety [*li*]."[16]

The Confucian *junzi* was superior to the extent that his attitudes and actions accorded with the dao of the *junzi*. It was the view of Confucius that everyone could follow the dao of the "superior man" to some extent, but that even the wisest, called a sage, could not follow it perfectly. In a later Confucian work, the *Doctrine of the Mean*, Confucius was quoted as having said, "The Way of the superior man has its simple beginnings in the relation between man and woman, but in its utmost reaches, it is clearly seen in heaven and earth."[17] And further:

> There are four things in the Way of the superior man, none of which I have been able to do. To serve my father as I would expect my son to serve me: that I have not been able to do. To serve my ruler as I would expect my ministers to serve me: that I have not been able to do. To serve my elder brothers as I would expect my younger brothers to serve me: that I have not been able to do. To be the first to treat friends as I would expect them to treat me: that I have not been able to do.[18]

Mencius (371?–289? B.C.E.) continued the systematic consideration of human nature begun by Confucius. Like Confucius, he wanted to restore the harmony and unity of Chinese society, and he understood human nature as those characteristics of consciousness needed to achieve that end. He considered love of others (human heartedness) and commitment to do what was right (righteousness) as necessary, but he recognized that, as developed by Confucius, they were no longer simple feelings or intentions, but had become guides to right conduct. Mencius called them virtues and he added two more: propriety and wisdom. According to Mencius, original human nature consisted of the beginnings of these virtues—the four beginnings and the four virtues. He found the beginning of human heartedness in the feeling of commiseration, saying: "All men have a mind which cannot bear [to see the suffering of] others. . . . If today men suddenly see a child about to fall in a well, they will without exception experience a feeling of alarm and distress."[19]

Mencius found the beginning of righteousness in the feeling of shame and dislike, the beginning of propriety in the feeling of respect and reverence, and the beginning of wisdom in the feeling of right and wrong.[20] (Those inclined to think that distinguishing right from wrong is always a matter of rational judgment should recall Hume's view that feelings of pleasure and pain are associated with observed good and evil.)[21] The four beginnings, according to Mencius, were not implanted by culture, but were part of the original nature of human beings. This is the origin of the predominant view throughout most of Chinese history that human nature is originally good.[22] Each person could develop, or ignore, the beginnings of virtue. If developed to the fullest, the result was a sage. If neglected, or blocked, the person lost natural goodness and became no better than an animal.[23]

Whereas Confucius had implicitly assumed that all human beings had the same feelings and would agree upon what social obligations were implicated by them, Mencius explicitly addressed the problem. He argued that human beings have the five senses in common with the animals, but uniquely possess a mind. Activation of one of the five senses stimulates a natural reaction. But in the human being the mind weighs the input from the senses in light of human heartedness, righteousness, propriety, and wisdom before selecting a course of action. This ability to think distinguishes a human being from an animal, and full development of this ability distinguishes the superior man (or sage) from the small man. Mencius argued that the human mind is tuned to the virtues as the senses are tuned to the essences of the phenomena they detect. He then said: "Men's mouths agree in having the same relishes; their ears agree in enjoying the same sounds; their eyes agree in recognizing the same beauty. Shall their minds alone be without that which they similarly approve?"[24] If all minds were the same, agreement could be reached on social obligations, thus making harmony and unity possible. But the minds had to be developed before important decisions could be entrusted to them.

According to Mencius the one who deserved the name king was the one who ruled in a kingly way, not the one who controlled the most territory. The true king had the mind of the sage and ruled through moral instruction and education. The military lord ruled by force and compulsion. The moral power of the true king was ultimately stronger than the physical force of the military lord.[25] Mencius said:

When one subdues men by force, they do not submit in their hearts, (and submit outwardly only because) their strength is insufficient. When one subdues men by virtue, in their hearts' core they are pleased and sincerely submit, as was the case with the seventy disciples in their submission to Confucius.[26]

Mencius also taught that the kingly way—of virtue rather than force—should extend to the distribution of land, which was the most important economic question in an agrarian society. He advocated a "well-field system," in which every square *li* (about a third of a mile) was divided into nine equal squares. The eight outer squares were the private land of eight families who tilled the middle square in common for the benefit of government.[27]

It was Mencius' view that extending the rule of virtue to economic matters would teach the small men to develop their own beginnings of virtue to the point where they would willingly cooperate in the division of labor, necessary to an effective society. Mencius said, "There is the business of the great man, and the business of lesser men. . . . Some labor with their brains and some with their brawn."[28] But this division of labor should be governed by virtue, not force. Mencius said:

When right government prevails in the world, persons of little virtue are submissive to those of great, and those of little worth to those of great. When bad government prevails in the world, persons of small power are submissive to those of great, and the weak to the strong.[29]

In arguing against a doctrine of universal love, propounded by the *Mo Jia* (which will be discussed below), Mencius further developed the Confucian view that the practice of *ren* should follow the natural affections that differ in accordance with such things as proximity and dependence. Mencius said that it was impossible to love a neighbor's child as much as a brother's child, or one's own child. Nevertheless, the feeling for close relatives was to be a standard for the treatment of others. He said, "Treat the aged in your family as they should be treated, and extend this treatment to the aged of other people's families."[30]

Because of his doctrine of the original goodness of human nature, his emphasis upon the full development of the moral nature of man, and his theory of government by moral suasion instead of physical force, Mencius became the leader of the idealist wing of the *Ru Jia*. Xun Zi (Hsuan Tzu) (298?–238? B.C.E.) was the leader of the realist wing of Confucianism. Xun Zi argued that man is born with the inherent desire for profit and sensual pleasure. However, he needs society in order to survive and prosper. Moreover, he has the intelligence to recognize that need and to meet it by adopting human heartedness, righteousness, obedience to law, and uprightness in order to establish *li*, rituals and rules of conduct, which reconcile conflicting demands for limited goods, and make society possible. Morality arises because men learn to obey *li*. Thus, Xun Zi attributes everything good in society to culture, not to human nature. Whereas Mencius said "that by developing one's mind to the utmost, one knows one's nature, and by knowing one's nature, one knows Heaven," Xun Zi said that "it is only the sage who does not seek to know Heaven."[31] According to Xun Zi man formed a trinity with heaven and earth. "Heaven has its seasons, Earth has its resources, man has his culture." The vocation of man was to utilize what was offered by heaven and earth and to create his own culture.[32]

Xun Zi thus substituted intellect for the emotional beginnings of moral virtue in his account of human nature. The intellectual capacity to make distinctions is the essence of human nature, and the greatest of distinctions are social. Social relations are the products of culture. Accordingly, Xun Zi held that prescriptive names were arbitrarily assigned to underlying ideal realities. But having become generally accepted through custom, the names were accurate guides to the attitudes and actions needed to attain those ideals. That is, the conventional names had become the daos of the entities to which they refer. Therefore, Xun Zi, like Confucius and Mencius, advocated rectification of names, and he denounced the *Ming Jia* (School of Names) for sophistries that used the assertedly arbitrary nature of names to cast doubt on the ideal nature of human beings and upon the process of moving them from the actualities of attitude and action toward the ideal.[33]

The *Mo Jia*

This school was named for Mo Zi (Mo Tzu) its founder, who lived during the hundred years from the death of Confucius to the birth of Mencius. Mo Zi was the chief rival of Confucius. During his lifetime his fame and influence were the equal of Confucius's and for a time Confucianism and Mohism were the dominant schools of Chinese philosophy.[34] During the feudal period literati, *ru*, and military specialists, *xie*, were attached to the households of kings, princes, and feudal lords. With the disintegration of feudalism the *xie* as well as the *ru* lost their positions.

Some found official positions as military specialists in the states that were becoming fully independent and were seeking to control the whole of China, during the Spring and Autumn and the Warring States periods. Mo Zi and his followers addressed themselves to the problem of restoring the harmony and unity of the social order, thus becoming philosophers. The perspective of the *xie* was quite different from that of the *ru*.

The *ru* were engaged in thinking and discussing. They were supported by the labor of others and protected by the military service of others. The *xie* were engaged in acting. Of the *xie*, the *Historical Memoirs* of the great Han historian, Sima Qian, and his father, says that, "Their words were always sincere and trustworthy, and their actions always quick and decisive. They were always true to what they promised, and without regard to their own persons, they would rush into dangers threatening others."[35] They were equal in the face of danger and, increasingly, they were equal in their lack of social status. As war changed from jousts between horse-drawn chariots to clashes between massed infantry, more and more members of the lower classes were drafted into the infantry. The lower classes, not being insulated from daily vicissitudes by the actions of others, were concerned with their own actions and resulting effects upon their material well-being and physical safety.

The approaches of Confucius and Mo Zi to the problem of social disorder were shaped by their different perspectives. Confucius searched the historical records for state policies, rituals, ceremonies, and rules of propriety of rulers during times of social harmony and prosperity. He found them in the reigns of the Western Zhou founders, Kings Wen and Wu, and the Duke of Zhou. He formulated two characteristics of consciousness that would account for these successes, which he called human heartedness and righteousness. He then proposed to teach all those who aspired to positions of social responsibility to cultivate these character traits in themselves and to discharge their responsibilities by moral suasion and education through policies, rituals, ceremonies, and rules of propriety like those of the Western Zhou rulers, but shaped by the guiding virtues to suit current problems, situations, and circumstances. This way of proceeding assumed the validity of humanism. Confucius was concerned with human consciousness because he believed that social relations were the product of that consciousness. To cure social disorder he sought to develop the aspects of that consciousness that would produce social relations of harmony and unity.

Mo Zi seemingly rejected humanism; he preached the old belief, perhaps still widely held by the common people, in a supreme god and a host of spirits who rewarded or punished human beings depending upon whether their actions conformed to the will of heaven. If he had been sincere in this belief, he would have had to seek to learn the will of heaven, by some means, such as sacrifice and divination. In fact, he assumed that human beings could discover the pattern of social relations that would restore harmony and unity. He called that pattern the will of heaven in order to induce compliance by those who genuinely believed in a supreme god and the spirits, and who would, therefore, be moved by the prospect of divine punishments and rewards.[36] He also sought to invoke political sanctions, arguing that the emperor, as the son of heaven, was the most reliable judge of what heaven required and, therefore, the decision of a superior on a question of right and wrong action should always be controlling. This is not surprising in view of the military perspective of Mo Zi. A passage in the *Book of Mo* says: "Upon hearing good or evil one shall report it to a superior. What the superior thinks to be right, all shall think to be right. What the superior thinks to be wrong, all shall think to be wrong."[37]

To restore the harmony and unity of the social order it was necessary to achieve a generally acceptable distribution of social obligations, and then get general compliance with those obligations. Confucius proposed to accomplish this by developing the guiding emotion of *ren*, human heartedness, and the motivating emotion of righteousness. Mo Zi proposed to put aside all emotions and rely upon actions calculated to achieve desired ends. The *Book of Mo* says: "One must get rid of joy and anger, pleasure and sadness, love and hatred. When hands, feet, mouth, nose, ears (and eyes) are employed for righteousness, one will surely become a Sage."[38] Righteousness, in that quotation, must be understood in accordance with Mo Zi's meaning. For Confucius, righteousness meant doing the right thing, regardless of whether any benefit came of it.[39] Mo Zi ridiculed this position. To him no action was right unless it produced a benefit.[40] Therefore, Mohist righteousness was acting for profit, or benefit. Similarly, for Confucius, human heartedness, *ren*, love of others, meant an emotion naturally attaching to those near to us, which was to be trained in accordance with the principle of the golden rule. For Mo, *ren* meant the intention to do those acts that would produce benefits for the people and the country.

Mo Zi recognized that judgments would differ about whether a given action was right and wrong, that is, whether it would produce a benefit. Therefore, he proposed three tests, two of which were (at least purportedly) empirical, and one of which was experimental, but never implemented. He said that every proposed action should be tested for its basis, its verifiability, and its applicability. It should be verified by the senses of hearing and sight of the common people. It should be applied by adopting it in government and observing its benefit to the country and the people.[41]

Mo purported to find that the ancient kings of the Xia dynasty had laid down all the social obligations of a perfect society, in which everything that would be needed would be produced and distributed without conflict or violence, and time, effort, and resources would never be wasted. (This bears a striking resemblance to the utopian society which that latter-day social empiricist Karl Marx called communism.) On this basis Mo denounced lavish and costly funerals, and extended periods of mourning that resulted in abstention from work. He exaggerated the loss of wealth caused by these rituals by assuming that Confucians advocated them for all people, instead of just the elite. Speaking of extended mourning rituals, the *Book of Mo* says:

> If farmers practise this they cannot start out early and come back late, to cultivate the land and plant trees; the artizans cannot build boats and vehicles, and make vessels and utensils; and the women cannot rise early and retire late to spin and weave.[42]

By his second test, verification by the eyes and ears of the common people, Mo meant that one should inquire among the common people whether anyone had ever heard of or seen an instance in which putting wealth into unproductive display and abstaining from work had ever benefited the people.[43] This enabled the Mohists to invoke the envy and antipathy of the common people for the extravagant expenditures of the *junzi*. The third test, applicability and observation of the results, depended upon the ruler of some state adopting a Mohist program, and so far as is known, none did.[44]

In addition to the loss of wealth through rituals and ceremonies, Mo Zi deplored the diversion of wealth into adornment, works of art, and the performance of music, none of which produced material benefit, or profit. Mo Zi said: "The levy of heavy taxes on the people to construct the big bell, the sounding drum, [and musical instruments] is of no help in endeavoring to procure the benefits of the world and destroy its calamities."[45] However, he did not consider economic harm the greatest cause of the current disorder. That cause, he said, was the incessant fighting of people and states among themselves.[46]

Mo Zi's procedures for empirical investigation of right and wrong action are weak indeed. But the fatal weakness of Mohism was its view of human nature. Human beings were essentially actors, with the capacity to learn the effects of actions, and to control their actions. Thus, human beings were capable of refraining from actions that would produce unwanted results. How did Mo Zi propose to get general agreement about right and wrong actions? By persuading everyone to adopt his standard, which he called "universal love," in contrast with his parody of Confucius's graded love of others, which he called "partiality." The *Book of Mo* quotes this argument:

> I say that when everyone regards the states of others as his own, who would attack the others' states? Others would be regarded like self. When everyone regards the capitals of others as his own, who would seize the others' capitals? Others would be regarded like self. When everyone regards the houses of others as his own, who would disturb the others' houses? Others would be regarded like self. Now, when states and capitals do not attack and seize each other, and when clans and individuals do not disturb and harm one another, is this a calamity or a benefit to the world? We must say that it is a benefit. When we consider the origins of the various benefits, how have they arisen? Have they arisen out of hate of others and injuring others? We must say not so. We should say that they have arisen out of love of others and benefitting others. If we should classify all those who love others and benefit others, should we find them to be partial or universal? We must say that they are universal.[47]

How could Mohists hope to restore effective cooperation in society by such a hortatory imperative? For centuries Chinese had understood themselves to be associated for cooperative activities in hierarchical family relations. A common consciousness within each family, clan, and state had been built up, consisting of shared meanings, shared values, shared intentions, and a commitment to guide and limit actions by shared principles and rules. The Mohists proposed to rebuild society *without any basis in common consciousness*—just a mass of individuals related to each other as equal benefit-seeking, action-directing creatures, who by harangue, and supernatural sanctions, assertedly could be induced to treat everyone with the same consideration they had for themselves.

So Mo Zi really did reject humanism. Not because he believed that the order of human society was supernatural, but because, in his view, human beings were incapable of *creating* the relations of human society.

His empirical method assumed that the relations of human society *existed*, and could be discovered by empirical investigation, exactly like the relations between entities in a physical system. For a time, Mohists' denunciation of excessive displays of wealth and the privileges of the elite must have attracted popular support. And their denunciation of aggressive violence must have earned them favorable regard among all those not engaged in it at the time. It is reported that upon hearing that a state was about to make war, Mo Zi would hasten to that state and try to dissuade the ruler. If unsuccessful in preventing war, Mo and his follow-ers would go to the state under attack and help in its defense.[48] Mohists were organized under a leader who exercised military type command and discipline.

The empirical method of the Mohists stood them in good stead in inventing new technologies of war. Mohists anticipated the use of mus-tard gas in the trench warfare of World War I by 2300 years. The pounded earth walls of ancient Chinese cities were vulnerable to tunneling by attacking forces. Mohists burned balls of dried mustard and other toxic vegetable matter in furnaces and pumped the resulting gas into the enemies tunnels by means of pipes and an ox-hide bellows. They also made bombs and grenades containing various poisons, which were hurled from the walls into the ranks of the attackers.[49]

The empirical method was appropriate for investigation of physical systems. Later Mohists made significant contributions to the logic of empirical investigation, the standardization of measurements, the under-standing of weight and force, levers and balance, the strength of materi-als, tension, breakage, and continuity, and a number of characteristics of light.[50] The anticipation of Newton's first law of motion by a Mohist has already been mentioned.[51]

The empirical method of the Mohists, which was a strength for the investigation of physical systems, disabled them for the task of recreating an effective social order. Therefore, Mohism died out completely as a philosophy soon after the end of the third century B.C.E., leaving only its considerable contributions to Chinese science, recently rediscovered by Needham.[52]

The *Ming Jia*

This is the School of Names, but its origin was in debaters, disputers, and arguers, who often practiced their specialty in aid of parties to a lawsuit. Of one of the most famous early members of this school it was said that, "[H]e succeeded in changing right into wrong and wrong into right, until no standards of right and wrong remained, so that what was regarded as possible and impossible fluctuated from day to day."[53] What the members of this school argued about was the meaning of names, because the Chinese view of reality was expressed in concepts that they called "names." Perhaps a short review of what has been said above about names, and other basic Chinese ideas, might be helpful at this point.

The Chinese were very aware of observable changes in all things. They understood a physical entity, such as a plant, in terms of sets of changes of form and substance throughout its life cycle. From many observations and from experiments in breeding and cultivation they developed a concept of what that plant could become if its full potential were realized and they gave this concept a prescriptive name. All individual plants that tended toward, but fell short of, the prescribed set of forms and sub-stances (indicated by the prescriptive name) were the actualities of that name. The forms and substances of a physical entity were passed from one generation to the next by the natural processes of genetics. As physical entities, members of the Ma family (for instance) received the genetic inheritance of that family. Additionally, as social entities, they also received, through the cultural processes of child training, family rituals, and education, the prescribed attitudes and actions (social dao) indicated by the Ma name. Actual social entities, as well as actual physical entities, were referred to by the same name as the prescriptive ideal. Millet, Ma, father, son, friend, referred to both the ideal and the actuality. Those concerned with physical cultivation or social regulation sought to induce the rectification of names, that is, to bring actualities into accord with the prescriptive name.[54]

Members of the School of Names were centrally concerned with this dual use of names. They tried to analyze the nature of each referent and the relations between them. But, because Chinese words refer to partic-ular, concrete sensed phenomena, it was very difficult for Chinese to conceive of a general, abstract, non-observable ideal entity. It was even more difficult for them to communicate their thoughts to others, who naturally expected every use of a word to refer to concrete particulars. Their statements, such as, "A white horse is not a horse," were paradox-ical to the hearer. No doubt they used their cachet of double meanings to confound their opponents. The Daoist *Book of Zhuang* says that the members of the School of Names "could overcome men's words but could not convince their minds."[55] The great Han historian Sima Tan (d. 110 B.C.E.) said: "The School of Names conducted minute examinations of trifling points in complicated and elaborate statements, which made it impossible for others to refute their ideas."[56]

The antipathy of contemporaries and historians to this school was not due solely to abusive uses of their analytical skills. It was due, in large part, to the fact that their skills *were analytical*, instead of practical. The development of associational science and the institutions of feudal society attest that the Chinese had become highly sophisticated in the conscious participation in the world. But, until the School of Names, this participation had not been *self*-conscious. They had new ideas and implemented them to develop more effective structures of human cooperation and more effective techniques and technologies for beneficial intervention in natural processes. The School of Names, alone, thought about thinking.[57]

Members of the School of Names have been called Logicians[58] and Dialecticians[59] in the West. But these names can be misleading. Their logic was not like that of the Greeks, proceeding deductively from an abstract, universal, first principle, or first cause, down to every concrete observable, particular.[60] Nor was their logic dialectical like Hegel's, proceeding by projection of ideas from the mind of superego into history and nature, alienation of superego from the embodied idea, reconciliation and movement to a new "moment" of projection, alienation and reconciliation until all knowledge has returned to superego as self-conscious knowledge.[61] Hegel's dialectical logic is another version of the One creating, guiding, and animating the Many. In Greek secular philosophy, in medieval European dialectical philosophy, logic has served to test the validity of the particular Many by whether they were properly derived from the universal One.

The Chinese took the world as they sensed it. But they observed opposing, interacting, complementary tendencies, principles, or forces, beginning with yin and yang, and found the resulting moderation beneficial. Therefore, their logic was that of a number of pairs of opposing principles operating spontaneously, like the interacting "causes" in the human endocrine system, as Needham suggested.[62] It was from this point of view that the Chinese Logicians analyzed names and actualities. Hui Shi (f. 350–260 B.C.E.) emphasized actualities, pointing out that they were particular, concrete, occupied space and time, and were, therefore, observable. He called attention to the fact that, compared with names, actualities were relative and constantly changing. He also observed that actualities have qualities, such as color, form, and hardness. Gong-sun Long (f. 284–259 B.C.E.) emphasized names, showing that they were universal, abstract, did not occupy space and time, and were, therefore, not observable. Universals, he said, were absolute, and unchanging. According to Gong-sun Long, universals in themselves have no existence, but they can participate in things that do have existence, and in Fung Yu-lan's words, "the combination of universals and their manifestation in time and space as things, is a spontaneous process not caused from without."[63]

This part of Gong-sun Long's analysis of names is inconsistent with the general view that names were prescriptive. He was famous for his "Discourse on the White Horse," in which he said, "A white horse is not a horse. . . . The word 'horse' denotes a shape, 'white' denotes a color. What denotes color does not denote shape. Therefore, I say that a white horse is not a horse."[64] He further explained that "white horse" specifies that which is white. Therefore, "white horse" refers to this or that white horse, an actuality, that can be sensed. Also, necessarily, the horse in "white horse" refers to this or that horse, an actuality. And, his argument goes, this or that white horse is not a particular manifestation of the universal "horse," because universal horse is (only) a shape. This or that white horse is a manifestation of the universal "horse" (shape) *plus* a manifestation of the universal "white" (color). It is clear, therefore, that Gong-sun Long's names (universals) were not the ideal entity—the perfect millet, Ma, father, son, friend, or horse—toward which every actuality bearing that name should move or be moved. The names (universals) of the Logicians were qualities—shape, color, hardness, softness, wetness, dryness—which could combine and manifest themselves in various actualities (particulars).[65]

Because their interests were purely intellectual the Logicians made no contribution to restoring harmony and unity in society. But they did make a very significant contribution to Chinese philosophy by discovering "that which lies beyond shapes and features." The "discovery" was purely logical. The existence of all of those things that have shapes and features could be verified by sensed observation. Their dualistic dialectic told them that there must be an opposing/interacting category of being without shapes and features.[66] It was left to the *Dao Jia* to explore the nature of that which lies beyond shapes and features.

The *Dao Jia*

Over the centuries this school has had an influence second only to that of Confucianism. The philosophers of other schools referred to the "way" of this or that entity. That usage has been transliterated with a lowercase initial letter and without italics as dao, in previous discussions. All daos of all entities has been referred to collectively as Dao. The concept to which the title of this school refers is something different from those usages. A capital initial letter and italics will be used to indicate the concept—*Dao*—but for the sake of convenience the school will be referred to as Daoism, and its members as Daoists.

There is a good deal of uncertainty about dates regarding this school. The first major figure, Yang Ju lived after Mo Zi and before Mencius, because Mencius said, "The words of Yang Zhu and Mo Ti [Mo Zi] fill the world."[67] Yang's remedy for war and social disintegration was in stark contrast with Mo's. Mo's remedy was to love everyone as yourself, and to act only for profit. Yang's remedy was each one for himself, and value life but despise things.[68] According to tradition, Lao Zi, the most important Daoist, was a little older than Confucius. Fung Yu-lan believes this to be an error, possible resulting from confusion of Lao Zi with a man named Lao Tan, who was an older contemporary of Confucius.[69] In any event, Fung is convinced that the book called *The Lao Zi*, or *Dao De Jing*, which is the bible of Daoism, was written after the Logicians Hui Shi and Gong-sun Long because it explores the meaning of that which lies beyond shapes and features.[70] The third great name in early Daoism was Zhuang Zi (Chuang Tzu) (c.369 – c.286 B.C.E.). He was a contemporary of Mencius and a friend of the Logician Hui Shi, but the book bearing his name, *Zhuang-Zi*, was probably compiled by a commentator about a century later.[71]

The originators of Daoism were recluses, like those met by Confucius in his travels, as recorded in the *Analects*. Most of these recluses were from the southern state of Chu, in the Yangzi basin. People in south China were not subject to the long, dry, bitterly cold winters, the catastrophic floods, and the frequent invasions of barbarian nomads that the people in north China had to cope with. Long-range planning and coordinated

actions over a very large area were required to grow and store crops for
use months later, to carry out monumental projects of canals and levees
to ameliorate flooding, and to constantly protect borders by fortifications
and standing armies. Therefore, the need for society and government was
self-evident to people in the north. On the other hand, people in the south
could grow up to three crops a year, winter was moderate and short, water
was plentiful but not a constant danger, and fruits and vegetables domesticated in the south were for immediate consumption. Life was much
easier, and concern only with immediate, local needs was unlikely to be
punished with death by freezing or starvation at the hands of nature, or
death or slavery at the hand of invaders.[72] The need for society and
government was not self-evident in the south. Furthermore, most of the
inhabitants of Chu were non-Chinese, who were not fully integrated into
the Chinese consciousness that had been developing in the north. Therefore, the value of society and government had neither been impressed
upon them by circumstance nor taught them by custom or education.

No one can say, on the basis of anything but conjecture, that these
differences between north and south China influenced the fundamental
beliefs of the founders of Daoism. It is fact however, that Daoism began
with south China recluses, and that Daoism turned away from a focus
upon society, which had dominated Chinese philosophy, to a focus upon
nature. In the first stage of Daoism, all obligation beyond the family was
rejected. It is recorded in the *Analects* that Zi Lu, a disciple temporarily
separated from Confucius, met a recluse and his two sons. Zi Lu said to
the sons:

> It is not right to refuse to serve in office. If the regulations between old and young in
> family life may not be set aside, how is it that he (your father) sets aside the duty that
> exists between a ruler and his ministers? In his desire to maintain his own personal
> purity, he subverts the great relationships of society.[73]

The recluse, however, had given up hope of achieving a good life through
reforming society and government. As an alternative, the recluse sought
to preserve his own life by withdrawal into nature. Mencius said of the
first Daoist, "The principle of Yang Ju is: 'Each one for himself.' Though
he might have profited the whole world by plucking out a single hair, he
would not have done it."[74] This was not hedonism. To give free rein to
desires would be to entangle one's self with others who could provide or
withhold satisfactions. By limiting desires one could avoid the dangers
and restrictions of society and government.

The second stage of Daoism, represented by Lao Zi, went beyond withdrawal and sought to understand the basic laws of nature, in order to preserve the quality of life by living in accordance with nature. In the Chinese view of reality, every entity had its actualities and its name. Actualities consisted of changing sets of form and substance, for physical entities, and changing sets of attitudes and actions, for social entities. Actualities were concrete particulars, which had observable characteristics, and which occupied space and time. Actualities, therefore, were said by the Logicians to have shapes and features. Following the dual symmetry of Chinese logic, Gong-sun Long said that in opposition/interaction with concrete, particular entities, which had shapes and features, were names, which were abstract and universal, and beyond shapes and features. However, Long said, names have "*zhi.*" *Zhi*, which literally means "finger," is that which points to, or indicates something.[75] This part of Long's analysis is consistent with the general Chinese view that name was prescriptive.

If names are prescriptive, pointing out what that entity ought to become, then human beings, as conscious entities, have the moral obligation to *do* something to rectify names by bringing actualities into accord with the ideal indicated by the name. The son has the obligation to bring his every attitude and action with respect to his father in accord with the ideal attitudes and actions indicated by "son." With respect to physical entities, also, human beings are obliged to be active. Breeding and cultivation can bring the actualities of millet closer to the ideal indicated by the name. Dao is the way of the son, or of the millet, the agenda of what must be done to rectify the name. The son, or the farmer, follows the dao by yin (passive) and yang (active) modes of animation, or motivation.

This brief summary of previous discussions will suffice to show that the Logicians' analysis of what lies beyond shapes and features was incomplete. Names of things were shown to be beyond shapes and features, but names of forces, or principles, such as guidance and animation, were not considered and it was not considered whether there was anything beyond names. Using the Chinese logic of dual symmetry, Lao Zi said that beyond names is the unnameable. Faced with the need to indicate the unnameable in some way, Lao Zi called it *Dao*, but specified that he meant something more unchanging, abiding, and undifferentiated than the names of things. The first chapter of the *Dao De Jing* says:

> The *Dao* that can be comprised in words is not the eternal *Dao*; the name that can be
> named is not the abiding name. The Unnameable is the beginning of Heaven and
> earth; the nameable is the mother of all things.[76]

And in chapter 32 the *Dao De Jing* says, "The *Dao* is eternal, nameless, the Uncarved Block. . . . Once the block is carved, there are names."[77]

The nature of the interaction between the undifferentiated nameless and everything nameable is not that of creation, nor is it the fulfillment of a divine purpose. "Like a garment it covers the ten thousand things and brings them up, but makes no claim to be master over them."[78] Chapter 21 of the *Dao De Jing* says:

> Dao [*Dao*] as a thing is impalpable, incommensurable. Incommensurable, impalp-
> able, yet latent in it are forms. Impalpable, incommensurable, yet within it there is an
> essence. This essence is extremely pure, but none the less efficacious.[79]

Here we have it—efficacy, the pure essence of energy. And it is not purposefully directed. It operates spontaneously.[80] *Dao*, spontaneous efficacy, enables everything to be what it is. *Dao* enables being to be being, guidance (Dao) to be guidance, animation (yin/yang) to be animation, millet to be millet, and son to be son.

Dao, which is undifferentiated efficacy, imparts to every entity, as it becomes an entity, the differentiated spontaneous efficacy needed to complete itself in accordance with its name. This is *de*. Most English translations of *Dao* and *de* make it impossible for the casual reader to discover that *Dao* and *de* are undifferentiated and differentiated efficacy. Because Dao is used by all other schools to mean the way, the *Dao* of Daoism is usually translated as the way. *de* is often translated as the "virtue" of a thing.[81] It is also referred to by Fung Yu-lan as the principle underlying each individual thing, but he says it "would be better translated as the 'efficacy' or 'power' inherent in a thing. . . ."[82] The *Dao De Jing* is enigmatic about *de*, saying of things, "*Dao* gave them birth. *de* reared them." And also, "Becoming things, they gained forms; through their tending forces they became completed. . . ."[83] The eleventh century C.E. commentator, Lu Huiqing, said:

> When they become things, there is simply a special shaping of them. . . . Once having
> forms, those which are to be naked cannot but be naked; those which are to have
> scales, claws, feathers and hair, cannot but have these scales, claws, feathers and hair.
> And the progression through infancy, maturity, old age and death, cannot be otherwise
> than this progression through infancy, maturity, old age and death. For all these, it is
> their tending forces which make them necessarily so.[84]

The doctrines of *Dao* and *de* make it clear that the Daoists departed from the general view that names are prescriptive. For them, instead of pointing out what an entity *ought to become*, name indicated what an entity *would become*, unless its inherent nature were blocked or frustrated. Conscious entities, human beings need not come to know the dao of a social entity and intervene with character development, education, constraining rituals, or threats of punishment, in order to move that entity toward the ideal attitudes and actions indicated by the name of Ma, father, son, friend. Such cultural interventions would substitute artificial, purposeful actions for the natural, spontaneous actions initiated by *Daode*. To introduce the good is also to introduce the evil, since the universe operated according to opposing/interacting principles. To follow one's *de* is to move beyond good and evil and live by the natural. Indeed, names are an impediment to achieving harmony of life in accordance with nature. *Dao* is nameless; the 10,000 things have names. But, since *de* operates naturally, it is not necessary to learn about an entity through its name in order to act correctly toward it. Lao Zi advocated a human society of "Unwrought Simplicity." "As soon as it is put under regulation, there are names." When names are introduced, "Only by knowing when it is time to stop can danger be avoided."[85]

In order to live by nature, instead of by culture, Lao Zi said that it was necessary to understand the "invariable." This master principle is: "Reversing is the movement of *Dao*." The Chinese character translated as "invariable" also means eternal, or abiding. The principle means that in the Chinese universe of dual symmetry of qualities, principles, and forces, whenever one extreme is approached movement will start returning to the opposite extreme. Here are quotations from the *Dao De Jing*: "It is upon calamity that happiness leans; it is upon happiness that calamity rests. . . ." "Be twisted and one shall be whole; be crooked and one shall be straight; be hollow and one shall be filled; be tattered and one shall be renewed; have little and one shall obtain; but have much and one shall be perplexed."[86]

To know the invariable law of reversal was to know what could be accomplished and what could not be accomplished. To know *Daode* was to know that only natural, spontaneous actions—moving with the invariable instead of against it—could have any effect. Therefore, even moral virtue was useless or even harmful. Lao Zi said:

When the *Dao* is lost, there is the *de*. When the *de* is lost, there is [the virtue of] human-heartedness. When human-heartedness is lost, there is [the virtue of] righteousness. When righteousness is lost, there are the ceremonials. Ceremonials are the degeneration of loyalty and good faith, and are the beginning of disorder in the world.[87]

Therefore, the sage kept his desires simple, and followed the principle of *wuwei*, nonaction—meaning no action against nature. Thus, he was able to accomplish all that could be accomplished in his circumstances, and he did not long for more. "To know how to be content is to avoid humiliation; to know where to stop is to avoid injury." And "The sage, therefore discards the excessive, the extravagant, the extreme."[88] Of the sage ruler, Lao Zi said:

Banish wisdom, discard knowledge, and the people will be benefitted a hundredfold. Banish human-heartedness, discard righteousness, and the people will be dutiful and compassionate. Banish skill, discard profit, and thieves and robbers will disappear. (Ch.19) [And] Do not exalt the worthies, and the people will no longer be contentious. Do not value treasures that are hard to get, and there will be no more thieves. If the people never see things that excite their desire, their mind will not be confused. Therefore, the sage rules the people by emptying their minds, filling their bellies, weakening their wills, toughening their sinews, ever making the people without knowledge and desire. (chap. 3)[89]

Lao Zi did not, in fact, advocate banishing all skill, only those skills that could be taught or learned. But there was a higher skill, which could only be acquired by one who had a particular "knack," or special sensitivity, to some aspect of nature. Given the knack, years of acute observation and practice could develop a mastery of a craft, or occupation. Perhaps the most famous of the "knack" stories is that of Ting the master butcher. The prince of Hui was watching Ting cut up a bullock. His every movement was in perfect harmony and his chopper never met any resistance. The prince congratulated Ting on his skill. Ting replied that he followed *Dao*, which was higher than mere skill. He said that after three years of intensive observation his spirit had no more need of control by the senses, but, following the natural structure of the bullock he separated it into its parts without even dulling the blade of his chopper. Ting said that a good cook changes his chopper once a year, because he cuts, an ordinary cook needs a new chopper once a month, because he hacks, but he, Ting, had used the same chopper for nineteen years and its edge was still as sharp as if it had just come from the whetstone.

"Excellent," cried the prince. "From the words of Ting the Cook we may learn how to nourish (our) life."[90]

In the Daoist literature there were many more such "knack-stories," concerning musicians, cicada catchers, boatmen, swimmers, sword makers, bellstand makers, arrow makers, wheelwrights, animal tamers, mathematicians, and buckle makers. These all have to do with physical entities, or aspects of physical reality. However, Daoists advocated the same approach to social entities. In one of the famous stories a master wheelwright asked a prince why he was reading the "words of the sages," which the wheelwright called the "dregs and refuse of bygone men." When the wheelwright told the prince about following the *Dao* of things, the prince accepted the advice, which was said to be:

> [I]nstead of looking in the books of dead Confucians, study the *Dao* of the people and acquire the knack of governing, leading from within. See as they see and hear as they hear. Do not interfere with the fulfillment of the people's natural human needs and desires. Do not set yourself above them, but return to the ideal of the Common Life.[91]

Their sensitivity to the *Dao* of things enabled the Daoists to contribute greatly to the development of Chinese associational science. The record of that contribution is extensively covered by Needham.[92] In the third stage of Daoism, represented by Zhuang Zi, the attempt was made to rise above the relative happiness of living in accordance with one's *de*, to a mystical awareness of the operation of *Dao* in the whole universe.[93]

The *Yin/Yang Jia*

This school grew out of the occult arts, including magic divination, astrology, the calendar, and the beginnings of alchemy.[94] It differed from these arts by rejecting supernatural forces and by seeking to understand the whole universe instead of seeking to predict, or beneficially control, particular events.[95] Because of their attempt to give a systematic account of the fundamental processes of the whole universe, members of this school will be referred to as Cosmologists. The Cosmologists assumed the reality of the sensed world, in which every entity was self-existing and self-directing, and yet none encroached on any other or failed to interact with any other, thus creating a natural, spontaneous order of harmonious interdependence. Entities were organic, more like processes than objects, moving through sets of forms and substances throughout their life cycles. Events occurring simultaneously were related to each other geometrically in space; those not occurring simultaneously were related to each other cyclically in time. Space and time were prescriptive, consisting of sites where and occasions when events should occur in order for each of the interacting entities to rectify its dao.[96]

In the Greek view of reality, with fundamental entities of fixed characteristics interacting with each other in invariant ways, attention is focused on the question, "What caused the fundamental entities to be what they are?" Therefore, the West has always struggled with the problem of creation. But in the Chinese view of reality all entities are constantly coming to be in the sensed world. That is, each entity's actual activities are always changing in accordance with its dao. In such a world, attention focused on the question, "What causes entities to do what they should?" The Cosmologists attempted to answer this question by developing the doctrine of yin and yang as primal forces, and by originating or developing the doctrine of Five Elements (Agents, Forces, Powers). Unfortunately, the Cosmologists did not distinguish between physical entities with their changing sets of form and substance and social entities with their changing sets of attitude and action. They ignored the cultural completely, mixed natural and human affairs, and therefore believed in historical forces that controlled human events as inexorably as supernatural forces.

The idea of two primal forces, or principles, is very ancient. It is found in the eight trigrams as broken and unbroken lines, which originally indicated positive and negative. Etymologically, and in the interpretations of the sixty-four hexagrams, they were light and dark. In the *Book of Changes*, the first two hexagrams, composed respectively of six unbroken and six broken lines, are referred to as Heaven and Earth, Father and Mother, Strong and Yielding. Through the interaction of these two hexagrams, all other hexagrams are formed, symbolizing the coming into being of everything in the universe.[97]

In the "Monthly Commands," a document of the *Yin/Yang Jia* found in a third century B.C.E. text (and included in the Han dynasty *Book of Rites*), the structure of the universe is described in terms of the *Yin/Yang Jia*. The four seasons are correlated with the four compass points: summer, south; winter, north; spring, east; autumn, west. The orients and the seasons are also correlated with the Five Elements: fire is dominant in the south and in summer; water in the north and in winter; wood (suggesting budding) in the east and in spring; metal (harsh and hard) in the west and in bleak autumn. The fifth power, earth (nourishing), was correlated with center and given a brief time between summer and autumn.[98] Natural phenomena were sought to be explained by the influences of the forces, but the main purpose was to tell the sovereign what he should do month by month, throughout the year.

In the first month of spring the Son of Heaven should live in the apartment on the left side of the Bright Green Hall; ride in a great belled chariot drawn by green dragon horses bearing green flags; wear green robes with green jade pendants; and eat wheat and mutton from coarse, open vessels. He should order the work of the fields to begin, order the inspectors of the fields to repair the boundaries of the fields, to inspect the paths and irrigation ditches, to examine closely the mounds and hills, slopes and heights, and plains and valleys to determine what lands are good and where the five grains should be sown, and order the inspectors to instruct the people who will be doing the work. In the first month of spring it was forbidden to cut down trees, to destroy nests, to kill young insects, the young yet in the womb or newborn, or fledgling birds. All young animals and eggs were to be spared. Multitudes of people were not to be summoned for any service, and no construction was to be done on walls or fortifications. All bones and corpses of those who had died by the wayside were to be buried. And it was forbidden to take up arms offensively in that month.[99]

An account of the Five Elements appears in a section of the *Book of History* known as the *Hong Fan* (Grand Norm). The Grand Norm was traditionally attributed to King Wu, a founder of the Zhou dynasty, but modern scholarship assigns it to the fourth or third century B.C.E. and attributes it to the *Yin/Yang Jia*.[100] In the Grand Norm, the nature of the Five Elements is explained in a way that is apt for Chinese associational science. The text, in Needham's translation is:

Water (is that quality in Nature) which we describe as soaking and descending. Fire (is that quality in Nature) which we describe as blazing and uprising. Wood (is the quality in Nature) which permits of curved surfaces or straight edges. Metal (is that quality in Nature) which can follow (the form of a mould) and become hard. Earth (is that quality in Nature) which permits of sowing, (growth), and reaping.

That which soaks, drips and descends causes saltiness. That which blazes, heats and rises up generates bitterness. That which permits of curved surfaces or straight edges gives sourness. That which can follow (the form of a mould) and then become hard, produces acridity. That which permits of sowing, (growth), and reaping, gives rise to sweetness.[101]

Needham sees these correlations as reflections of the chemical interest of the Cosmologists, or Naturalists as he calls them. He suggests that the association of saltiness with water might have arisen from primitive experiments and observations on solution and crystallization; the association of bitterness with fire might imply the use of heat in preparing medicinal decoctions from plants; the association of sourness with wood was natural because vegetal substances become sour with decomposition; the association of acridity with metal would suggest itself because smelting operations give off acrid fumes, such as sulfur dioxide; and the association of sweetness with earth might have occurred because of the generally sweet taste of cereals.[102]

From these observations of Needham it is clear that the methods of investigation of the Cosmologists would contribute directly to Chinese associational science by directing attention to interactions between juxtaposed entities, such as lowering the temperature needed to melt iron ore by putting in "black earth" (in fact, iron phosphate), or blowing a constant stream of air against cast iron, oxidizing it into steel or wrought iron.[103] Indeed, Needham discusses this school not in a chapter headed by the name of the school, as he does with other schools, but in a chapter headed "The Fundamental Ideas of Chinese Science."[104]

The Cosmologists also contributed to the development of numerical categories to indicate the proper distribution of phenomena in space and time, and the proper proportions in things created by artisans.[105] For the Cosmologists, numbers had no quantitative, cardinal, ordinal, or distributive significance.[106] A number was a symbol that referred to a group of sensed phenomena, or geometrical proportions. In the construction of the chariot, which represented the structure of the universe, the Cosmologists and their subsequent followers made extensive use of geometrical representations of imperfect triangles that were employed in determining the relation of the square base, the curved canopy, and the supporting pole to the circumference, diameter, and radius of the wheel. These triangles were imperfect in that the square of the hypotenuse plus or minus one was equal to the sum of the squares of the two sides. The most important of the imperfect triangles were:

$$5^2 + 5^2 = 7^2+1;\ 8^2 + 9^2 = 12^2+1;\ 8^2 + 4^2 = 9^2-1;\ 7^2 + 4^2 = 8^2+1.^{[107]}$$

The discovery of incommensurability in some triangles astounded the Greeks because, for them, numbers referred to real material objects, the smallest of which, atoms, were believed to be indivisible. It was, therefore, logically necessary for every line to be composed of a whole number of units. Democritus tried to save his atomic theory by saying that the incommensurability was only in the apparent, sensed world, not in the real, rationally known world. The distinction between apparent and real worlds became a hallmark of Western thought, but its application to perfect and imperfect triangles was unsound. The West abandoned the atomic theory until the modern period.[108] For the Chinese, however, numbers referred to batches of sensed phenomena, which were more process than material objects, and which were under constraint of their inherent natures to find their place in space and time in harmonious juxtaposition with all creatures and things. The play of numbers served to adjust relationships, and the fact that the squares of the hypotenuses differed by only one unit from the sums of the squares of the two sides presented the opportunity to equate this unity with the One Man of the long-established theory of the emperor as the clear channel between heaven and earth. Having no quantitative dimensions as gnomon he "served to adjust concrete dimensions to the [ideal] proportions of the universe."[109] This ineradicably established the interaction between natural and human events and brought into the very heart of universal order the sovereign as supreme, regulating gnomon, acting not by physical force but by funneling Daoist efficacy from heaven into earth thereby causing natural and human events to occur where and when they should. If the sovereign's dress, demeanor, food, and sacrifices were correct, rain, sun, wind, and water would be in due measure and proper sequence; crops would flourish, and the state would be free from danger. If, however, he followed autumn regulations in the spring there would be great pestilences, violent wind, beating rain, and the growth of weeds.[110]

Zuo Yan, who lived after Mencius, was the most famous of the Cosmologists. Only fragments of his own writing have survived, but he is discussed in a chapter of the *Historical Memoirs* written by Sima Qian in the second or first century B.C.E.[111] Sima says that Zuo Yan examined deeply into the increase and decrease of the yin and yang, wrote essays about their strange permutations, and about the cycles of the great sages; Zuo first spoke about modern times, and then went back to the time of the legendary Yellow Emperor; he followed great events in the rise and fall of the ages, recorded their omens and institutions; and, starting "from the time of the separation of Heaven and earth," he made citation of the revolutions and transformations of the Five Powers, and the different ways of government and different omens appropriate to each.[112]

On the basis of this study Zuo Yan produced a theory of dynastic succession that made him extremely influential. According to this theory, a dynasty ruled by the power of one of the Five Elements, and the dynasties rotated in accordance with the order that the elements were able to overcome each other. The Yellow Emperor was said to have ruled by virtue of the power of earth and so he took yellow for the color of his vestments and flags. Wood was said to be able to overcome earth and its color was green and, therefore, these were the element and color of the Xia dynasty. Shang was said to have overthrown the Xia by virtue of metal, whose color is white. Fire overcomes metal and, therefore the Zhou dynasty ruled by virtue of fire and its color was red.[113] According to Sima Qian, the theory of dynastic succession continued:

> Water will inevitably be the next force that will succeed Fire. Heaven will first make the ascendancy of Water manifest. The force of Water being in ascendancy, black will be assumed as its color, and Water will be taken as the pattern for affairs. . . . When the cycle is complete, the operation will revert once more to Soil.[114]

This theory had contending rulers salivating all over China. Whereas Confucius had been ignored, in his travels, Zuo Yan was treated as an honored guest everywhere he went. Every ruler hoped to unite China and found a new dynasty. All he needed was to appropriate the force of water and invoke the will of heaven. Perhaps Zuo Yan, the great historian and prophet could help him. Zuo Yan was highly regarded in his home state of Qi. When he went to Liang, King Hui went to the suburbs to welcome him, "and acted toward him with all the etiquette of a host to a guest." In Zhao, Prince Pingyuan personally brushed the dust from his mat. In Yan, King Zhao acted as his advance guard, built him a palace and sat as a disciple to receive instruction.[115]

However, a cyclical theory of history, while it may be plausible as an explanation of past events, is not a practical guide to causing desired future events. Sima Qian said: "Kings, dukes and great officials, when they first witnessed his arts, fearfully transformed themselves, but later were unable to practise them."[116] So, it was not the *Yin/Yang Jia* that showed the way to unification, or to restoration of social harmony, but it had lasting impact upon Chinese philosophy. The interdependence of natural and human events, the correlation of everything in the universe by means of numerical symbols, the rotating influence of the Five Elements, and the cyclical theory of history were absorbed into Confucian orthodoxy beginning in the Han dynasty. When the last emperor renounced the throne in 1912 his official title was still "Emperor through [the Mandate of] Heaven and in accordance with the Movements [of the Five Powers]."[117] The great contribution of the *Yin/Yang Jia* to Chinese science has already been indicated above.

The *Fa Jia*

This school developed in response to changing conditions resulting from the disintegration of feudalism. "Fa" means a command that carries the threat of punishment. It is translated as "law." The name of the school is usually translated as Legalist School, and members are referred to as Legalists. This name was not used until 90 B.C.E., but the doctrines of the school had been developing for several hundred years. The Legalists were more technicians of power than philosophers.[118] Under the Western Zhou dynasty, feudalism obtained within states as well as between the feudal rulers and the Zhou king. The head of state did not rule directly over all persons within the boundaries of his state, even though the territory was not large. Noble families held fiefs and organized and regulated all activities therein. For the most part this organization and regulation was accomplished by *li*, the customs, mores, rituals, and rules of propriety of the family, and was, therefore, personal, moral, educational, and inspirational. Only the small men (*xiao ren*), such as the serfs who actually tilled the fields, were given specific commands and corrected by punishments (*xing*). Accordingly, it was said that "the *li* do not go down to the common people; the *xing* do not go up to the ministers."[119]

This mode of government was feasible under feudalism because the members of the noble families, the *junzi*, participated in the Chinese consciousness; they understood in accordance with shared meanings, desired in accordance with shared values, intended in accordance with shared purposes. Therefore, they were willing and able to guide and limit their attitudes and actions in accordance with principles transmitted by family precept and example. As the consolidation of states proceeded many of the noble families lost their ministerial positions and their lands. Members of the noble families were forced to seek positions on the basis of individual effectiveness in the techniques of war, taxation, trade, or commerce. Their status and welfare came to depend upon the favor of some person holding political, military, or economic power. At the same time, small men, who had not been permitted to participate in the Chinese consciousness, were coming into positions of responsibility. The *li* of the noble families, having become irrelevant, became corrupt. The new men did not understand *li* and had not learned the moral responsibility needed for it to function effectively.[120]

Confucius sought to revivify *li* and preserve the family as the basic unit of society by building social morality out of emotions of human heartedness and righteousness. The resulting social obligations, which were to be graded in accordance with proximity and dependence, would be objective because all men had the same emotions by nature and would cultivate the same morality. The Mohists rejected all family-oriented *li*, called for all emotions to be set aside, and sought to establish a universal standard of right and wrong actions based on empirical experience about the ends of action. Mo Zi called the necessary disposition to obey that standard "universal love," but he really hoped to induce the disposition by appealing to common sense, the authority of ancient sage kings, and the threat of divine punishment. Actions that would produce a benefit in material possessions or physical safety were said to be right; those that would not were wrong. Mo ignored the emotive and moral aspects of human nature and relied only upon the ability to calculate the general tendency of actions. He assumed that people could be induced to avoid actions that would be personally advantageous in the individual instance but disastrous if people generally acted in that way. The Legalists did not even seek to establish a general standard of right and wrong, let alone to develop the moral aspects of human nature. They were interested in the specific and the immediate. As ministers, or advisers to ministers, it was their job to go get things done so that their state would become richer and more powerful.

The first important Legalist was Guan Zhong (d. 645 B.C.E.) who was prime minister of the state of Qi. The book *Guan Zi*, which is sometimes attributed to him but was compiled later, probably in the third century B.C.E., contains writings of the Legalists, and others.[121] Shang Yang, also known as Lord Shang (d. 338 B.C.E.), as prime minister of Qin, helped that state to acquire the power that enabled it, in the next century, to unify the whole of China.[122] *The Book of Lord Shang* is a compilation of various

Legalist writings.[123] Shen Buhai (d. 337 B.C.E.) was prime minister of the state of Han. Li Si (d. 208 B.C.E.) was the chief minister of the first emperor of the Qin dynasty.[124] Legalists, such as Shen Dao (d. 275 B.C.E.?), and Han Feizi(d. 233 B.C.E.), who did not hold office, nevertheless addressed themselves to the problem of how to strengthen government.[125]

Li Si and Han Feizi had been pupils of Xun Zi, the leader of the realist wing of the Confucianists, who taught that human nature is evil.[126] It became the premise of the Legalists that human nature is entirely selfish: human beings move toward that which is beneficial and away from that which is harmful. In the Legalist's conception, human beings do not also have intellect that, according to Xun Zi, enables them to understand the necessity of ordering society in accordance with *li*.[127] Neither did the Legalists' view of human nature include the ability to calculate the general tendency of actions so as to put understanding of benefit and harm on a long-range basis, as the Mohists advocated.[128] Instead, the Legalists' human being was able to choose only between immediately offered alternatives of doing what would earn reward or doing what would earn punishment. This view of human nature applied to the vast majority. A few, who were qualified to rule, possessed something more, but not much.

What they possessed was the ability to get others to do things. For this purpose, the Legalists judged wisdom to be useless. Han Feizi said:

> What is called wisdom consists of subtle and unfathomable doctrines. [Perhaps the Daoists, or Logicians]. Such subtle and unfathomable doctrines are difficult even for men of highest intelligence to understand. If what men of highest intelligence find to be difficult is used to become laws for the people, the people will find them impossible to understand.[129]

Character development and moral goodness were also considered useless for the practical purpose of governing. Han Feizi said that people everywhere loved Confucius' doctrine of human heartedness and praised his doctrine of righteousness, but only seventy disciples tried to live as Confucius taught. On the other hand, he said Duke Ai, who was not devoted to human heartedness or righteousness, became a ruler because he knew how to manipulate power.[130]

Power to get others to do things, which the Legalists called authority (*shi*), was one of the three essential elements of Legalism. A second element was law (*fa*), by which they meant positive law. "A law is that which is enacted into the statute books, kept in government offices and proclaimed to the people."[131] Specific, coercive, unchanging commands—law—told the people what to do. The third element arose from the complexity of knowing what needed to be done and multiplicity of doers. It was assumed that what needed to be done would be urgent and evident, and probably this was true after five hundred years of internal turmoil and international war. Nevertheless, one man could not know about all affairs everywhere in the kingdom, and so he could not know every command that should be given, nor could he be everywhere at once in order to see that his commands were obeyed. Therefore, the exercise of power had to be bureaucratized. Managing this bureaucracy was the third element of Legalism. It was called *shu*, which meant statecraft, methods of government, ways of handling men.

Shi, fa, shu! That was the Legalists solution for the social disorder. They considered it impossible to teach men to be good. What was feasible was to prevent men from doing evil, by telling them what to do and rewarding them if they did it or punishing them if they did not do it. Whoever aspired to rule, therefore, had to have the power to reward or punish. People had to know what they were expected to do. Therefore, laws were published. Publication of the laws was also a check on the officials of the bureaucracy. If the officials did not reward or punish the people strictly in accordance with the law it could only be because the responsible officials were corrupt. The ruler, then, could remove them from office and punish them. This was an important part of the statecraft.[132] Probably the most important device for preserving the power of the ruler over officials and the people was indirect rule.

In their doctrine of indirect rule the Legalists adapted concepts borrowed from the Daoists and others. The ruler they said, should govern through nonaction, and actualities should always be kept in accordance with names. The king was inactive, but all-controlling. Anyone aspiring to become an official would be asked what needed to be done. If his proposals were plausible, the ruler would appoint him to an office to carry them out, but hold him accountable for the success of the policies in accordance with the Legalists' version of rectification of names. By "*names*" the Legalists meant the titles of the offices to which officials were appointed. "Actualities" meant accomplishment of the results that the official had claimed would result from his policies. When the accomplishment met the claim, the official was rewarded; when they did not, he was punished, usually by execution. Strictness and severity were considered essential to preserving the power of the ruler. Han Feizi said, "If the ruler has won the hearts of the people, they will exhort themselves without being pressed." But, it was assumed that what would impress the hearts of the people was punishment strictly in accordance with published laws.[133] He also said, "The severe household has no fierce slaves, but it is the affectionate mother who has spoiled sons."[134]

Most of the Legalists stressed one of the elements of Legalism. Shen Dao, (d. 275 B.C.E.?), who was strongly influenced by the Daoist concept of efficacy, emphasized *shi*. According to Shen, authority (power) was not something accorded to the sage king who ruled through moral instruction and education, as the Confucianists taught. A would-be ruler either had *shi* or he did not. If he did not, no amount of talent, goodness, and wisdom would enable him to govern. If he did, even Confucius himself would submit to him, though he was a man of little talent or moral worth.[135] Lord Shang (d. 338 B.C.E.) was the most prominent of those Legalists who stressed *fa*. He extended the idea of uniformity to every activity in the kingdom, fixing models and measures for everything so that disputes were minimized, expectations were fulfilled, and no one worked at cross purposes with others. The resulting increase in satisfaction and confidence greatly strengthened the state of Qin, which in the next six generations conquered all the other feudal states and established the empire.[136] Shen Buhai (d. 337 B.C.E.) was the leader of those who emphasized *shu*, but his works are lost. Presumably he adapted the doctrine of rectification of names to methods of government. Of *shu*, Han Feizi said: "In using the method of maintaining uniformity, names are of primary importance. When names have been rectified, things undergo change. Therefore the Sage holds to uniformity and rests in quiescence."[137] Han Feizi (d. 233 B.C.E.) synthesized the three elements of *shi*, *fa*, and *shu*, and his book is the fullest statement of the doctrines of the school.

Han Feizi's synthesis came at the peak of the Legalists influence. The state of Qin absorbed the territory of the last Zhou king in 256 B.C.E. In a series of campaigns from 231 to 221 B.C.E. Qin destroyed and absorbed all its opponents. In 221 B.C.E. the king of Qin proclaimed himself the first emperor of a unified China.[138] Li Si was a principal minister of the state of Qin and became the chief minister of the new empire.[139]

Notes

1. Fung Yu-lan, *A Short History of Chinese Philosophy* (New York: Macmillan Co., 1958), p. 32; Hsu Cho-yun, *Ancient China in Transition* (Stanford, Calif.: Stanford University Press, 1965), p. 99.
2. Hsu, *Ancient China in Transition*, pp. 26–52; Wolfram Eberhard, *A History of China* (Berkeley: University of California Press, 1969), pp. 51–57.
3. Fung, *A Short History of Chinese Philosophy*, pp. 30–39.
4. Ibid., pp. 30–33, 38–39.
5. Ibid., pp. 38–40.
6. Fung Yu-lan, *A History of Chinese Philosophy*, vol. 1 (Princeton, N.J.: Princeton University Press, 1983), pp. 43–59, 62–66.
7. Ibid., pp. 59–62.
8. Wing-tsit Chan, *A Source Book in Chinese Philosophy* (Princeton, N.J.: Princeton University Press, 1963), pp. 14–15.
9. Ibid., p. 15.
10. Wm. Theodore de Bary et al., *Sources of Chinese Tradition*, vol. 1 (New York: Columbia University Press, 1960), p. 18–19.
11. Gray L. Dorsey, *Jurisculture: Greece and Rome* (New Brunswick, N.J.: Transaction Publishers, 1989), pp. 54–55.
12. Fung, *A History of Chinese Philosophy*, vol. 1, pp. 66–71.
13. Fung, *A Short History of Chinese Philosophy*, pp. 44–45.
14. Chan, *A Source Book in Chinese Philosophy*, p. 28.
15. Ibid., p. 23.
16. Ibid., p. 104.
17. Ibid., p. 100.
18. Ibid., p. 101.
19. Fung, *A History of Chinese Philosophy*, vol. 1, p. 120.
20. Ibid., p. 121.
21. David Hume, *A Treatise of Human Nature* (Cleveland: Meridian Books, 1962), pp. 43–51.
22. Chan, *A Source Book in Chinese Philosophy*, pp. 53–55.
23. Ibid., Fung, *A History of Chinese Philosophy*, vol. 1, pp. 121–25.
24. Fung, *A History of Chinese Philosophy*, vol. 1, p. 123.
25. Fung, *A Short History of Chinese Philosophy*, p. 74.
26. Fung, *A History of Chinese Philosophy*, vol. 1, p. 112.
27. Fung, *A Short History of Chinese Philosophy*, p. 75.
28. Fung, *A History of Chinese Philosophy*, vol. 1, pp. 113–14.
29. Ibid.
30. Fung, *A Short History of Chinese Philosophy*, pp. 71–72.
31. Ibid., p. 144.
32. Ibid.
33. Ibid., p. 49; Chan, *A Source Book in Chinese Philosophy*, pp. 211, 232–43.
34. Chan, *A Source Book in Chinese Philosophy*, p. 211–31.
35. Fung, *A Short History of Chinese Philosophy*, p. 50; Charles O. Hucker, *China's Imperial Past* (Stanford, Calif.: Stanford University Press, 1975), pp. 223–24.
36. Fung, *A History of Chinese Philosophy*, vol. 1, pp. 96–100.
37. Ibid., p. 100.
38. Ibid., p. 91.

39. Fung, *A Short History of Chinese Philosophy*, pp. 44–46.
40. Fung, *A History of Chinese Philosophy*, vol. 1, pp. 84–85.
41. Fung, *A Short History of Chinese Philosophy*, p. 54.
42. Fung, *A History of Chinese Philosophy*, vol. 1, pp. 88–89.
43. Joseph Needham, *Science and Civilisation in China*, vol. 2 (Cambridge: Cambridge University Press, 1956), p. 169.
44. Fung, *A Short History of Chinese Philosophy*, pp. 49–59; Chan, *A Source Book in Chinese Philosophy*, pp. 211–13.
45. Fung, *A History of Chinese Philosophy*, vol. 1, p. 90.
46. Ibid., pp. 91–94.
47. Ibid., p. 92.
48. de Bary et al., *Sources of Chinese Tradition*, p. 35.
49. Robert Temple, *The Genius of China: 3000 Years of Science, Discovery and Invention* (New York: Simon & Schuster, 1989), pp. 215–16.
50. Needham, *Science and Civilisation in China*, vol. 4, part 1, pp. 15–55; Fung, *A Short History of Chinese Philosophy*, pp. 118–28.
51. See above, chap. 8, text at note 30.
52. Chan, *A Source Book in Chinese Philosophy*, p. 212; Needham, *Science and Civilisation in China*, vol. 2, p. 165.
53. Fung, *A Short History of Chinese Philosophy*, pp. 80–81.
54. See above, chap. 2, and chap. 6, concerning obedience.
55. Fung, *A History of Chinese Philosophy*, vol. 1, p. 193, 204.
56. Fung, *A Short History of Chinese Philosophy*, p. 81.
57. Fung, *A History of Chinese Philosophy*, vol. 1, pp. 1–2; Chan, *A Source Book in Chinese Philosophy*, pp. 232–33.
58. Chan, *A Source Book in Chinese Philosophy*, p. 232; Needham, *Science and Civilisation in China*, vol. 2, p. 185.
59. Fung, *A History of Chinese Philosophy*, vol. 1, p. 192.
60. Dorsey, *Jurisculture: Greece and Rome*, pp. 56–57.
61. Hegel, G.W.F. *Hegel: Highlights: An Annotated Selection*, Wanda Orynski, ed. (New York: Philosophical Library, 1960), pp. 1–137.
62. Needham, *Science and Civilisation in China*, vol. 2, p. 289.
63. Fung, *A Short History of Chinese Philosophy*, pp. 83–90; Fung, *A History of Chinese Philosophy*, vol. 1, 211.
64. Fung, *A History of Chinese Philosophy*, vol. 1, p. 204.
65. Ibid., pp. 203–12.
66. Fung, *A Short History of Chinese Philosophy*, pp. 91–92.
67. Ibid., p. 61.
68. Ibid., p. 67.
69. Ibid., p. 93–94.
70. Ibid.
71. Fung, *A Short History of Chinese Philosophy*, p. 104.
72. Fung, *A History of Chinese Philosophy*, vol. 1, pp. 175–76; see above, chap. 1.
73. Ibid., p. 136.
74. Fung, *A Short History of Chinese Philosophy*, p. 61.
75. Fung, *A History of Chinese Philosophy*, vol. 1, pp. 205–6, 209–12.
76. Fung, *A Short History of Chinese Philosophy*, pp. 94–95.
77. Ibid., p. 95.
78. Fung, *A History of Chinese Philosophy*, vol. 1, p. 177.
79. Ibid., p. 179.

80. Ibid., pp. 177-78.
81. Ibid., p. 179; de Bary et al., *Sources of Chinese Tradition*, vol. 1, pp. 55, 60; Chan, *A Source Book in Chinese Philosophy*, p. 790.
82. Fung, *A History of Chinese Philosophy*, vol. 1, p. 179.
83. Ibid., p. 180.
84. Ibid.
85. Ibid., p. 187.
86. Ibid., p. 183.
87. Fung, *A Short History of Chinese Philosophy*, p. 101.
88. Ibid., p. 100.
89. Ibid., p. 102.
90. Needham, *Science and Civilisation in China*, vol. 2, pp. 45-46.
91. Ibid., pp. 121-22.
92. Ibid., pp. 33-164.
93. Fung, *A Short History of Chinese Philosophy*, pp. 104-17.
94. Ibid., pp. 129-30; Needham, *Science and Civilisation in China*, vol. 2, pp. 239-40.
95. Chan, *A Source Book in Chinese Philosophy*, p. 245; Fung, *A Short History of Chinese Philosophy*, p. 130.
96. Needham, *Science and Civilisation in China*, vol. 2, pp. 279-91; Granet, *La Pensée Chinoise*, (Paris: Éditions Albin Michel, 1950), pp. 86-114.
97. Hellmut Wilhelm, ed., Richard Wilhelm and Cary F. Baynes, trans., *The I Ching, or Book of Changes*, 3rd ed. (Princeton, N.J.: Princeton University Press, 1967), pp. 1, 287, 369-97; Needham, *Science and Civilisation in China*, vol. 2, pp. 273, 276-77.
98. Fung, *A Short History of Chinese Philosophy*, pp. 133-34; Fung, *A History of Chinese Philosophy*, vol. 1, pp. 159-69.
99. de Bary et al., *Sources of Chinese Tradition*, vol. 1, pp. 208-09.
100. Fung, *A Short History of Chinese Philosophy*, pp. 131-32; Fung, *A History of Chinese Philosophy*, vol. 1, p. 163.
101. Needham, *Science and Civilisation in China*, vol. 2, p. 243.
102. Ibid., p. 244.
103. See above, chap. 8, text at notes 23, 24.
104. Needham, *Science and Civilisation in China*, vol. 2, pp. 216-52.
105. Granet, *La Pensée Chinoise*, pp. 149-208, 249-76.
106. Ibid., p. 151.
107. Ibid., pp. 249-73.
108. Dorsey, *Jurisculture: Greece and Rome*, pp. 35-37.
109. Granet, *La Pensée Chinoise*, pp. 260-76.
110. Fung, *A History of Chinese Philosophy*, vol. 1, pp. 164-65.
111. Ibid., pp. 159, 414.
112. Needham, *Science and Civilisation in China*, vol. 2, pp. 232-33; Fung, *A Short History of Chinese Philosophy*, pp. 136-37.
113. Fung, *A Short History of Chinese Philosophy*, pp. 136-37.
114. Ibid.
115. Fung, *A History of Chinese Philosophy*, vol. 1, p. 161.
116. Needham, *Science and Civilisation in China*, vol. 2, p. 233.
117. Fung, *A Short History of Chinese Philosophy*, p. 138.
118. Fung, *A History of Chinese Philosophy*, vol. 1, p. 312; Chan, *A Source Book in Chinese Philosophy*, p. 252; de Bary et al., *Sources of Chinese Tradition*, vol. 1, pp. 122-23.

119. Fung, *A History of Chinese Philosophy*, vol. 1, p. 312; Fung, *A Short History of Chinese Philosophy*, p. 155.
120. Hsu, *Ancient China in Transition*, pp. 28-52, 78-106; Wolfram Eberhard, *A History of China* (Berkeley: University of California Press, 1969), pp. 51-57.
121. Chan, *A Source Book in Chinese Philosophy*, p. 252; Fung, *A History of Chinese Philosophy*, vol. 1, p. 112.
122. J. J. L. Duyvendak, trans. *The Book of Lord Shang* (Chicago: University of Chicago Press, 1963), pp. 1-3.
123. Chan, *A Source Book in Chinese Philosophy*, p. 252; Fung, *A History of Chinese Philosophy*, vol. 1, p. 414.
124. Chan, *A Source Book in Chinese Philosophy*, p. 252; de Bary et al., *Sources of Chinese Tradition*, vol. 1, p. 122.
125. Chan, *A Source Book in Chinese Philosophy*, p. 252.
126. Fung, *A Short History of Chinese Philosophy*, p. 154.
127. Ibid., pp. 145-47.
128. Ibid., pp. 53-55.
129. Chan, *A Source Book in Chinese Philosophy*, p. 259.
130. Ibid., p. 258.
131. Ibid., p. 256.
132. Fung, *A History of Chinese Philosophy*, vol. 1, p. 321.
133. Ibid., pp. 323-26; Chan, *A Source Book in Chinese Philosophy*, pp. 254-55.
134. Chan, *A Source Book in Chinese Philosophy*, p. 253.
135. Fung, *A History of Chinese Philosophy*, vol. 1, pp. 318, 155.
136. Duyvendak, *The Book of Lord Shang*, pp. 2-7.
137. Fung, *A History of Chinese Philosophy*, vol. 1, p. 324.
138. Hucker, *China's Imperial Past*, pp. 40-41.
139. See Derk Bodde, *China's First Unifier: A Study of the Chin Dynasty As Seen in the Life of Li Ssu (280?-208 B.C.)* (Hong Kong: Hong Kong University Press, 1967).

10

Legalism in Action

The assumptions, strategies, and procedures of Legalism succeeded in unifying and (for a short time) pacifying China. This is a carefully ambiguous statement in two respects. In the first respect, unification and pacification are something short of the social harmony and unity that has been a lodestar throughout Chinese history. In the second respect, unification and pacification were accomplished not by Legalist philosophers, but by practitioners of government, whose successful assumptions, strategies, and procedures came to be called Legalism when systematically stated, especially by Han Feizi. The practitioners were retroactively called Legalists. However, for convenience and in accordance with custom, the following discussion will speak of the role of Legalism and Legalists in the acquisition of the wealth and power that enabled the state of Qin to conquer all of its rivals and create the first Chinese empire.

Legalism in the State of Qin

Qin was a small state on the Wei River, west of the Western Zhou capital near Xian. It was not one of the Western Zhou feudal states. Much of its population, including the ruling class, had Turkish and Tibetan as well as Chinese ancestors.[1] At the end of the Western Zhou period, in 771 B.C.E., Duke Xiang of Qin was enfiefed in recognition of his help to the Zhou in the attack by Rong tribes that resulted in the loss of the Western capital and the beginning of the Eastern Zhou dynasty at the new capital near Luoyang. Qin received much of the formerly royal lands around the abandoned Western capital. Nevertheless, as late as 361 B.C.E., Qin was not considered sufficiently civilized to participate in the conferences held by the other feudal lords of China.[2] And nearly one hundred years later, in 266 B.C.E., a noble of the state of Wei said, "Ch'in [Qin] has the same customs as the Jung [Rong] and the Ti [Di]. It has the heart of a tiger or a wolf. It is avaricious, perverse, eager for profit, and without sincerity. It knows nothing about etiquette (*li*), proper relationships (*i*) [*yi*], and virtuous conduct (*te hsing*) [*de xing*], and if there be an opportunity for material gain, it will disregard its relatives as if they were animals."[3]

The people of Qin were not sufficiently civilized because they did not participate sufficiently in the Chinese consciousness. Over the centuries that consciousness had come to include proper behavior with respect to the five human relationships—between sovereign and family head, husband and wife, parent and child, older and younger siblings, and between friends. In the first document in the *Book of History*, the prescribed attitudes and actions for each of these relationships are referred to as the Five Codes.[4] The Five Codes had been developed gradually as an important part of the shared Chinese consciousness.

The states of the Eastern Zhou dynasty considered Qin uncivilized because the five sets of *li* had not been fully developed there, but in the states where li had become fully developed it was becoming ineffective. The normative content of the five aspects of li and the social and political structure of feudalism had developed together. In the Spring and Autumn period (770–481 B.C.E.) and the Warring States period (481–221 B.C.E.) feudalism was disintegrating. This resulted in a great deal of social mobility. The personal relationships of lineage became insufficient to assure official position. Noble families lost their power, status, and wealth, and members had to live by personal competence. Men of common origins but high competence became ministers and even rulers.[5] In this situation the li of the *junzi*, the noble families, could no longer function as the organizing and ordering norms of the state, as it had in the past. It was a time of change and crisis in which the schools of philosophy developed as various solutions were offered to the problem of social disorder.[6]

The solution of Confucianism was to revivify the five aspects of li and make them applicable to all instead of just the noble families. Confucius proposed to do this by invoking reverence for the ancient sages, but in fact basing li on the moral principles of human nature. Confucianists would teach the new li to anyone, and they said that anyone who followed the way of moral goodness could become a superior man (*junzi*), whereas superiority had previously depended upon descent from noble ancestors. The Legalists made a virtue out of the lack of noble ancestors and ignorance of the ancient sages. They said, "Why look to the old. It has failed. Take advantage of new opportunities." Position, status, and wealth were coming to depend solely upon individual competence, not upon lineage or knowledge of ancient lore. The new opportunity was to control by centralized power. This was much more feasible in Qin than in the states where feudalism and the Five Codes of li had flourished.

In 361 B.C.E. Shang Yang, later known as Lord Shang, went from his native state of Wei to Qin, whose ruler, Duke Xiao, was looking for competent ministers even if they came from other countries. Shang Yang earned the confidence of Duke Xiao and his measures made him one of the greatest of the Legalists. He divided Qin into thirty-one counties, each administered by a centrally appointed magistrate, thus facilitating direct rule by the duke and curtailing the political power of hereditary land owners. Then he ended the system of hereditary land holding, under which peasants were attached to the land. Labor service was replaced by taxation. New methods of laying out fields were adopted and land could be bought and sold. The hope of acquiring their own land encouraged peasants from other states to immigrate to Qin, thus increasing the pool from which infantry could be conscripted.[7] Status on the basis of family lineage was replaced by a hierarchy of honorary ranks based on meritorious conduct.[8] Shang Yang stimulated internal migration to uncultivated areas and undermined the authority of families and clans by doubling the taxes of persons having two or more adult sons living with them and forbidding fathers, sons, and brothers from living the in the same room.[9]

To communicate the will of the king to the multitude of increasingly independent individuals, and to ensure that the individuals obeyed, Shang Yang relied upon one code of law, *fa*, instead of five codes of *li*. The laws were posted on pillars in prominent places so that all could know them. Punishment was strict and severe. Shang Yang organized people into groups of five and ten who were responsible for each other. They were required to report each other's crimes and if they failed to do so they suffered the same punishment as the guilty person. For some crimes relatives of the five or ten men were also punished.[10] The laws were administrative as well as criminal. Very recent excavations have discovered Qin laws and legal texts from the next century after Shang Yang. Eighteen headings deal with matters such as arable lands, stables, parks, and granaries. Also discovered were legal catechisms that explained laws and legal procedures by means of questions and answers, and "patterns" formulated as guides to officials for carrying out legal procedures, such as questioning suspects.[11]

The lack of traditional Chinese culture in Qin also created the opportunity for the Legalists to make an extensive use of quantitative requirements, records, and statistics in their administrative efforts to increase their wealth and strength. In the *Book of Changes*, the calendar, and associational science, the Chinese made a symbolic use of numerical categories to indicate orientation, anticipate changes, and discover symbiotic associations. The goal was to live in harmony with nature. The Legalist administrators in Qin sought beneficial control of nature in order to increase the wealth and power of the state. One of the recently discovered Qin administrative statutes specified how much seed was to be used for planting different grains, pulses, and textile crops. Another required every county to maintain records covering the planting and growing of grain, including the amounts of precipitation and the acreage of crops affected, the occurrence and consequences of droughts, hurricanes, floods, insect pests, and other disasters. Reports based on these records had to be sent to the Qin capital before the end of the eighth month. Other statutes specified the exact dimensions of pieces of hemp cloth that were used as a medium of exchange. Standard weights and measures were specified and fines were to be imposed for violations. Great precision and efficiency were required for administrative actions.[12]

In order to maintain public acceptance the laws had to be perceived to be impartial and directed toward the good of all. Therefore, it was important that ministers should not be seen to favor some over others or to be pursuing private interests. Shang Yang was said to have been exemplary in this respect. Duyvendak quotes one account that said that the strength that enabled Qin to annex all the feudal states was the result of the plans laid by Shang Yang (the Lord of Shang). The account continued:

> Indeed the Lord of Shang worked with his whole person and had only one thought. He was entirely devoted to the public weal and did not think of himself; at home, he caused the people to be active in the work of agriculture and weaving, in order to enrich the state, and abroad, to attach importance to the rewards for fighting, so as to encourage brave soldiers; his laws and orders were enacted rigorously; in the capital he did not flatter nobles and favorites, and in the province he was impartial with regard to those who were distant, with the result that, when his orders were issued, forbidden actions stopped, when his laws were published, crime ceased.[13]

Another means of keeping the confidence of the people was to punish persons in high office the same as anyone else for violations of law. Shang Yang even insisted that a law violation by the crown prince should not go unpunished. The emperor would not allow the crown prince to be punished, but he permitted the punishment of his tutor and his teacher. It was said that, "The following day, the people of Ch'in [Qin] all hastened into (the path of) the law."[14]

Qin was also deficient in Chinese culture with respect to warfare. Military expeditions of Chinese feudal states began with decisions made in the ancestral temple of the clan, after divination and sacrificial invocation of the support of the ancestors, and the results of the expedition were reported in the temple. The ancestral tablet of a renowned warrior ancestor was always carried on a military expedition. The expedition was expected to yield honor to the family, not merely victory in battle. Ancestors were arbiters of right and wrong, and when displeased could bring about defeat in battle.[15] Battles between Zhou feudal states in the Spring and Autumn period were conducted according to codes of chivalry and humanity. Combat was mainly between nobles riding in bronze chariots.[16] Gallantry in the face of danger was greatly admired. One charioteer, hotly pursued, used his last arrow to kill a stag, which he then presented to his pursuers who, thereupon, permitted him to return safely to his own lines. On the battlefield, propriety was more frequent than savagery.[17] Captured troops were held for ransom or enslaved. If territory was annexed, few of the defeated nobles were killed and the royal line was never extinguished.[18]

To Shang Yang, Chinese culture poisonously distracted warriors from their duty. He said that the people should be trained to engage in agriculture in accordance with the law and in battle in accordance with the orders of the generals. If the people learned integrity, sincerity, righteousness, benevolence, and filial piety, they would have alternative standards of conduct. The people should be kept simple and ignorant and constantly engaged in agriculture or warfare. If they learned anything else they would be useless to the state.[19] The lowest could achieve status and office through merit, but a life of luxury was open only to those who excelled in warfare. The prosperity of its well-managed agriculture, the peasant immigrants attracted by the possibility of land ownership, and the productiveness of its land created a very large pool of manpower available for conscription. Qin kept a standing army of one million infantry. The Legalists' amoral view of the state vitally affected the conduct of battle and the treatment of the vanquished. Soldiers who faltered and generals who made one mistake were executed. Savagery replaced chivalry on the battlefield. The vanquished were slain; the Qin would not have to fight them again on another day. The *Historical Memoirs* says that in a battle with the state of Zhao in 260 B.C.E., Zhao lost 50,000 men killed in battle. Of the 400,000 who surrendered Qin slaughtered all but 240. The combined casualties inflicted by Qin upon its enemies in 130 years was said to be 1,489,000.[20]

Qin enjoyed a favorable geographic location on the Wei River; it was nearly impregnable to attack because entry had to be through a few easily guarded passes. Qin was also farsighted in carrying out extensive irrigation and flood control projects in its own region and in the Chengdu plain in an annexed area to the south. Qin was also fortunate in having long-lived rulers. However, in a recent reevaluation of the reasons for the triumph of Qin in *The Cambridge History of China*, Derk Bodde concludes that the "decisive factors were the programs of administrative efficiency, agricultural reform, and single-minded pursuit of political and military power that Shang Yang had bequeathed to Ch'in [Qin]."[21]

Legalism in the New Empire

During the Spring and Autumn period (770–481 B.C.E.) there were fourteen major states contending for supremacy in China.[22] In the Warring States period (481–221 B.C.E.) the number of major contending states had been reduced to seven. These included Qin on the Wei River, west of the great bend in the Yellow River as it came down from the north and turned east towards the sea, Zhao, Wei, and Han in north central China, Yan and Qi in the northeast, and Chu in the south.[23] In 256 B.C.E., Qin destroyed the Zhou ruling house and annexed its small domain.[24] King Zheng came to the throne under a regency in 246 B.C.E. at the age of thirteen and began to rule in his own right upon reaching the age of twenty-one in 238 B.C.E. Qin conquered the north central states of Zhao, Wei, and Han from 230 to 225 B.C.E., the southern state of Chu in 223, and the northeastern states of Yan and Qi in 222 and 221.[25]

King Zheng, now in control of the whole of China, adopted the title Shihuangdi, First August Emperor. History knows this first emperor as Qin Shihuangdi. The "di" harked back to the Lord on High worshiped by the Shang. Now the task began of ruling what had been conquered. The emperor's chancellor, Wang Guan, urged him to place the more distant territories in control of sons of the Qin family. Li Si, the Legalist, who with Han Feizi had studied originally under the realist Confucian Xun Zi, pointed out that this was the feudalism that had failed the Zhou dynasty. The emperor rejected the advice of his chancellor and took the advice of Li Si, who had been Justice Minister of the Qin state. Shihuangdi made Li Si his Grand Councillor and depended so consistently upon his advice that Bodde has called Li Si, rather than the emperor, the "First Unifier of China."[26]

Legalism was the guiding influence of Shihuangdi's reign. The principle of centralized power was immediately implemented. The entire territory of the new empire was divided into thirty-six commanderies, which were subdivided into counties. At the head of each commandery was a civil governor, a military commander, and an imperial inspector, who was the immediate representative of the emperor. Each county was administered by a magistrate, who was appointed at the imperial level, had a fixed salary, and was subject to recall at any time.[27] The former rulers, nobles, and officials of the conquered states—120,000 families in all—were removed from their homes, where they might have made trouble, to the imperial capital at Xianyang, where they were provided with palatial accommodations but kept under surveillance. Weapons were collected throughout the empire, brought to Xianyang, melted down, and cast into bells and statutes.[28]

Shihuangdi standardized writing. Written graphs were originally simplified pictures of the thing referred to, such as man, woman, child, sun, moon, and tree.[29] In time, these pictographs became stylized, and thousands of graphs were invented to refer to things that could not be seen, such as emotions, relations, and obligations. For most graphs, therefore, its form was a mere convention, without any natural relationship to an aspect of reality, but serving to indicate that aspect for all who accepted the convention. However, as Xun Zi pointed out, persons cannot understand each other unless they use the same name for the same reality.[30] During the nearly nine hundred years of Zhou dynasty, changes had occurred that made the perceptions and experience of peoples of previous periods or different regions inaccessible. It was essential to the Legalists' form of government that everyone, everywhere, understand the published laws in the same way. According to Legalism, meanings should not be left to chance or custom. The ruler could select any name he wished, but, once established in the law and orders of the ruler, name should be everywhere the same and unchanging.[31] Accordingly, Shihuangdi appointed a panel of experts to standardize the script, eliminating anachronisms and differences and simplifying for clarity.

The resulting "Small Seal" script, which emerged from this process, lent itself to the use of the newly introduced writing brush, thereby giving aesthetic pleasure along with uniformity and clarity. This script, further simplified in Han times, was used until the Chinese Communist simplification of recent decades, and is still in use in Taiwan. The unity of written language in the face of great differences in regional spoken dialects is generally credited with preserving Chinese cultural unity and contributing to political unity.[32] The standardization of writing is probably the greatest accomplishment of the Qin dynasty.

The Legalist doctrine of uniformity by imperial decree was generally applied. Weights and measures were standardized throughout the empire. Two types of coin were issued, yellow gold and bronze, circular with a square center hole. All other objects, including pearls, jade, tortoise shell, cowrie shells, silver, and tin, were prohibited as media of exchange. The meaning of "money" was fixed. A standard gauge for the axles of vehicles was established, not to bring them into accord with the symbolic dimensions of the universe, but for the practical purpose of running freely in the same set of ruts in the pounded earth roads.[33] The law code of the Qin state, with its principles of collective responsibility and strict punishments, was extended to the whole empire. Minor infractions were punished with fines and forced labor. Punishments for serious offenses were calculated to instill deterring fear. In addition to tattooing the face, amputating a hand, foot, genitals, or the nose, punishments included beheading, "chiselling the crown," "extracting ribs," boiling in a cauldron, cutting in two at the waist, pulling apart with chariots, and combinations of death-causing and mutilation-causing punishments.[34]

Public works, military campaigns, and support of agriculture grew to gigantic proportions, chewing up hundreds of thousands of lives through frenzied work, harsh conditions, and impossible requirements. Beginning in 220 B.C.E., a series of imperial highways were built radiating from Xianyang toward the north, northeast, east and southeast. Of pounded earth, the roads were wide and tree-lined. Also in the first year of the empire, construction was begun on a great wall to protect against barbarian invasions from the north and northwest. A famous general, Ming Tian, had 300,000 men constantly at his disposal, with whom he was charged with driving off the Rong and Di tribes and building the wall, which was 2,600 miles long. Undesirable persons, as well as persons convicted of crime, were sentenced to forced labor on the wall. So many died that Chinese historians have referred to the great wall as the "Longest Graveyard in the World." In 212 B.C.E., General Ming was ordered to simultaneously build a straight road from the capital of Xianyang to the northern border. The royal roads built during the short reign of Shihuangdi covered about 4,250 miles, exceeding by 500 miles the road system that Rome later built in Europe. Three massive canal and irrigation projects were also completed, which increased agricultural production and provided transport for grain and goods—all of which are still in use today. When the Ordos region in the north was secured, 30,000 families were sent into the region to colonize it. Another 30,000 families were sent to the south side of the Shandong peninsula.[35]

Legalism provided no guidance with respect to sacrifices, rituals, and ceremonies of the imperial court. Rather than forego these things, Shihuangdi drew eclectically upon tradition and philosophers. He sacrificed to eighteen mountains and seventeen rivers, and worshiped at hundreds of shrines in the vicinity of the capital. There were shrines to the gods of the sun, the moon, and the planets, to wind and rain, and other natural forces. He had three hundred observers of the heavens to assure the accuracy of the imperial calendar, and he created an academy of seventy (the number of Confucius' disciples) men of wide learning from various schools of philosophy. He made grand tours to various parts of the empire, worshiping at local shrines, erecting monuments with inscriptions proclaiming his benevolence and virtue, and asserting his care for the people. His court ceremonies like those of the ancient sage-kings were linked to the rhythm of life and order of natural and human events.[36] Following the theory of dynastic succession of Zou Yan, the Yin/Yang philosopher, Shihuangdi took water as the element under whose aegis he ruled and black as the color of his clothes and emblems, and he called the Chinese the Blackhaired people.[37]

The Legalist theory of controlling people's thoughts was much more difficult to implement in the empire than it had been in the state of Qin. Confucianism was widely known and taught and its primacy of familial obligations was directly contrary to the Legalist primacy of state obligations. The great majority of the people in the former Chinese states, and the 120,000 aristocratic families brought to the Qin capital, adhered to the traditional culture of China as developed by the schools of philosophy.[38] The problem came to a head in 213 B.C.E. when, at a banquet celebrating the emperor's birthday, a Confucian member of the academy dared to tell the emperor that previous dynasties had survived for so long because land was distributed to family members and that the survival of Qin depended upon its ability to learn from this past experience.

The challenge to centralized power could not have been more direct or audacious. Li Si replied that the Qin dynasty was a new era when "all the laws and all decrees issue from a single source, when the 'Blackhaired people' support themselves by farming and handicrafts and students study only the laws and prohibitions."[39] Then Li Si attacked non-Legalist scholars, saying:

> They study the past in order to criticize the times in which we live and sow confusion among the Blackhaired people. Speaking frankly, and on pain of death, I cannot but say that in the past, when the world was torn by chaos and disorder, no one could unify it.

> That is why so many would-be rulers arose, using the past to denigrate the present, burying reality in their empty arguments and rhetoric.[40]

Li Si warned the emperor against those who resisted his laws and orders, debating them in accordance with their own school of thought, opposing them in their hearts and disputing them openly in the streets, thereby lowering the prestige of the sovereign and leading to the formation of factions. Li Si thereupon proposed that all of the official histories of the contending states, except for the annals of Qin, should be burned, and that anyone who possessed copies of the Confucian classics, the *Book of Poetry* and the *Book of History*, or the philosophical discourses of any of the schools of philosophy, should present them within thirty days for burning; that anyone who failed to turn over the forbidden texts within thirty days should have his face tattooed and be sent to do forced labor on the Great Wall; and that anyone who discussed them in public should be executed. Shihuangdi agreed, the decree was issued, and the books were burned.[41] Millions of persons adhered to beliefs that could no longer be discussed in public. But rebellion did not break out until the imperial center had become weaker.

Shihuangdi's power was waning; he became nervous and irritable. For nearly ten years he had been trying to create a new social and political reality, superseding the five sets of reciprocal obligations indicated by the social names of ruler-family head, husband-wife, father-son, older brother-younger brother, and friend-friend, and sweeping everyone in the empire into a single set of unilateral obligations indicated by the new social names of emperor-subject. Furthermore, deprived by Legalism of any guidance or reinforcement from a common consciousness of meanings, values, and purposes, he had to rely solely upon his own calculation and personal experience. The psychological strain must have been very great. Also, his work load was unbelievably heavy. Because of the absence of community standards he could not delegate any decision making. He is reported to have processed 120 pounds of documents each day. Small wonder that he began to confuse his interests with those of the state. Indeed, in Legalist theory, the two may have been identical; Li Si asserted that the ruler was the reason for the existence of the state.[42] In any event, Shihuangdi increasingly pursued his own comfort and glory.

Shihuangdi began to seek immortality in 219 B.C.E. On an imperial tour to the east coast, some magicians proposed that they make an expedition to the offshore islands that were said to be the home of the Immortals, in order to capture the elixir of immortality. Shihuangdi eagerly agreed to the expedition and ordered "thousands of youths and maidens" to go with the magicians. If the expedition ever occurred it was unsuccessful. (According to legend the young people sent on this expedition were the beginning of the Japanese race.)[43]

Shihuangdi returned to the east in 218 and again in 215 B.C.E. He became increasingly impatient with his magicians and alchemists for not finding or synthesizing the elixir of immortality. He gave vent to his anger when his boat was endangered by high winds and heavy rain as he was crossing the Yangzi River. He ordered 3,000 convicts to destroy all the trees and vegetation on the mountain where the river deity was said to dwell and then he had the whole mountain painted a bright red, the color worn by criminals.[44] After the tour of 215 B.C.E., he remained in his capital until a final tour in 211 B.C.E., but he started more construction on a grandiose scale. He ordered a huge new imperial palace to be built on the south bank of the Wei. It was 675 meters by 112 meters, with galleries that could hold 10,000 men and accommodate banners fifty feet high. He began, or greatly accelerated, work on his tomb at Mount Li. More than 700,000 men were put to work on the two projects.[45] Recently discovered, the tomb is eight miles in circumference. Partial excavation has revealed an entire army of life-size terra cotta figures, including more than 7,500 soldiers with armor and weapons, and also horses and chariots. Each human face is distinctive and many different hair styles are depicted.[46] When a magician told him that he should keep out of sight so that evil spirits could not thwart his quest for the elixir of immortality, he ordered the construction of 270 palaces connected by secret passages and covered roadways and only a few servants and officials ever knew where he was.[47]

Fear and vindictiveness began to grip the palace. Shihuangdi's servants and officials were afraid to tell him the truth. His three hundred astronomers did not report unfavorable omens. Members of the court began to talk secretly of his cruelty. There was speculation that he was going mad. One day, looking down from the palace upon Li Si's huge retinue, Shihuangdi remarked that Li Si was becoming too proud. When Li reduced his retinue, the emperor knew that someone has reported his remark to Li Si. He had everyone who had been with him that day executed.[48]

In 212 B.C.E., when two court magicians left without permission, Shihuangdi said:

> Now I learn that these many magicians have departed without warning, having spent millions with no results. I have showered them with honors and yet they slander me, reproaching me with my faults.
>
> I have had enquiries made about the scholars who consorted with these magicians and find that they are spreading vicious rumors in the capital to confuse the Black-haired people.

Shihuangdi called all the magicians and scholars together and demanded an explanation. When they accused each other he personally selected 460 of them to serve as examples and had them executed, reputedly by being buried alive from the neck down.[49] Shihuangdi's eldest son, Fu Su, opposed the execution of the scholars, saying that it would destroy the dynasty. His father's response was to banish Fu Su to the Great Wall.[50]

At about this time, 212 B.C.E., Shihuangdi gave himself a nominal victory in his search for immortality by referring to himself as "Pure Being" instead of the royal "We."[51] The term was borrowed from the

Daoist Zhuang Zi. The Chinese made no clear distinction between a material body and a numinous essence. Some Daoists, who were experimenting with alchemy, believed that it was possible to gradually "lighten" the body until it contained only the pure element of life, which could then exist indefinitely.[52] Zhuang Zi called persons who had achieved this immortality "pure beings."[53]

In 211 B.C.E., Shihuangdi undertook another journey to the east coast, accompanied by Li Si and a newly favored son, Hu Hai. Not yet fifty, he was worn out, but he was still obsessed with finding the elixir of immortality. He continued to be met with excuses. On his return journey, Shihuangdi fell ill. No one dared to discuss with him funeral arrangements or the succession. Shihuangdi issued a decree to Fu Su ordering him to return from the Great Wall and meet the funeral cortege at Xianyang and bury him there. The implication was that Fu Su was to succeed. Shao Gao, the eunuch responsible for transmission of imperial decrees, was also the tutor of Hu Hai.[54]

In this crucial situation, the Legalist rejection of community standards was again significant. In the first place, no ties of natural subordination, conscience, or good faith bound officials and servants to the emperor. Legalism rejected any basis of obligation except hope of reward or fear of punishment. Neither could be expected from the dying Shihuangdi. In the second place, Legalism rejected any normative standard for determining who was qualified to become emperor. Based on non-Legalist Chinese culture, the standard might have been that the person was in tune with the order of the universe, or possessed moral superiority. The Legalists said that one who had authority should be the sovereign. But since the Legalists defined authority as possession of the power to make people obey, the criterion was factual only. Therefore, on Legalists' premises, it cannot be said that what followed was treachery. But it certainly exposed a fatal weakness in the Qin dynasty.

Zhao Gao did not send the decree to Fu Su. Shihuangdi died. Li Si, Zhao Gao, and other eunuchs plotted to make Hu Hai the next emperor. They concealed Shihuangdi's death by a charade of food going to his covered litter and missives coming from it. They forged a letter from Shihuangdi to Fu Su ordering him to kill himself. He did. Upon the return to the capital another decree was forged proclaiming Hu Hai the Second Sovereign Emperor.[55]

Hu Hai had his brothers, half-brothers, and even sisters killed. He executed his father's ministers whom he distrusted. He allowed Zhao Gao to conduct most affairs of state. Li Si proffered counsel, but Zhao Gao ignored it and Hu Hai refused to grant him audience. Hu Hai pressed with great vigor the completion of his father's tomb and the new palace he had started. When Li Si criticized Hu Hai for exorbitant expenditures and heavy taxes, Hu Hai had him executed, after torture. Following completion of the tomb Hu Hai entered upon a purge of officials and generals whom he suspected of disloyalty.[56]

Imperial authority rapidly evaporated. Hu Hai did not seriously try to make officials and generals obey his orders and decrees. Zhao Gao sought to exercise the power but in place of amoral calculation of imperial interests and strict and uniform punishment of violations, he engaged in connivance and intrigue in pursuit of personal interests. Therefore, he never gained credibility, and when he sought to assume the throne himself not one minister would support him.[57] The descent into chaos and corruption continued as Qin armies were trying to put down rebellion. Distrust of Zhao Gao caused Zhang Han, one of the most successful Qin generals, to join the rebels. In 207 B.C.E. 200,000 Qin troops were slaughtered by rebel forces at the approaches to the capital. In October of that year Zhao Gao engineered Hu Hai's suicide. He then arranged the succession of Zi Ying, a nephew of Hu Hai, but Qin prospects were so far diminished that Zi Ying was invested only with the title of king, not emperor. Forty-six days later Zi Ying abjectly surrendered to a rebel force under Liu Bang.[58]

The Collapse and Its Causes

Two types of men led rebellions against the Qin. One type comprised common men driven to desperation by the harsh rigidities of Qin Legalism. Chen She, who has been celebrated as the first breath of the whirlwind that swept away the Qin, was of this type. A farmer, he was one of nine hundred conscripts sent to do garrison duty. Because of heavy rains it became impossible for the party to arrive on time. The Qin penalty for failure to make a rendezvous was execution. No extenuating circumstances were considered. Deciding that they might as well try for liberty, Chen She and Wu Guang killed the officers and rallied the other conscripts to join them in rebellion.[59] Liu Bang was also a peasant farmer.

He decided upon rebellion while leading a party of convicts to work.[60] Xiang Yu was of the second type, composed of men from families that had held high office in the former independent states. The Xiangs had held high commands in armies of the southern state of Chu. When Xiang Yu and his uncle Xiang Liang reconstituted the state of Chu and put a grandson of the former king on the throne, Liu Bang and his supporters threw in their lot with the Xiangs.[61]

Rebellions also broke out in the former central and northern states of Wei, Han, and Zhao, and the former eastern states of Qi and Yan. An expedition under Zhang Han, one of Qin's best generals, undertook to crush the insurgents and recover lost territories. When the Qin army attacked the key city of Ju Lu in Zhao, the rebels of Qi and Yan sent reinforcements. The new king of Chu also sent relieving forces under the overall command of General Song Yi, with Xiang Liang and Xiang Yu as subordinate commanders. Xiang Liang was killed. Xiang Yu had Song Yi killed, assumed command of Chu forces, relieved the siege of Ju Lu, took the surrender of Zhang Han and other Qin generals, and emerged as the foremost general in China. In the meantime, other Chu forces, under command of Liu Bang, penetrated one of the passes into the western homeland of the Qin, advanced on the capital of Xianyang, with its collapsing central administration, and took the surrender of Zi Ying, ending the Qin dynasty in 206 B.C.E. Liu Bang replaced the harsh Qin code with a simple code of only three articles, specifying the punishments for injury, theft, and murder. Liu Bang also sealed the palaces and armory to prevent looting and violence, but he did not have Zi Ying executed and did not allow the capital to be sacked. Two months later, however, Xiang Yu arrived and, as Liu's superior, took command. Xiang ordered the capital sacked, had Zi Ying executed, and permitted his soldiers to desecrate Shihuangdi's tomb.[62]

Until this century, it was generally believed that the causes of the precipitate collapse of the Qin dynasty were those stated by Jia Yi (201–169 B.C.E.) shortly after the event in an essay entitled, "The Faults of Qin." Jia wrote:

> For a while after the death of the First Emperor the memory of his might continued to awe the common people. Yet Ch'en She [Chen She], born in a humble hut with tiny windows and wattle door, a day laborer in the fields and a garrison conscript, whose abilities could not match even the average, who had neither the worth of Confucius and Mo Tzu [Mo Zi] nor the wealth of T'ao Chu [Tao Zhu] or I Tun [Yi Dun], stepped from the ranks of the common soldiers, rose up from the paths of the

fields and led a band of some hundred poor, weary troops in revolt against the Ch'in [Qin]. They cut down trees to make their weapons, raised their flags on garden poles, and the whole world in answer gathered about them like a great cloud, brought them provisions, and followed after them as shadows follow a form. In the end the leaders of the entire east rose up together and destroyed the House of Ch'in [Qin].[63]

Why was it, Jia Yi asked, that the Qin, who had defeated the professional armies of the Six States and become the master of the whole empire, could be defeated by such a ragtag and bobtail force and become the laughing stock of the whole world? Jia Yi answered: "Because it failed to rule with humanity [human heartedness] and righteousness and to realize that the power to attack and the power to retain what one has thereby won are not the same."[64]

Jia Yi also said that the first emperor was self-satisfied, unwilling to seek advice, and unready to change after committing a fault, the second emperor followed the same pattern, and Zi Ying was feeble and stood alone. He also criticized the Qin for not giving fiefs to meritorious ministers, like the ancient sage-kings.[65] Until this century, it was the moral deficiencies, especially the burning of the books and the brutal execution of the scholars, that the Chinese gave as the reasons for the collapse of the Qin. Chinese Communist scholars, in recent decades, have explained the collapse in terms of social institutions and the class struggle.[66] Bodde, in the recent *Cambridge History of China*, suggests that overextension of resources was a significant factor in the collapse. He also says that perhaps the Qin dynasty was not worse than other states might have been if they had possessed the same power.[67]

From the perspective of jurisculture, the causes of the collapse of the Qin dynasty were that the directing consciousness (Legalism) of that dynasty existed in the minds of only a few people, and that consciousness was at odds with the prevailing Chinese consciousness at the most fundamental level. When the Legalist Li Si was ostracized and then executed, there was no one at the center capable of providing consistent, principled direction. Hu Hai was weak and inexperienced, the eunuch Zhao Gao was conniving and treacherous, Zi Ying was doubtless bewildered. But, aside from deficiencies of intellect and character, without the guiding ideology of Legalism none of them was capable of coherent policy-making. On the other hand, Qin policies that clearly were directed by Legalism were the cause of the popular outrage that irrupted in rebellions. The reason for that outrage was that Legalism violated the understanding most Chinese had of themselves and the world they lived in.

The Chinese believed that the real world is the world of sensed experience, provided the sensed phenomena are correctly ordered. The Chinese written language preserved the uniqueness and particularity of sensed experience. It was the task of the calendar to prescriptively order all sensed phenomena by means of numerical symbols, each of which referred directly to a batch of concrete phenomena associated in the space/time continuum. Prescriptive ordering of human activities presented a special problem. Human individuals were not limited to a single set of activities for which they had been prepared by genetics, morphology, and behavioral control. Because of great plasticity of thought and action, human individuals could perform many kinds of activities, some of which might be, in a given circumstance, destructive or obstructive. Social names indicated the attitudes and actions prescribed for any individual who, at a given time and place, was included in a certain set of individuals. The most inclusive set was humanity, which was thought to be synonymous with "Chinese," and which referred to all those who participated in the emerging civilization in the north China plain. The next most inclusive set consisted of individuals who, at a time and place, or with respect to certain other individuals, were under the influence of yin, or yang. These names first referred to the complementary groups that divided between themselves the various jobs of an agricultural village.[68]

Social names greatly increased in number as society became more complex and more thoroughly delineated. At one time, family names and generational names may have sufficed to organize daily life. All who shared genealogical ties through the male lineage bore the same name. At one time, "father" and "mother" referred to the most respected male and female members of that generation, not to a biological parent. Later, as intrafamily relationships became more fully delineated, more names were needed, and more than one hundred family relationships were indicated by separate names, most of which have no English equivalent. For society as a whole, five binomes developed that designated the master relationships of Chinese society: sovereign-family head, parent-offspring, husband-wife, elder sibling-younger sibling, and friend-friend. *Social names indicated relationships that carried reciprocal obligations of attitude and action.*[69] The sets of attitudes and actions for these five master relationships were developed in family, clan, and court ceremonies and rituals, and became the Five Codes of *li*.

The relatedness of human beings was not an idea that could be rejected if its implications were inconvenient. It had seeped into the consciousness of so many people that it had become a fundamental belief, reality itself, in the only way that human beings can grasp reality.[70] In fact, nothing was more fundamental in the Chinese view of reality than the relatedness of things. No thing was a discrete entity, identified by fixed attributes of weight, density, and dimension, or by possession of an immortal soul, or the capacity to reason. Every thing was organic, moving through sets of changes of form and substance, or attitude and action, and interacting with other organic entities closely associated in prescriptive space and time through resonant or rhythmic causal stimulation. Every organic thing functioned in harmonious interaction within the organic universe. Every organic thing was identified by a prescriptive name, which indicated what it should become, and possessed an agenda of the changes (dao) necessary for it to "rectify" its name. It also possessed the motivational energy (yin/yang) to follow that agenda. Every thing in the sensed world also had a numinous essence, which could not be immediately sensed. This numinous essence often became the object of worship.[71]

The three paragraphs immediately above summarize the view of reality of the Chinese common consciousness as it had evolved prior to the age of philosophy. None of the schools of philosophy explicitly rejected that view of reality. Most of them explicitly affirmed one or another aspect of it as the basis of that school's program for restoring social unity and harmony. Confucius asserted that human nature is relational. He said that human heartedness is a natural emotion. *Ren*, which is translated human heartedness, is composed of the character meaning "man" combined with the character meaning "two." Confucius taught that one who was not *ren* did not have a genuine nature.[72] Mo Zi carried the obligations implied by the relatedness of human beings to the extreme of advocating a universal love that did not distinguish between those near and dear and distant strangers. The Logicians of the School of Names (*Ming Jia*) made no significant suggestions for restoring social unity and harmony, but their development of a Chinese logic of opposing principles operating spontaneously assumed an inherent relatedness in nature and human affairs. The Daoists asserted not only an ideal order in the universe but also a natural, spontaneous efficacy (*Dao*), which would produce that order provided human beings did not interfere. The Cosmologists of the *Yin/Yang Jia* contributed the theory of dynastic succession to the search for ways of restoring social unity and harmony, but their main efforts were directed to understanding the processes of interaction arising from the juxtaposition of sensed phenomena in prescriptive space and time. The great contributions of this school to Chinese associational science attest to its assumption of an inherent relatedness in the phenomena.[73]

Legalists implicitly rejected the relatedness of human beings by assuming that the ruler was completely free to create, by his command, any obligations he considered necessary in order to serve the interests of the state. In the Chinese common consciousness, and in Confucianism, the social name "father" carried with it obligations to protect, educate, and direct the activities of one bearing the social name of "son" who, reciprocally, bore the obligations to obey, care for, serve, mourn, and ultimately worship the "father." Acting under the influence of the Legalist Shang Yang, the Qin state levied double taxes upon the extended family households, and prohibited fathers, sons, and brothers from living in the same room. In the Qin state and empire, the traditional relation between sovereign and the head of a family, who had intrafamily authority and was responsible for the actions of family members, was replaced by a sovereign-subject relation between the king or emperor and every individual. The son owed obedience directly to the ruler, and a father was required to report his son's criminal actions.

All of the other traditional relations of the five social binomes were also set at nought by the Qin, superseded by a direct relation between sovereign and subject. This new relationship did not carry reciprocal obligations. Under Legalism, the purpose of the state was no longer the traditional one of serving the people. The purpose of the state was to increase the power and wealth of the state. Therefore, the obligation of the ruler was to increase the power and wealth of the state—which increasingly became indistinguishable from the ruler himself. The obligation of every person was to increase the power and wealth of the state. The ruler had authority to create all the subject obligations that he deemed necessary to serve the interests of the state. These obligations were promulgated as laws, which were published, strictly interpreted, and severely enforced. In return for their obedience, the ruler owed the people nothing, except as they might be said to benefit from the power and wealth of the state. The obligations between ruler and subject were unilateral.

The Legalists also implicitly rejected the relatedness in nature by assuming that human activities were not subject to any general principles or forces of nature. In the Chinese common consciousness, and in Daoism and other schools, the activities of all things are subject to the operation of opposing, interacting principles or forces, which become alternately dominant, so that as one extreme is approached movement is reversed and proceeds toward the opposite objective. Thus, everything in the universe had natural limits to its domain of life, and all functioned in harmony within the organic universe. Acting under the influence of the Legalist Shang Yang, the Qin state began the quantitative use of numbers to facilitate the maximum agricultural yield instead of using numbers symbolically to harmonize agricultural activities with the interactions of soil, water, and the weather generated by the movements of the heavenly bodies and the influences of the numinous aspects of nature. The rulers of the Qin state and empire began to imagine themselves to be more powerful than the forces of nature. When winds and waves threatened to sink his boat as he crossed the Yangzi, Shihuangdi ordered the mountain where the river god dwelled to be denuded and painted red like the head of a criminal. The contingencies of nature were not accepted in exculpation for failure to complete a mission on time. Chen She and the other conscripts were threatened with execution for failure to make a rendezvous, even though they had been held up by heavy rains. No thought was given to limitations of human endurance or physical obstacles. The Great Wall, the network of roads, and irrigation projects undertaken simultaneously by Shihuangdi, under the influence of Li Si, were each prodigious, and the very short time within which their completion was demanded, increased geometrically their immoderation. The threat of execution for failure, and the hope of reward for success, caused officials in charge of these projects to drive workers to, and beyond, the limit of their endurance.

All those who lived and worked under Legalist-style direction and supervision were in a constant state of tension, and few could escape that direction and supervision. Education, except for training in the activities that would serve the state, was prohibited. Engaging in commerce, or some other disapproved activity, could lead to a sentence to do forced labor on the Great Wall. Daoism, which offered the peace of withdrawal from society, could not be discussed in public. Nor could Confucianism, with its message of human heartedness and righteousness. There was not a dispersion of effort and thought to a wide range of activities, as determined by the self-interested decisions of many persons. All energies of all persons in the whole empire were marshalled into the activities that one person, the emperor, decided would serve the interests of the state. And these activities were conducted at a frenetic level of intensity.

Legalism also put a heavy burden upon the emperor. Charged with making all of the decisions for the whole empire, the emperor was deprived of any common consciousness of right and wrong that had grown out of cumulative, collective wisdom and experience. There was literally no meaning to such things as limit, moderation, mercy, or justice. There were no institutions to check him; he was answerable to no one on earth, and he was answerable to the gods only in accordance with his own understanding. Under Western Zhou feudalism, blood relationship was the community standard for qualification to make social and political decisions, and the rules developed in the course of family and clan regulation of activities were the measure of right and wrong decisions. These standards were rejected by the Legalists on the ground that feudalism had long ceased to function effectively. Confucianism offered moral superiority as the standard for qualification and the measure of right and wrong decisions. The Legalists rejected this standard on the grounds that it was another appeal to past, outdated wisdom, and that it was impractical because few could be controlled by morality. The Legalists also rejected agreement with nature as the standard for right and wrong decisions. This standard had been pervasive in Chinese common consciousness from earliest times. It was the standard of the culture specialists who developed the written language, the prescriptive calendar, the lore of the *Book of Changes*, and the techniques and technologies that became Chinese associational science. That human activities should be in harmony with nature was also fundamental to the Daoists, the Logicians (*Ming Jia*), and the Cosmologists (*Yin/Yang Jia*), and was implicitly assumed by the Confucianists.

All alone, devoid of any warrant to govern except effective coercion, deprived of any guidance from Chinese consciousness, as it had been or was becoming, the emperor according to Legalism was charged with making all decisions with respect to all activities of everyone solely on the basis of his own character and experience. No wonder that the strong

Shihuangdi sought immortality, indulged in personal aggrandizement, and became suspicious and querulous. No wonder that the inexperienced Hu Hai should shun the office. No wonder that the unscrupulous Zhao Gao should think himself qualified. No wonder that central power faded so quickly that Zi Ying was enthroned only as king, not as emperor.

Empire and emperor, polity and office, under the aegis of Legalism were monstrosities, unnatural, uncivilized, un-Chinese. That is why the Qin dynasty collapsed in fifteen years. That is why Legalism has always been despised in China.

Notes

1. Wolfram Eberhard, *A History of China* (Berkeley: University of California Press, 1969), p. 62; Derk Bodde, *China's First Unifier: A Study of the Ch'in Dynasty as Seen in the Life of Li Ssu* (Hong Kong: Hong Kong University Press, 1967), p. 2.
2. Herlee G. Creel, *The Origins of Statecraft in China*, vol. I (Chicago: The University of Chicago Press, 1970), p. 248; Bodde, *China's First Unifier*, pp. 2, 6.
3. Bodde, *China's First Unifier*, p. 3.
4. Fung Yu-lan, "The Philosophy at the Basis of Traditional Chinese Society," in F. S. C. Northrop, *Ideological Differences and World Order* (New Haven, Conn.: Yale University Press, 1949), p. 25; K. C. Wu, *The Chinese Heritage* (New York: Crown Publishers, 1982), p. 75.
5. Cho-yun Hsu, *Ancient China in Transition: An Analysis of Social Mobility, 722–222 B.C.* (Stanford, Calif.: Stanford University Press, 1965), chaps. 2, 3, 4, 5.
6. Eberhard, *A History of China*, p. 57.
7. Derk Bodde, "The State and Empire of Ch'in," in *The Cambridge History of China*, vol. 1, *The Ch'in and Han Empires, 221 B.C. – A.D. 220*) (Cambridge: Cambridge University Press, 1986), pp. 34–36; Arthur Cotterell, *The First Emperor of China: The Greatest Archeological Find of Our Time* (New York: Holt, Rinehart and Winston, 1981), p. 109.
8. Bodde, "The State and Empire of Ch'in," p. 37.
9. Ibid., pp. 36–37.
10. Ibid.
11. Ibid., pp. 49–52.
12. Ibid., pp. 51–52.
13. J. J. L. Duyvendak, trans., *The Book of Lord Shang: A Classic of the Chinese School of Law* (Chicago: The University of Chicago Press, 1928), pp. 3–4.
14. Ibid., p. 16.
15. C. K. Yang, *Religion in Chinese Society* (Berkeley: University of California Press, 1961), pp. 40–41; Herlee G. Creel, *The Birth of China* (New York: Reynal and Hitchcock, 1937), pp. 175, 336–39.
16. R. W. L. Guisso, Catherine Pagani with David Miller, *The First Emperor of China* (New York: Birch Lane Press, 1989), p. 50.
17. Ibid., pp. 50–53; Cotterell, *The First Emperor of China*, p. 96.
18. Guisso et al., *The First Emperor of China*, p. 52.
19. Duyvendak, *The Book of Lord Shang*, pp. 85–86.

20. Guisso et al., *The First Emperor of China*, pp. 64-65, 75.
21. Bodde, "The State and Empire of Ch'in," pp. 46-48, 49.
22. Cotterell, *The First Emperor of China*, p. 92.
23. Ibid., p. 102.
24. Bodde, "The State and Empire of Ch'in," p. 38.
25. Ibid., pp. 40, 45.
26. Ibid., pp. 53-54; Bodde, *China's First Unifier*, pp. 21-22, 121-23; Cotterell, p. 139; David Keightley, "The Religious Commitment: Shang Theology and the Genesis of Chinese Political Culture," in *History of Religions*, vol. 17, (May 1978), pp. 211-13.
27. Bodde, "The State and Empire of Ch'in," p. 54.
28. Ibid., pp. 55-56.
29. Cotterell, *The First Emperor of China*, p. 169.
30. Fung Yu-lan, Derk Bodde, trans., *A History of Chinese Philosophy*, vol. 1, *The Period of the Philosophers* (Princeton, N.J.: Princeton University Press, 1983), pp. 305-11.
31. Ibid., pp. 321-23.
32. Cotterell, *The First Emperor of China*, pp. 168-71; Guisso et al., *The First Emperor of China*, pp. 90-91; Bodde, "The State and Empire of Ch'in," pp. 56-58.
33. Bodde, "The State and Empire of Ch'in," pp. 59-60.
34. Ibid., p. 58.
35. Ibid., pp. 59-66; Guisso et al., *The First Emperor of China*, pp. 144-46, 166.
36. Bodde, "The State and Empire of Ch'in," pp. 66-68; Guisso et al., *The First Emperor of China*, pp. 126, 134, 138-40.
37. Bodde, "The State and Empire of Ch'in," p. 77; Guisso et al., *The First Emperor of China*, p. 86.
38. Bodde, "The State and Empire of Ch'in," pp. 55-56, 73-77.
39. Guisso et al., *The First Emperor of China*, pp. 162-64; Cotterell, *The First Emperor of China*, pp. 163-64.
40. Guisso et al., *The First Emperor of China*, pp. 164-65.
41. Ibid.; Bodde, "The State and Empire of Ch'in," p. 69.
42. Cotterell, *The First Emperor of China*, p. 166.
43. Guisso et al., *The First Emperor of China*, pp. 127, 132.
44. Ibid., p. 136.
45. Ibid., pp. 178-79; Bodde, "The State and Empire of Ch'in," p. 82; Cotterell, *The First Emperor of China*, chap. 1.
46. Bodde, "The State and Empire of Ch'in," p. 82; Guisso et al., *The First Emperor of China*, pp. 178-85.
47. Guisso et al., *The First Emperor of China*, pp. 154-56.
48. Ibid., pp. 166, 168.
49. Ibid., p. 166.
50. Ibid.
51. Ibid., p. 104.
52. Joseph Needham, *Science and Civilisation in China*, vol. 2, *History of Scientific Thought* (Cambridge: Cambridge University Press, 1956), pp. 139-43, 153-54.
53. Guisso et al., *The First Emperor of China*, p. 104.
54. Ibid., pp. 172, 174-75.
55. Ibid., pp. 174-75.
56. Ibid., pp. 36-37, 176.
57. Ibid., p. 187.

58. Ibid., pp. 186-87.
59. Charles Hucker, *China's Imperial Past: An Introduction to Chinese History and Culture* (Stanford, Calif.: Stanford University Press, 1975), p. 46; Bodde, "The State and Empire of Ch'in," p. 83; Wm. Theodore de Bary, Wing-tsit Chan, Burton Watson, *Sources of Chinese Tradition*, vol. 1 (New York: Columbia University Press, 1960), p. 153.
60. Michael Loewe, "The Former Han Dynasty," in *The Cambridge History of China*, vol. 1, *The Ch'in and Han Empires, 221 B.C. – A.D. 220* (Cambridge: Cambridge University Press, 1986), p. 113; Nishijima Sadao, "The Economic and Social History of Former Han," in *The Cambridge History of China*, vol. 1, *The Ch'in and Han Empires, 221 B.C. –A.D. 220* (Cambridge: Cambridge University Press, 1986), pp. 545, 552.
61. Loewe, "The Former Han Dynasty," pp. 103, 113-14.
62. Ibid., pp. 114-15.
63. de Bary, *Sources of Chinese Tradition*, vol. 1, pp. 150-52.
64. Ibid., p. 152.
65. Bodde, "The State and Empire of Ch'in," pp. 86-87.
66. Ibid., pp. 87-89.
67. Ibid., 85-90.
68. See chap. 5, above.
69. Ibid.
70. See chap. 3, above.
71. See chaps. 2 and 5, above.
72. Fung, *A History of Chinese Philosophy*, vol. 1, p. 69.
73. See chap. 9, above.

11

The Cultivar Chinese Society

The Han dynasty, which succeeded the Qin, was founded in 202 B.C.E. and came to an end in 220 C.E. It was interrupted from 9 to 23 C.E. by the Xin dynasty of the usurper Wang Mang.[1] The earlier period is called the Former Han and the later period is call the Later Han. During the four hundred years of these dynasties the cultivar Chinese society came into existence in the Chinese common consciousness. This ideal society exerted a prescriptive influence upon events in China for the next seventeen centuries. The cultivar was shaped by ancient beliefs, ideas from the schools of philosophy, and experience.

The Chinese people decisively rejected the Qin dynasty, but subsequent history shows that they did not reject empire and imperial dynasties. Chinese history is periodized by imperial dynasties instead of centuries—until the abdication of the Qing in 1912 C.E. Several dynasties lasted from 250 to 400 years, and interregnums between dynasties were periods of struggle for reunification.[2] The impulse to harmony and unity never waned. However, the rebellion against the Qin certainly raised the issue of popular dissatisfaction. The following brief review of chapter 3 will show the significance of that issue.

Society builds on evolution. Evolution is the story of increasingly complex organisms, from one-cell organisms to human beings. Increased complexity of organization enables organisms to exploit more effectively the life opportunities of various habitats and environments on earth. Society extends organization to the relations between organisms. Sets of individuals perform auxiliary and complementary activities. Each of the activities, performed by some, benefits all, thus increasing the effectiveness of the social group above the result attainable by independent efforts. Nonhuman societies (insect and animal) are organized and regulated by natural processes of structural development and stimulation and inhibition of behavior. These processes prepare individuals for a limited

number of activities, which they cannot refuse to perform. Human beings
have generalized structure and a highly developed central nervous system. We can do many things and can refuse to do any of them. We, not
"nature," decide how we will organize ourselves into the sets of individuals that will perform the auxiliary and complementary activities of
society.

Human beings organize society by the cultural processes of knowing,
desiring, and acting. Our brains are not preset to any mode of cooperative
action. We can disagree about every aspect of knowing, desiring, and
acting. We can avoid misunderstanding, conflict, and chaos and form an
effective society only by building a common consciousness, which is
composed of beliefs. The product of an individual consciousness is an
idea, which can be doubted, argued with. When an idea has seeped into
the consciousness of many persons so pervasively that, for them, it has
become reality itself, which must be reckoned with, like it or not, it has
become a belief. By a common consciousness a human society can
achieve some of the reliability and effectiveness that natural systems
achieve by necessity because the individuals involved understand in
accordance with shared meanings, desire in accordance with shared
values, intend in accordance with shared purposes, and guide and limit
actions in accordance with shared principles and rules.

A human society exists in the common consciousness and in the sum
total of the actions of its members. If a member does not do what is
expected, other members will try to correct that member's consciousness
or actions. Determining what is to be expected of each, that is, organizing
society, distributes the benefits and duties of that society. Correcting
consciousness or actions, that is, regulating society, seeks to close the
gap between ideal and actual society. A society in which all members
voluntarily did what was expected of them would be the most efficient
and effective. The lower the level of voluntary compliance, the less
efficient and effective the society. As voluntary compliance goes down,
the use of force to secure compliance tends to go up and at some point it
becomes ineffective.

It is to be expected that dissatisfaction with the distribution of benefits
and duties would result in less voluntary compliance. The experience of
India indicates that dissatisfaction with one's lot is not a problem if it is
believed that the organization of society is not within human competence.
In India, it was believed that the benefits and duties of each station in

society were determined by immemorial custom. What station one occupied in the current incarnation was determined by one's good or bad deeds in previous incarnations. Accordingly, political authority did not extend to organizing (or reorganizing, e.g., by decree or law) society. Kings regulated society by punishing for failure to do whatever one's social status required one to do.[3]

The experience of Greece and Rome indicates that when it is believed that the organization and regulation of society are, to some extent, within human competence, dissatisfaction with one's lot is not a problem if social and political authority is accorded to those persons generally believed to be most capable of exercising it for the benefit of all. The common consciousness authorizes decision making by those persons. In early Greece, that authority was accorded to the eponymous heads of patriarchal families, and city-states, who possessed some of the gods' power to control events. As long as it was believed that the paterfamilias was most capable of organizing and regulating the activities of the family, or city-state, for the benefit of all, dissatisfaction with the social order was not a problem.[4] When the Greek natural philosophers dissolved the world in which gods controlled events, and substituted a world charac-terized by a rational order, knowable through the exercise of human reason, authority to organize and regulate society passed to those who demonstrated competence in reasoning. Plato said only the few philoso-pher-kings who could grasp pure truth through speculative reason should rule. The Stoics trusted practical reason, possessed (they said) by all, which could distinguish between true and false sensed experience, and could understand that experience in terms of premises and principles given by speculative reason.

When the ideas of the Stoic philosophers became beliefs, Roman society was transformed and Roman private law was created on the basis of individual responsibility and rational assent. Individuals were deemed to have legal capacity by virtue of possessing reason. Each owed certain obligations to all others, such as to avoid injuring another or depriving another of that which was his. Obligations to particular persons were created by agreement or by breach of a general obligation. Individuals were expected to pursue their own interests and competing claims were adjudicated in accordance with rules derived from basic premises and principles by exercise of a public, objective, canon of reasoning. Certain specialists, called jurisconsults, were trained in that reasoning. The law, therefore, operated objectively, unaffected by personal preferences or interests. It was fair to all and partial to none. People who were subject to Roman law were happy with it, and people who were not subject to it wanted to be. It became the law of the whole mediterranean world. In modern times, after Roman private law was rediscovered in the Renaissance, it was adopted as law in all the countries of Western Europe.[5] Therefore, placing authority to organize and regulate the activities of members of the society in persons deemed capable of exercising what Cicero called "right reason" was highly satisfactory in the West.[6] The common consciousness authorized decision making by those persons.

In ancient China, the universe was organic, ever-changing, and observable. Entities were not so much beings, as processes. Name, such as "millet," or "father," was prescriptive. Millet indicated the most desirable characteristics of form and substance of which that plant was deemed capable, that is, the cultivar. Beginning with the wild cultigen, and aware of observable continuity, contingency, the potentialities of change, and the causal interactions with soil, water, and weather, the farmer moved millet toward an actuality as close as possible to the name. Father indicated the most desirable characteristics of attitude and action for the head of a family. It was the task of one who became head of a family to rectify the name by developing the indicated characteristics. One who had grown up in a farm family, who remembered the instructions of his father, who took seriously the admonitory influences of family ancestors, and who was committed to serving the interests of the family could best be entrusted with organizing and regulating the activities of the family. Something like this seems to have been assumed about the capability of the heads of independent farm families in early China.

As amalgamation occurred, the heads of clans, towns, and countries were apparently assumed to have the same capability *ex officio*, that is, complete knowledge, rather than specialized knowledge, reverence for ancestors, awe of other numinous influences, and commitment to serve the interests of the group. The heads of families, clans, towns, and countries, apparently were also capable of observing the emotions that evoked, in themselves and in other members of the familial group, willingness to comply with assigned duties. Ceremonies and rituals were devised to evoke and refine these emotions. In time, the emotion-inducing rituals, *li*, merged with the substance of the obligation and *li* came to mean the proper attitude and action, or propriety. From this process emerged the five codes of *li*, covering the five master categories of relations in an essentially familial society. In time *li* became customary. At the level of kingdoms, comprising several countries, organization and regulation of society were symbolically represented as occurring spontaneously; as long as the ruler's virtue was clear he could serve as the channel through which the order of heaven flowed into everything on earth. Functionally, as a supplement to the *ex officio* capability, the king utilized culture specialists who devised new techniques and technologies and, as administrators, made appropriate social changes.

Xia and Shang kingdoms were relatively small. When the Western Zhou tried to rule a very large territory,[7] a limitation on *ex officio* authority to organize and regulate society became evident. The exercise of that authority was not explicit enough to be written down, step by step, and taught, learned, and transmitted.[8] Therefore, the Western Zhou could not rule such a large territory directly. They turned to feudalism. Members of the Zhou family (or persons assimilated to family members) were appointed to rule states that were expected to be subordinate. It was inevitable, however, that the heads of these states had knowledge of their own state but not the whole Zhou kingdom, showed greater reverence for their own ancestors than for the Zhou ancestors, and were committed to serving the interests of their own state rather than the kingdom as a whole. The Western Zhou feudal kingdom began to fall apart. In the Spring and Autumn and the Warring States periods, feudalism collapsed and philosophy flourished. Philosophers concerned themselves with the social and ethical implications of ideas, instead of ideas themselves.

Confucius admired the exercise of *ex officio* capability by the founders of the Western Zhou dynasty, and often recommended their ceremonies and rituals. But he understood that a prescriptive order, at least with respect to human affairs, was a moral order and he laid the foundation for a *moral* capability to organize and regulate society. This foundation was the idea that the emotions of human heartedness (*ren*) and righteousness (*yi*) could be developed so that the moral standard of the Chinese Golden Rule ("Do to others what you wish yourself; do not do to others what you do not wish yourself")[9] could be used to determine the proper attitudes and actions for each person in a relationship. Confucius called one who could do this a *junzi* (superior man). Members of the School of Names studied the relation between names and actualities, thus developing Chinese logic, but they made no direct contributions to a solution of the problem of social chaos. Members of the *Yin/Yang Jia* systematically developed the traditional view of the interrelatedness of things, contributing greatly to Chinese associational science.

The *Ru Jia* (Confucianists), *Dao Jia* (Daoists), *Ming Jia* (School of Names), and the *Yin/Yang Jia* (Cosmologists) systematically reexamined one or another aspect of the common consciousness that had developed in the Ancient Period. They did not contradict any part of that tradition, but sought to enrich it and find new implications for organizing and regulating society. The *Mo Jia* (Mohists) rejected the family as the basic social unit, saying that favoring those close meant harming those at a distance, which inevitably led to waste and conflict. The Mohists urged everyone to have equal love for all. This was contrary to common experience, and Mohism had no practical impact, except upon military technology.

Legalism (*Fa Jia*) both contradicted basic elements of the traditional consciousness and proved to be useful in the chaos and conflict of the Warring States period. The elements of Legalism were *Shi*, the power of being obeyed; *Fa*, clear and simple commands that would be strictly interpreted and severely punished; and *Shu*, the management of officials by means of punishment and reward. *Shi*, *Fa*, and *Shu* were said to be all that was needed in order to govern. Implicitly rejected was the belief that a prescriptive order is part of the inherent nature of organic society, and the belief that the ruler should serve the interests of the people. The Legalists assumed that names were merely conventional; the ruler could give them any meaning he chose, and alter the structure of society accordingly. Meanings would then be kept constant by law enforcement. The Legalist ruler was dedicated to increasing the wealth and power of the state at whatever cost to the people. The human capability relied on by the Legalists for organizing and regulating society was pure power, the *puissant* capability. Kings of the Qin state used *puissant* authority to organize and conduct foreign conquests and did not meet with popular resistance. However, the people of the Qin state did not fully share the Chinese common consciousness. In the Qin empire, of course, most of the people did share the Chinese common consciousness, and that consciousness simply did not authorize the emperor to nullify the organic nature of Chinese society and reorganize it to serve the interests of the state (and himself) and regulate it by command and punishment. When he ignored shared meanings, shared values, and shared purposes, he could not expect the people to guide and limit their actions by his principles and rules.

Emperors of the Han dynasty, which began in 202 B.C.E., came from a family of farmers in central China, which undoubtedly shared the traditional Chinese consciousness.[10] Early Han emperors turned to Confucianists, not because of the ideas of Confucius himself, but because the *Ru Jia* was the school of the literati who had preserved, transmitted, interpreted, and taught the ancient texts, ceremonies, and rituals. The first Han emperor, Liu Bang, whose imperial name was Gaodi, made knowledge of the traditions taught by the Confucianists the qualification for administrative positions.[11] Ch'en Ch'i-yün says in the new *Cambridge History of China*:

> By the time of Yüan-ti [Yuandi, r. 49–33 B.C.E.] not only did the emperor have a thorough Confucian education, but most of the high officials as well came from the Confucian school, and numerous lesser Confucian students were placed in middle- and low-ranking government positions. Even local magnates, heads of powerful families and clans, big landlords, successful merchants, or local warlords of significant influence and popular appeal began to model themselves after the Confucians.[12]

Han Confucianism included texts and rituals from the Ancient Period, ideas from Confucius and other members of the *Ru Jia*, commentaries on ancient classics (especially the *Book of Changes*), and many ideas borrowed from the Daoists and the Cosmologists (*Yin/Yang Jia*). The intent was primarily eclectic, appealing to any ideas that would help to justify the pragmatism of the Han emperors who wanted the efficiency of central administration without harsh Legalist measures of enforcement.[13] But it was also syncretic, ending the exclusive emphasis upon ethics, calling attention to a Daoist natural world of spontaneous, harmonious interactions, and placing both human activities and natural events in relation to heaven, the totality of all prescriptive essences. Dong Zhongshu (Tung Chung-shu) was the most important of the Han eclectic/syncretic philosophers.[14] On the basis of this version of the Chinese common consciousness it could reasonably be expected that the reaction to the *puissant* authority asserted by the Qin would be a return to the *ex officio* authority of ancient tradition. But *ex officio* authority, while not provoking popular rebellion, had failed to provide unity and harmony. The Confucian germ of a third human capability for organizing and regulating society has been noted. That capability was moral development, the capability of the "superior man" or *junzi*.

The method of exercising *junzi* capability to organize and regulate society was systematically developed by Confucianists of the Qin and Han dynasties. It is set out in two remarkably succinct works, the *Zhong Yong* (*Chung Yung*) or *Doctrine of the Mean*, and the *Da Xue* (*Ta Hsüeh*) or *Great Learning*. Together they constitute a chapter in the *li Ji* or *Book of Rites* (*Rituals*), one of the six Confucian classics. From 1313 to 1905 C.E., the *Doctrine of the Mean*, the *Great Learning*, the *Analects* of Confucius, and the *Book of Mencius* were referred to as the "Four Books," which were the core texts for Chinese education and the basis of civil service examinations.[15] As subsequent discussion will show, the *junzi* capability, like the *ex officio*, required complete knowledge of factual situations. But the *junzi* capability substituted for the commitment to the interests of a group, commitment to the principle of *ren*, human heartedness.

According to Confucius, the ideal order of human affairs was moral. That order was not the product of human thought and action (as the Legalists had assumed). The moral order was metahuman. To know that order and follow it, and to help others to know and follow it, was to participate in organizing and regulating (actual) society. Exercise of *junzi* capability identified optimal behavior and challenged the individual to live up to it. Therefore, as Confucius proposed, the Chinese Golden Rule was the appropriate standard. The *Mean* and the *Learning* provided the canon of moral reasoning for applying this standard.

The *Doctrine of the Mean* consists of two short paragraphs to which thirty-two quotations from Confucius were appended. The full text, without the appended quotations is:

> What heaven (*T'ien*, Nature) imparts to man is called human nature. To follow our nature is called the Way (Tao) [Dao]. Cultivating the Way is called education. The Way cannot be separated from us for a moment. What can be separated from us is not the Way. Therefore the superior man is cautious over what he does not see and apprehensive over what he does not hear. There is nothing more visible than what is hidden and nothing more manifest than what is subtle. Therefore the superior man is watchful over himself when he is alone.

> Before the feelings of pleasure, anger, sorrow, and joy are aroused it is called equilibrium (*chung* [*zhong*], centrality, mean). When these feelings are aroused and each and all attain due measure and degree it is called harmony. Equilibrium is the great foundation of the world, and harmony its universal path. When equilibrium and harmony are realized to the highest degree, heaven and earth will flourish.[16]

The *Great Learning* consists of just three paragraphs, with ten short chapters of commentary appended. The full text, without the appended commentaries is:

> The Way of learning to be great (or adult education) consists in manifesting the clear character, loving the people, and abiding (chih) in the highest good.
>
> Only after knowing what to abide in can one be calm. Only after having been calm can one be tranquil. Only after having achieved tranquillity can one have peaceful repose. Only after having peaceful repose can one begin to deliberate. Only after deliberation can the end be attained. Things have their roots and branches. Affairs have their beginnings and their ends. To know what is first and what is last will lead one near the Way.
>
> The ancients who wished to manifest their clear character to the world would first bring order to their states. Those who wished to bring order to their states would first regulate their families. Those who wished to regulate their families would first cultivate their personal lives. Those who wished to cultivate their personal lives would first rectify their minds. Those who wished to rectify their minds would first make their wills sincere. Those who wished to make their wills sincere would first extend their knowledge. The extension of knowledge consists in the investigation of things. When things are investigated, knowledge is extended; when knowledge is extended, the will becomes sincere; when the will is sincere, the mind is rectified; when the mind is rectified, the personal life is cultivated; when the personal life is cultivated, the family will be regulated; when the family is regulated, the state will be in order; and when the state is in order, there will be peace throughout the world. From the Son of Heaven down to the common people, all must regard cultivation of the personal life as the root or foundation. There is never a case when the root is in disorder and yet the branches are in order. There has never been a case when what is treated with great importance becomes a matter of slight importance or what is treated with slight importance becomes a matter of great importance.[17]

The metahuman, moral order of society was, of course, prescriptive. The prescriptive name of each social entity, such as father, mother, son, indicated the characteristics of attitude and action that entity should have with respect to every other social entity, in every life situation. The dao of an entity was the set of characteristics indicated by the name. Social daos, therefore, distributed the benefits and duties of Chinese society, and that society would be fully regulated when all names were rectified, and son was son, father was father, ruler was ruler, minister was minister. Therefore, to cultivate one's moral character in order to know and follow one's dao was to participate in organizing and regulating society. Let us take a particular instance of such cultivation by means of the moral reasoning in the *Mean* and the *Learning*.

Suppose that a son proposed to discover his dao with respect to his mother. He would probably need some help in understanding some preliminary matters in the *Mean* and the *Learning*. The first paragraph of the *Mean* says that our nature cannot be separated from us; it is with us even when we see or hear nothing. The son might intuitively understand that our nature is within us, and is something we bring to experience. He might know that rituals had regulated and refined feelings for hundreds of years, and so he would not be surprised to be told that human nature consists of feelings (pleasure, anger, sorrow, joy), which can be quiescent or aroused. Doubtless he would need help with the assertion in the first sentence of the *Learning* that learning to be great consists in loving the people and abiding in the highest good. The appended commentary cites King Wen as the exemplar of abiding in the highest good: "As a ruler he abided in humanity. As a minister, he abided in reverence. As a son, he abided in filial piety. As a father, he abided in deep love."[18] However, these are ideal attitudes for particular relationships, whereas the first sentence in the *Learning* says that "only in knowing what to abide in can one be calm," which indicates a preconditioning of the self in order to begin the self regulation delineated in the *Mean* and the *Learning*.

At this fundamental level, knowing what to abide in surely refers to the Confucian premise that the essential nature of human beings is *ren*, or human heartedness. The graph for *ren* is composed of the graph meaning man and the graph meaning two. Confucius said that one who is *ren* and who desires to develop himself develops others, and that one who is without *ren* does not have a genuine nature.[19] Abiding in *ren* would be an appropriate precondition for becoming calm, tranquil, and in peaceful repose so that one could undertake to cultivate oneself from which regulation of the family, the state, and the world would follow, according to the *Learning*. Loving the people could be the feeling that would cause one to enter upon such an undertaking.

Having got past the preliminary matters and preconditioned himself, the son would be dependent upon sufficient order in the state and his family to afford him an education and leisure for contemplation. Now, he is called on to cultivate his personal life by rectifying his mind. What is meant by this? The *Mean* indicates that human nature consists of feelings. But the *Mean* is a systematic statement about the regulation of human feelings and, therefore, it assumes a human capacity to reason about feelings. Would it conduce to a clear understanding of one's feelings to be under the influence of one or another of those feelings, or to be free from any such influence? Clearly, the latter. Therefore, the *Mean* contributes at this point to the enterprise of the *Learning*. "Before the feelings of pleasure, anger, sorrow, and joy are aroused it is called equilibrium." Zhu Xi commented that when one is affected by wrath, fear, fondness, worries, or anxieties, one's mind is not correct.[20]

To stave off the influence of feelings in order to reason clearly about feelings, the *Learning* says that one must make one's will sincere. What better way to eliminate all pretense, sham, equivocation, and dissembling than by an unshakable commitment to the premise that one is *ren*—not a discrete entity but a member of the family, which is the smallest unit in an organic society that includes all civilized persons?[21] Then, with rectified mind and sincere will, one is ready to investigate things. Since the enterprise is to regulate the person, the family, and the state in order to bring peace to the world, the "things" to be investigated must be human relationships, behavior, and motivations.[22]

The investigation of things in order to regulate the behavior of a son toward his mother required two kinds of knowledge, knowledge by introspection and knowledge by experience. Introspection would yield knowledge about one's feelings, and experience would yield knowledge about the activities and situations in which son and mother were both involved. A grown son would know most of the activities and situations within the family. Therefore, it would be feasible for him to reconsider his behavior with respect to his mother by asking himself, "If I were a mother, how would I want my son to treat me?" If he did this with respect to every activity and situation of their relationship, he probably would find instances in which his previous behavior fell short of what he would wish from a son. Then he would need to consider his feelings. Suppose he found that he felt love, gratitude, and respect for his mother, but did not feel tenderness or concern for her health, was impatient with her, and was ashamed of her appearance. He probably would conclude that stifling his impatience and shame, stimulating his tenderness and concern for his mother's health, and retaining his love, gratitude, and respect would elicit from him the behavior that would meet the moral standard. The result of his "investigation of things" would be *knowledge* of the feelings, in due measure and degree, that would constitute the filial piety owed by this son to this mother. And, if he had reasoned correctly and if the assumption stated by Mencius was correct, that all minds are the same,[23] that set of feelings, in due measure and degree, would constitute the filial piety owed by any son to any mother.

The purpose of the first set of sorites in the *Learning* would now be accomplished, namely, *knowledge* of the filial piety owed by son to mother. The son would then move on to the second set of sorites. This time, making his will sincere would not mean committing himself to *knowing* what filial piety required of him with respect to his mother, but committing himself to *manifesting* that filial piety. Rectifying his mind would mean not freeing his mind from all feelings but filling his mind with the proper feelings in due measure and degree so that by thought, demeanor, actions, and restraints he would *manifest* that filial piety. Then his personal life would be cultivated with respect to his mother. When the personal life of every member of the family had been cultivated with respect to every other member of the family, the family would be regulated. When every family was regulated the state would be in order and there would be peace in the world.

The scenario just suggested shows that, as Confucius said in a quotation appended to the *Mean*, men and women of simple intelligence could share the knowledge of the way of the superior man and put it into practice, and yet many things were beyond the capabilities of ordinary people.[24] As to those things, ordinary people needed the help of one who was a superior man, a *junzi*. Moral sensitivity was required to know how to put human feelings in due measure and degree in order cultivate the personal life—which would lead to regulation of the family, and ordering of the state. But the Golden Rule standard was applied to factual situations, and therefore the *junzi* had to possess dual capabilities, of moral sensitivity and accurate knowledge about all kinds of human activities and the kinds of situations that arise between persons in different stations and having different functions. This dual capability was the reason why the way of the *junzi*, delineated in the *Mean* and the *Learning*, yielded practical wisdom, immediately applicable to real life problems. This was to be expected, of course, because Chinese philosophy was not interested in ideas for their own sake, nor even in discussion of ideas, but was interested in the application of ideas to social problems.

Within the family, a clan elder was most likely to have the factual and moral capabilities of a *junzi*. He would have knowledge of the activities of all the families in the clan, and all of the factual situations that had arisen in the relations between family members. In addition, he would have access to the records of the clan and the advice of ancestors, who continued to have an organic relationship with the living members of the family.[25] Thus, the experience that once had been the basis of pragmatic, incidental decisions, and had hardened into customary *li*, would be reconsidered in accordance with the systematic moral reasoning of the *Mean* and the *Learning*. Similarly, state policies, recorded in the annals of the various states in the pre-Imperial period, could be systematically reconsidered with the assistance of a *junzi* who had sufficient knowledge of those policies through a study of the records.

To the Western mind, this history of the three types of authority to organize and regulate Chinese society suggests a dialectical process: *ex officio* authority, having proved inadequate to provide unity and harmony, was succeeded by *puissant* authority, which achieved unity but not harmony, and now would be succeeded by *junzi* authority. Therefore, the cultivar, the prescriptive image, of society that emerged from Han Confucianism would be understood to be an empire in which the activities of human society would be organized and regulated by *junzi* authority. But to the Chinese mind, no one principle, force, or capability is correct for every situation, purpose, and relationship. Every principle needs to be countered by another, so that nothing is pressed to the extreme. Therefore, Han Confucianism should be understood as adding *junzi* authority, without eliminating *ex officio* authority or *puissant* authority. With the addition, cumulatively, of experience, which would determine whether *ex officio*, *puissant*, or *junzi* authority was appropriate for a particular situation, purpose, or relationship, the prescriptive image of Chinese society that would guide and inspire various, cyclical, instances of Chinese society for nearly two millennia was in place.

The obvious situation for exercise of *puissant* authority was the struggle for reunification during an interregnum between dynasties. Defeating all opponents and founding a dynasty required effective use of force. One who is not obeyed cannot organize and regulate force. Therefore, the power to command (and be obeyed), which the Legalists called *shi*, was the *puissant* capability. Such power cannot be acquired by wisdom or moral goodness. Han Feizi said that Confucius, for all his wisdom and goodness, could command only his seventy disciples, whereas no one in the kingdom of Lu dared to disobey the ruler, Duke Ai, although he was an inferior ruler.[26] The position of ruler helps to put people in awe and tends to induce them to obey. But one needs to get into the position. In extreme situations, some persons are accepted as leaders and some are not. The presumed leadership ability, which is the basis of that instinctive acceptance is reinforced if it is believed to be beyond human acquisition. In Western theology it was called charisma and was reputed to be of divine origin. In ancient China, the ability to lead was thought to be conferred by the Lord on High (Shang dynasty), and then by heaven (Zhou dynasty).[27] From the time of the Zhou to the end of the empire in 1912, the authority of the ruler was justified by his asserted possession of the mandate of heaven.[28] Zhou and Han texts established a tradition that the founder of the Shang dynasty, and the mythical sage-emperors Shun and Yu, had been selected by heaven.[29] Catering to that tradition, the founder of the Han dynasty, Gaodi, who was from a family of humble farmers, had a fraudulent genealogy concocted in order to claim descent from the ancient sage-rulers.[30]

Emphasis upon the power of the founder of a dynasty was appropriate in terms of the Chinese view of society as an organism. Organisms have a life cycle, as nearly everything in the Chinese tradition attests. Looking back on Chinese history, this was certainly true of dynasties. The dao of an empire was there in the Chinese consciousness, that is, the organization and regulation of society needed to rectify the social name, empire. There was a rationale of legitimate succession within dynasties.[31] But an infusion of life force was needed to found a dynasty. Therefore, the power to command, which the Legalists made one of the three elements of their theory of government, is plausibly understood, in terms of the ancient consciousness, as the inspiriting life force (yang) that ended the quiescent, regenerative, phase of an organism's existence and began, again, the active, dynamic phase. This gives more than symbolic significance to the ruler as the clear channel through which the order of heaven flows into everything in the earth. This understanding of the founding emperor as exercising vivifying force would also help to explain what Fairbank has called the "transcendental role" of the emperor in the Chinese belief system.[32]

Probably the most significant thing about founding a dynasty is that no peaceful process for that purpose had been developed in Chinese consciousness. Therefore, the question of who would become emperor was left to the arbitrament of force. The other situations in which *puissant* authority was similarly appropriate were the control of the army and of the imperial bureaucracy. Relations with other peoples, on the borders of

China, were not covered by the five categories of relationships of Chinese society. There was no guidance for relations with strangers. Thus, *puissant* authority was appropriate and the emperor had the final word, but *puissant* authority was countered by *junzi* authority through the influence of Confucian-educated advisers and officials.[33] The management of skills and talent (of officials) by manipulation of rewards and punishments, which the Legalists called *shu*, was a major element in Qin rule. Exercise of *puissant* authority in this situation was still appropriate under the Han syncretic consciousness, because the relationship between the emperor and an official had not been familial since feudalism and, therefore, was not subject to the formidable disciplinary influences of family. However, in the situation and relationship of controlling bureaucrats, the emperor's exercise of *puissant* authority was strongly countered by *junzi* authority exercised by the Confucian-imbued advisers and the officials themselves, although, again, the emperor had final authority, including even the summary beheading of an offending official.[34]

The obvious situation for the exercise of *ex officio* authority by the emperor was performance of the daily ceremonies and rituals that manifested the respect and reverence conducive to the free flow of all the numinous influences of heaven and earth, strengthening space and renewing time, evoking by resonance or cyclical rhythm the occurrence of every activity, human or natural, in accordance with the inherent nature of the acting organism, and thus, producing unity and harmony. This responded to the belief in the interdependence of heaven, man, and nature in the Han syncretic consciousness. Furthermore, any irregularity in natural events, such as floods or earthquakes, were understood as the weakening of the emperor's "virtue" (quickening and sustaining power), and therefore an omen that the dynasty was coming to an end. Manipulation of omens was a principal part of the leverage of Confucian scholar-officials in asserting *junzi*-based alternatives to counter any excessively self-serving assertions of authority by the emperor.[35]

In the organization and regulation of all those activities generally referred to as civil, to distinguish them from military, criminal, and public, the emperor, with the help of his experts of all kinds, exercised *ex officio* authority, based on complete knowledge, ancestral filiality, numinal reverence, and the imperial view of the people's interests. If his view of the people's interests became too self-serving, he was constrained by his officials' exercise of *junzi* authority, based on complete knowledge, ancestral filiality, numinal reverence, and the moral reasoning of the *Mean* and the *Learning*.

The greatest impact of *junzi* authority, however, was in the relationship between the central administration and regional or local centers of authority. This relationship was the point at which Zhou feudalism had failed. Exercising *ex officio* authority, the king had knowledge of the whole kingdom and perceived royal interests, whereas, the feudal lords had knowledge only of their own state and perceived their own interests. Therefore, the attempt was made by the Qin to have all organizing and regulating decisions made at the imperial level and only administration and enforcement of those decisions were to be done regionally or locally. Developments during the Han dynasties made it possible to decentralize, to a significant extent, organization and regulation of the activities of Chinese society. These developments were the dominance of what came to be called gentry families, and the remarkable objectivity of the moral reasoning process underlying *junzi* authority.

The powerful families that exercised great influence over regional and local affairs in Han times may have been continuations of the aristocratic families of pre-Imperial times. However, some time from the Han dynasties to the Song (960–1279 C.E.) gentry families became dominant in Chinese society. The gentry family is characterized by land holding and degree holding. The wealth acquired from the land (most of which was rented out) gave members the leisure to study and take the imperial exams, success in which led to the granting of degrees. Degree holders, identified by items of dress, entered positions of influence in imperial service or in their home communities. The dominant position of gentry families lasted into the twentieth century.[36]

Objectivity in moral reasoning is an oxymoron in the modern West. In his *Principia Ethica*, in 1903, G. E. Moore said that "the good" is consciousness of pleasure or beauty, and only the "naturalistic fallacy" of treating a pleasurable state of consciousness as an attribute of the external object or event that evoked it led people to think that a social ideal could be determined by rational knowledge and analysis.[37] When moral relativity is opposed in the West it is usually on theological grounds that depend upon authority, revelation, or grace. It should be a source of astonishment, therefore, to the modern Western scholar that examinations could determine, with any reasonable degree of credibility, competence for civic responsibilities on the basis of Confucian education, which was entirely moral. Nevertheless, as we have seen, Confucianists, relying upon emotions, or feelings, rather than a posited faculty of reason, worked out a canon of reasoning from premises and fundamental principles to specific obligations in a variety of situations and relationships; this canon was open to the scrutiny of all, and was repeatable so that it could be checked for error. This Chinese canon of moral reasoning compares very favorably with the canon of reasoning of the jurisconsults of Roman private law with respect to objectivity.

Within the gentry family, within the provincial communities in which these families were the guiding influence, and at the capital where members of these families became imperial teachers, tutors, advisers, ministers, and officials, the Confucian method of determining moral duty was propagated, reiterated, and emphasized by success or failure. It was no wonder that with *junzi* authority as a counter to the *ex officio* authority of the heads of great and powerful families, emperors found it possible to let local activities be organized and regulated locally without undue concern for loss of uniformity, frustration of imperial policies, or separatism. The gentry families mediated between the imperial bureaucrats and the peasants. Local gentry manifested their filiality to the emperor by dealing with "flood and famine, incipient rebellion, a multitude of minor criminal cases, and projects for public works."[38]

The gentry also managed the land use system, which was extremely complicated and largely customary. Gentry also collected taxes, supervised local markets, and acted as wholesalers and brokers for tradesmen.[39] Imperial officials could accomplish their function only by cooperating with local gentry. The decentralization of government permitted the number of imperial officials to be kept quite small, considering the size of the country. From the Han to the Qing dynasty, which abdicated in 1912 C.E., the number of imperial officials remained at about 18,000 while population increased sixfold. Fairbank says, "in a country of over 400 million people, a century ago, there were fewer than 20,000 regular imperial officials but roughly 1.25 million scholarly degree-holders."[40]

As a result of the power of the gentry families and the remarkable objectivity of Confucian moral reasoning, culminating in the *Mean* and the *Learning*, the cultivar of Chinese society became an empire in which the emperor had supreme, but not exclusive, power, and gentry families organized and regulated society at the local level. The empire was founded on force and protected by force, but the emperor's *puissant* authority was constrained by moral (*junzi*) authority through his own education and the advice and leverage of his advisers and officials. The emperor had *ex officio* responsibility to align human activities with the events of heaven and earth and he met his responsibility by conducting daily ceremonies and rituals that showed the proper awe and respect for all numinous essences and invited the causal interactions of an organic universe. The emperor's *ex officio* authority over civil society was self-limited to empirewide activities. The exercise of *ex officio* authority over local activities of civil society by the heads of gentry families was sufficiently constrained by their own *junzi* authority that they did not unduly serve their own interests at the expense of imperial interests, did not frustrate imperial policies by local divergences, and did not seek separatism. In short, the cultivar Chinese society was the result of a balance of power, interest, and morality.

Daoism continued to be a significant part of the Chinese consciousness and, beginning in the first century of the Christian era, Buddhism had a great impact on that consciousness. However, Daoism is principally, and Buddhism is completely, directed to development of the self, rather than to organizing and regulating society. Daoism has always been the mental refuge of the Chinese scholar who is out of office.[41] Buddhism, in the centuries after its introduction to China, contributed to a loss of social cohesion, as it had when it was first formulated in India.[42]

In the actual societies, which were guided by the cultivar society over the centuries, the ordinary Chinese person lived in a world characterized by continuity, contingency, and change, in which the Creative, the Receptive, the Arousing, the Abysmal, the Keeping Still, the Gentle, the Clinging, and the Joyous interpenetrated in ever-changing permutations, producing every organic entity, inspiriting it with life force, imprinting it with the dao it must follow in order to be what it should, and harmonizing the rhythms of the stars, the snails, and everything in between. He was in, and of, that world, and could lay hold of particular parts of it by sight, touch, sound, smell, or taste. He could learn that every particular part was connected geometrically in space and sequentially in time with every other part and by use of permutations of numerical symbols representing batches of particular phenomena he could discover new and useful interactions. He lived in a world of remarkable achievements of associational science. The period from the Han through the Song

dynasties was particularly fruitful of discoveries and inventions, including the cofusion method of making steel (invented in 1863 in the West
as the Siemens method), segmental arch bridges, the chain drive, printing
(including use of movable type), multimast ships with watertight com-
partments and stern rudder posts, paddle-wheel boats, and pound canal
locks.[43] When natural gas from "fire holes" drilled as deep as 4800 feet
by the use of iron drilling bits, and bamboo cables could be captured in
a leather bag and carried a hundred miles and then lighted to produce
heat and light, and paper could be made so strong and impenetrable that
it made excellent body armor, nothing would seem to be too wonderful
to be possible.[44]

The ordinary Chinese person lived a life of hard work, but of justifiable
optimism. What he knew from observation and practical experience was
enriched and reinforced by scholars. There was no elite engaged in
disproving premises and criticizing settled beliefs. Nor did the Chinese
person need to be contentious to gain or retain his share of the benefits
of society. The idea of a right, which could be vindicated by a judicial
proceeding, was utterly foreign to the Chinese consciousness. And
"standing up for one's rights," which is necessary to the functioning of
what is called corrective justice in the West, would have been condemned
in China as disruption of the harmony that ought to prevail between the
parties involved.[45] There were no courts, no lawyers, and, of course, no
legislatures. Duties were the stuff of one's moral nature; knowing and
doing them developed that nature. Pressure to do what one should came
from one's own nature (social dao), from peers, superiors, ancestors,
other numinous essences, and only lastly from the threat of punishment.

When punishment was inflicted it was not for breach of obligation
determined by deductive reasoning from general principles stated in
terms of abstract concepts. Jones has shown that this sort of logical
structure, typical of Western law, was missing in China.[46] This volume
shows why it was missing. The Chinese did not understand the world in
terms of general concepts abstracted from the particular sensed phenomena and related by logic. They stayed with the myriad sensed phenomena
and related them by geometrical and sequential association. This way of
understanding resulted in the structure of the Chinese written language,
the numerology of the trigrams and hexagrams, the unique role of the
calendar, and the associational nature of Chinese science.[47] The Tang,
Ming, and Qing (and perhaps other) dynasties issued sets of orders that

are called law codes in the West. These orders, which were enforced by administrative officials, were limited to the activities of the governmental bureaucracy and the control of crime. Imperial control of these activities was an exercise of the emperor's *puissant* authority by the Legalist means of command and punishment. However, the Legalist conceit of controlling all activities of society by these means did not survive the collapse of the Qin dynasty. This remnant of Legalism became auxiliary to Confucian moral education, suasion, and familial discipline, which controlled all the other activities of Chinese society.[48]

The Western nations, which began to impinge upon China in the last three hundred years, must have been a mystery to the Chinese. A Chinese person could not have had a sense of country, state, or nation. He or she lived in (what they believed to be) the only civilized society. The cooperative activities of society were organized and regulated primarily at the local level, and by familial institutions. To the Westerners, China appeared to be a "sheet of loose sand."[49]

China, to a remarkable degree, cohered and functioned effectively because of the internal stimulus of morality, not because of the external coercion of law. And, because the Chinese always sought practical wisdom instead of pure truth, the *cultivar society was not an abstract, pure ideal.* Morality was practical, allowing for a sensible consideration of the realities of power and the desirabilities of interest. The Chinese cultivar society, exuberant, reasonably good, acquainted with grief, but capable of joy, had a remarkable career from Han times to the present century. And who knows whether the organic society it prescribes is dead or merely quiescent?

Notes

1. Denis Twitchett and Michael Loewe, eds., *The Cambridge History of China*, vol. 1, *The Ch'in and Han Empires, 221 B.C. – A.D. 220*, (Cambridge: Cambridge University Press, 1986), pp. xxxix–xli; Hans Bielenstein, "Wang Mang, the Restoration of the Han Dynasty, and Later Han," in *The Cambridge History of China*, vol. 1, *The Ch'in and Han Empires, 221 B.C. – AD. 220*, (Cambridge: Cambridge University Press, 1986), pp. 223, 229, 232.
2. John K. Fairbank, *China: A New History* (Cambridge, Mass.: Harvard University Press, 1992), pp. 24, 47; K. C. Chang, *Art, Myth and Ritual* (Cambridge, Mass.: Harvard University Press, 1983), pp. 1–2.
3. Gray L. Dorsey, *Jurisculture: India* (New Brunswick, N.J.: Transaction Publishers, 1990), pp. 67–101.

4. Gray L. Dorsey, *Jurisculture: Greece and Rome* (New Brunswick, N.J.: Transaction Publishers, 1989), pp. 2–12; José Ortega y Gasset, *Concord and Liberty*, Helene Weyl, trans. (New York: W. W. Norton and Co., 1946), pp. 19–21, 39–47.

5. Dorsey, *Greece and Rome*, pp. 14–30, 33–51, 54–63.

6. Cicero, *De Republica, De Legibus*, Clinton W. Keyes, trans. (Cambridge, Mass.: Harvard University Press, 1948), p. xxiii.

7. Herlee G. Creel, *The Origins of Statecraft in China*, vol. 1 (Chicago: The University of Chicago Press, 1970), p. 101.

8. Ibid., pp. 419–25.

9. Fung Yu-lan, *A History of Chinese Philosophy*, vol. 1, Derk Bodde, trans. (Princeton, N.J.: Princeton University Press, 1983), p. 71.

10. Michael Loewe, "The Former Han Dynasty," in *the Cambridge History of China*, vol. 1, *The Ch'in and Han Empires, 221 B.C. – AD. 220* (Cambridge: Cambridge University Press, 1986), pp. 113, 119; Yu Ying-shih, "Han Foreign Relations," in *The Cambridge History of China*, vol. 1, *The Ch'in and Han Empires, 221 B.C. – A.D. 220* (Cambridge: Cambridge University Press, 1986), pp. 377, 378.

11. Robert Kramers, "The Development of the Confucian Schools," in *The Cambridge History of China*, vol. 1, *The Ch'in and Han Empires, 221 B.C. – A.D. 220* (Cambridge: Cambridge University Press, 1986), pp. 747, 752–53.

12. Ch'en Ch'i-yun, "Confucian, Legalist, and Taoist Thought in Later Han," in *The Cambridge History of China*, vol. 1, *The Ch'in and Han Empires, 221 B.C. – A.D. 220* (Cambridge: Cambridge University Press, 1986), pp. 766, 769.

13. Ibid., p. 767.

14. Fung Yu-lan, *A Short History of Chinese philosophy* (New York: Macmillan Co., 1958), pp. 183–87, 191–203; Michael Loewe, "The Religious and Intellectual Background," in *The Cambridge History of China*, vol. 1, *The Ch'in and Han Empires, 221 B.C. – A.D. 220* (Cambridge: Cambridge University Press, 1986), pp. 649, 653–60, 683–90, 693–713; Kramers, "The Development of the Confucian Schools," pp. 752–56; Wing-tsit Chan, *A Source Book in Chinese Philosophy* (Princeton, N.J.: Princeton University Press, 1963), 271–88; Wm. Theodore de Bary, et al., *Sources of Chinese Tradition*, vol. 1 (New York: Columbia University Press, 1960), pp. 184–210.

15. Wing-tsit Chan, *A Source Book in Chinese Philosophy*, p. 95; Fung, *A History of Chinese Philosophy*, vol. 1, pp. 361–63, 369–71.

16. Wing-tsit Chan, *A Source Book in Chinese Philosophy*, p. 98.

17. Ibid., pp. 86–87.

18. Ibid., p. 88.

19. Fung Yu-lan, *A History of Chinese Philosophy*, vol. 1, Derk Bodde, trans. (Princeton, N.J.: Princeton University Press, 1983), pp. 69–70.

20. Wing-tsit Chan, *A Source Book in Chinese Philosophy*, p. 90.

21. Ibid., pp. 104–5.

22. Joseph Needham, *Science and Civilisation in China*, vol. 2 (Cambridge: Cambridge University Press, 1956), p. 578, note d.

23. Fung, *A History of Chinese Philosophy*, vol. 1, p. 123.

24. Wing-tsit Chan, *A Source Book in Chinese Philosophy*, p. 100.

25. Benjamin Schwartz, *The World of Thought in Ancient China* (Cambridge, Mass.: Harvard University Press, 1985), p. 21.

26. Wing-tsit Chan, *A Source Book in Chinese Philosophy*, p. 258.

27. David Keightley, "The Religious Commitment: Shang Theology and the Genesis of Chinese Political Culture," in *History of Religions*, vol. 17 (February-May 1978), pp. 212-13; Chang, *Art, Myth and Ritual*, pp. 44-45.
28. Creel, *The Origins of Statecraft in China*, pp. 44-45; de Bary, et al., *Sources of Chinese Tradition*, vol. 1, pp. 5-6.
29. Chang, *Art, Myth and Ritual*, p. 34; de Bary et al., *Sources of Chinese Tradition*, vol. 1, pp. 176-77.
30. Bielenstein, "Wang Mang, the Restoration of the Han Dynasty, and Later Han," p. 225.
31. Hok-lam Chan, *Legitimation in Imperial China: Discussions Under the Jurchen-Chin Dynasty (1115-1234)* (Seattle: The University of Washington Press, 1984), pp. 21-23.
32. Fairbank, *China*, p. 69.
33. Hok-lam Chan, *Legitimation in Imperial China*, p. 19.
34. Fairbank, *China*, pp. 68-69.
35. Ibid., pp. 64-66.
36. Wolfram Eberhard, *A History of China* (Berkeley: The University of California Press, 1969) (China), pp. 71-75; Charles O. Hucker, *China's Imperial Past* (Stanford, Calif.: Stanford University Press, 1975), pp. 128-40, 159-63; Fairbank, *China*, pp. 101-7.
37. G. E. Moore, *Principia Ethica* (Cambridge: Cambridge University Press, 1956), pp. 1-58, 183-225.
38. Fairbank, *China*, p. 104.
39. Ibid., pp. 103-5.
40. Ibid., p. 106.
41. Ibid., p. 53.
42. Ibid., pp. 72-76; Dorsey, *India*, p. 37.
43. Robert Temple, *The Genius of China: 3000 Years of Science, Discovery and Invention* (New York: Simon and Schuster, 1989), pp. 68-72, 110-16, 185-91, 192, 196.
44. Ibid., pp. 78-84.
45. Gray L. Dorsey, "The Influence of Philosophy on Law and Politics in Western Civilization," in Charles Moore, ed., *Philosophy and Culture; East and West* (Honolulu: University of Hawaii Press, 1968), pp. 533, 543-44.
46. William C. Jones, "Studying the Ch'ing Code—The Ta Ch'ing Lü Li," *The American Journal of Comparative Law*, vol. 22 (1974), pp. 330-35.
47. See chaps. 5 and 8.
48. Thomas B. Stephens, *Order and Discipline in China: The Shanghai Mixed Court 1911-27* (Seattle and London: University of Washington Press, 1992), pp. 3-43.
49. Sun Yat-sen, *San Min Chu I: The Three Principles of the People*, Frank Price, trans. (Taipei, Taiwan: China Cultural Service, 1953), pp. 2-5.

Bibliography

Barraclough, Geoffrey, ed. *The Times Atlas of World History.* London: Times Books Limited, 1978.

Bielenstein, Hans. "The Institutions of Later Han," in *The Cambridge History of China*, vol. 1. Cambridge: Cambridge University Press, 1986, p.491.

Biot, Eduoard. *Le Tcheou-Li*, vols. 1-3. Paris: A L'imprimerie Nationale, 1851.

Bodde, Derk. *China's First Unifier: A Study of the Ch'in Dynasty as Seen in the Life of Li Ssu, 280?-208 B.C.* Hong Kong: Hong Kong University Press, 1967.

_____ . *Essays on Chinese Civilization.* Princeton, N.J.: Princeton University Press, 1981.

_____ . "The State and Empire of Ch'in," in *The Cambridge History of China*, vol. 1., *The Ch'in and Han Empires, 221 B.C. – A.D.220.* Cambridge: Cambridge University Press, 1986.

Bodde, Derk, and Clarence Morris. *Law in Imperial China.* Cambridge, Mass.: Harvard University Press, 1967.

Chai Ch'u and Winberg Chai, *The Humanist Way in Ancient China.* New York: Bantam Books, 1965.

_____ . *Li Chi: Book of Rites*, vols. 1, 2. New Hyde Park, N.Y.: University Books, Inc. 1967.

Chan, Hok-Lam. *Legitimation in Imperial China: Discussions Under the Jurchen-Chin Dynasty (1115–1234).* Seattle: The University of Washington Press, 1984.

Chan, Wing-tsit. "The Individual in Chinese Religion," in *The Chinese Mind*, ed. Charles Moore. Honolulu: The University of Hawaii Press, 1967.

_____ . *A Source Book in Chinese Philosophy.* Princeton, N.J.: Princeton University Press, 1963.

Chang, K.C. *Early Chinese Civilization: Anthropological Perspectives.* Harvard-Yenching Institute Monograph Series, vol. 23. Cambridge, Mass.: Harvard University Press, 1976.

_____ . *Shang Civilization.* New Haven, Conn. and London: Yale University Press, 1980.

_____ . *Art, Myth, and Ritual: The Path to Political Authority in Ancient China.* Cambridge, Mass.: Harvard University Press, 1983.

Chen, Phillip. *Law & Justice: The Legal System in China, 2400 B.C. to 196 A.D.* New York: Dunellen Publishing Co., 1973.

Ch'en Ch'i-yun. "Confucian, Legalist, and Taoist Thought in Later Han," in *The Cambridge History of China*, vol. 1. Cambridge: Cambridge University Press, 1986, p. 766.

Ch'u Tung-tsu. *Han Social Structure.* Seattle: The University of Washington Press, 1972.

Cicero. *De Re Publica, De Legibus,* trans. Clinton Walker Keyes. Cambridge, Mass.: Harvard University Press, 1928.

Cohen, Jerome Alan, R. Randle Edwards and Fu-mei Chang Chen, eds. *Essays on China's Legal Tradition.* Princeton, N.J.: Princeton University Press, 1980.

Cotterell, Arthur. *The First Emperor of China.* New York: Holt, Rinehart and Winston, 1981.

Creel, Herrlee G. *The Birth of China.* New York: Reynal and Hitchcock, 1937.

_____ . *The Origins of Statecraft in China*, vol. 1. Chicago: University of Chicago Press, 1970.

Crump, J.I. *Chan Kuo-ts'e.* Oxford: Oxford University Press, 1970.

Dawson, Raymond, ed. *The Legacy of China.* London: Oxford University Press, 1964.

_____ . *The Chinese Experience.* New York: Charles Scribner's Sons, 1978.

de Bary, Wm. Theodore, Wing-tsit Chan and Burton Watson. *Sources of Chinese Tradition*, vol. 1. New York: Columbia University Press, 1960.

de Bary, Wm. Theodore, Wing-tsit Chan and Chester Tan. *Sources of Chinese Tradition*, vol. 2. New York: Columbia University Press, 1960.

Dorsey, Gray L. "The Influence of Philosophy on Law and Politics in Western Civilization," in *Philosophy and Culture: East and West*, ed. Charles A. Moore. Honolulu: University of Hawaii Press, 1968, p. 533.

_____ . *Jurisculture: Greece and Rome.* New Brunswick, N.J.: Transaction Publishers, 1989.

_____ . *Jurisculture: India.* New Brunswick, N.J.: Transaction Publishers, 1990.

Duyvendak, J. J. L., trans. *The Book of Lord Shang: A Classic of the Chinese School of Law.* Chicago: The University of Chicago Press, 1963.

Eberhard, Wolfram. *A History of China.* Berkeley: University of California Press, 1969.

Edelson, Edward. "Buckyball, the Magic Molecule." *Popular Science*, August 1991, p. 52.

Embree, Ainslee, ed. *Encyclopedia of Asian History*. New York: Charles Scribner's Sons, 1988.

Fairbank, John King. *China: A New History*. Cambridge, Mass.: Harvard University Press, 1992.

Fairbank, John, Edwin O. Reischauer and Albert M. Craig. *East Asia: Tradition and Transformation*. Boston, Mass.: Houghton Mifflin, 1973.

Fang, Thomé. *The Chinese View of Life*. Hong Kong: The Union Press. 1957.

Fitzgerald, C. P. *China: A Short Cultural History*. New York: Praeger, 1950.

Forrest, R. A. D. *The Chinese Language*. London: Faber & Faber, 1948.

Fung Yu-Lan. "The Philosophy at the Basis of Traditional Chinese Society," in *Ideological Differences and World Order*, ed. F. S. C. Northrop, New Haven, Conn.: Yale University Press, 1949, p. 18.

_____ . *A Short History of Chinese Philosophy*. New York: Macmillan Co., 1958.

_____ . *A History of Chinese Philosophy*, vols. 1,2., trans. Derk Bodde. Princeton, N.J.: Princeton University Press, 1983.

Gittings, John. *China Changes Face: The Road from Revolution 1949–89*. London: Oxford University Press, 1989.

Goodrich, L. Carrington. *A Short History of the Chinese People*. New York: Harper & Row, 1943.

Granet, Marcel. *Fetes et Chansons Anciennes de la Chine*. Paris: Editions Ernest Leroux, 1919.

_____ . *Danses et Legendes de la Chine Ancienne*, vols. 1,2. Paris, Librarie Felix Alcan, 1926.

_____ . *LaPensée Chinoise*. Paris: Editions Albin Michel, 1950.

_____ . *Chinese Civilization*, trans. Kathleen Innes and Mabel Brailsford. New York: Meridian Books, 1958.

_____ . *The Religion of the Chinese People*, trans. Maurice Freedman. Oxford: Basil Blackwell, 1975.

Grosvenor, Melville Bell, ed. *National Geographic Atlas of the World*. Washington, D.C.: National Geographic Society, 1963.

Guisso, R. W. L., Catherine Pagani, with David Miller, *The First Emperor of China*. Toronto: Birch Lane Press, 1989.

Hansen, Chad. *Language and Logic in Ancient China*. Ann Arbor: University of Michigan Press, 1983.

Hegel, G. W. F. *Hegel: Highlights: An Annotated Selection*, ed. Wanda Orynski. New York: Philosophical Library, 1960.

Howells, W. W., and Patricia Jones Tsuchitani, eds. *Paleoanthropology in the People's Republic of China*. Washington, D.C.: National Academy of Sciences, 1977.

Hsu, Cho-yun. *Ancient China in Transition*. Stanford, Calif.: Stanford University Press, 1965.

_____ . *Bibliographic Notes on Studies of Early China*. Chinese Materials Center, 1982.

Hsu, Cho-yun, and Katheryn Linduff, *Western Zhou Civilization*. New Haven, Conn.: Yale University Press, 1988.

Hu, Chang-tu. *China: Its People, Its Society, Its Culture*, ed., Hsiao Hsia. In collaboration with Samuel C. Chu, Leslie L. Clark, Jung-pang Lo, Yuan-li Wu. New Haven, Conn.: HRAF Press, 1960.

Hucker, Charles O. *China's Imperial Past*. Stanford, Calif.: Stanford University Press, 1975.

Hulsewe, A. F. P., trans. *History of the Former Han Dynasty*. Leiden: E. J. Brill, 1955.

_____ . "Ch'in and Han Law," in *The Cambridge History of China*, vol. 1, ed. Denis Twitchett and Michael Loewe. Cambridge: Cambridge University Press, 1986, p. 520.

Hume, David. *A Treatise of Human Nature*. Cleveland: Meridian Books, 1962.

Huxley, Julian. *Evolution, The Modern Synthesis*. New York and London: Harper & Brothers, 1943.

Jones, William C. "Studying the Ch'ing Code—The Ta Ch'ing Lü Li," *The American Journal of Comparative Law*, vol. 22 (1974), p. 330.

Kalupahana, David J. *Buddhist Philosophy: An Historical Analysis*. Honolulu: University of Hawaii Press, 1976.

Karlgren, Bernhard. *Philology and Ancient China*. Cambridge, Mass.: Harvard University Press, 1926.

Keightley, David. "The Religious Commitment: Shang Theology and the Genesis of Chinese Political Culture," in *History of Religions*, vol. 17 (February-May 1978).

_____ , ed. *The Origins of Chinese Civilization*. Berkeley: University of California Press, 1983.

Kramers, Robert. "The Development of the Confucian Schools," in *The Cambridge History of China*, vol. 1. Cambridge, Mass.: Cambridge University Press, 1986, p. 747.

Lai, T.C. *To the Yellow Springs*. Hong Kong: Joint Publishing Co. and Kelly & Walsh, 1983.

Latourette, Kenneth Scott. *A History of Modern China*. London: Penguin Books, 1954.

Lee, Orlan. *Legal and Moral Systems in Asian Customary Law: The Legacy of the Buddhist Social Ethic and Buddhist Law*. San Francisco: Chinese Materials Center, 1978.

Legge, James, trans. *The Chinese Classics*, vols. 1–4. Hong Kong: n.p. 1865–1892, 1966 reprint.

_____ . *The I-Ching; The Book of Changes*. New York: Dover Publications, 1963.

_____ . trans. *The Four Books*. New York: Paragon Reprint Corp., 1966.

Lévy-Bruhl, Lucien. *How Natives Think*, trans. Lilian A. Clare. New York: A. Knopf, 1926.

Li, Chi. *The Beginnings of Chinese Civilization*. Seattle: University of Washington Press, 1957.

Li Yu-ning. *The First Emperor of China*. White Plains, N.Y.: International Arts and Sciences Press, 1975.

Li, Xueqin. *Eastern Zhou and Qin Civilization*, trans. K.C. Chang. New Haven, Conn.: Yale University Press, 1985.

Loewe, Michael. *Records of Han Administration*. 2 vols. Cambridge: Cambridge University Press, 1967.

_____ . "The Former Han Dynasty," in *The Cambridge History of China*, vol. 1. Cambridge: Cambridge University Press, 1986, p. 103.

_____ . "*The Religious and Intellectual Background*," in *The Cambridge History of China*, vol. 1. Cambridge: Cambridge University Press, 1986, p. 649.

McEvedy, and R. Jones. "Figure 6.2," in *Atlas of World Population History*. Middlesex, U.K.: Penquin, 1978.

Michael, Franz. *China Through the Ages: History of a Civilization*. Boulder, Colo.: Westview Press, 1986.

Monod, Jacques. *Chance and Necessity*, trans. A. Wainhouse. New York: Alfred A. Knopf, 1971.

Moore, G. E. *Principia Ethica*. Cambridge: Cambridge University Press, 1959.

Muller, Max, ed., *The Sacred Books of the East*, vol. 28, "The *Li Ki*" London: Oxford University Press, 1926.

Munro, Donald J. *The Concept of Man in Early China*. Stanford, Calif: Stanford University Press, 1969.

Needham, Joseph. *Science and Civilisation in China*. 7 vols. Cambridge: The University Press, vol. 1, 1954; vol. 2, 1956; vol. 3, 1959.

_____ . "The Guns of Kaifeng-fu: China's Development of Man's First Chemical Explosive," *Times Literary Supplement*, 11 January 1980, pp. 39–41.

Newton, Sir Isaac. *Newton's Philosophy of Nature*, ed. H.S. Thayer. New York: Hafner Publishing Company, 1953.

Nishijima Sadao. "The Economics and Social History of Former Han," in *The Cambridge History of China, Vol. 1. The Ch'in and Han Empires, 221 B.C.–A.D. 220*. Cambridge: Cambridge University Press, 1986, p. 545.

Northrop, F. S. C. *Science and First Principles*. New York: Macmillan, 1931.

_____ . "The Complementary Emphases of Eastern Intuitive Philosophy and Western Scientific Philosophy," in *Philosophy, East and West*, C.A. Moore, ed. Princeton, N.J.: Princeton University Press, 1946. p. 187.

_____ . *The Meeting of East and West*. New York: Macmillan, 1946.

_____ , ed. *Ideological Diffreences and World Order*. New Haven, Conn.: Yale University Press, 1949.

Ortega y Gasset, José. *Concord and Liberty*, trans. Helene Weyl. New York: W.W. Norton, 1946.

Pan Ku, H.H. Dubs, trans. *History of the Former Han Dynasty*. 3 vols. Baltimore: Waverly Press, 1938.

Radhakrishman, S. *Eastern Religions and Western Thought*. New York: Galaxy Books, Oxford University Press, 1959.

Rand McNally. *The New International Atlas*. Chicago: Rand McNally & Company, 1980.

Schell, Orville. *Discos and Democracy: China in the Throes of Reform*. New York: Pantheon Books, 1988.

Schwartz, Benjamin. *The World of Thought in Ancient China*. Cambridge, Mass.: Harvard University Press, 1985.

Shigeki Kaizuko. *Confucius*, trans. Geoffrey Bownas. London: George Allen & Unwin, 1956.

Steele, John. *The I-Li*. Taipei, Taiwan: Ch'eng-wen Publishing Co., 1966 reprint.

Stephens, Thomas B. *Order and Discipline in China: The Shanghai Mixed Court 1911–27*. Seattle and London: University of Washington Press, 1992.

Sun Yat-sen. *San Min Chu I: The Three Principles of the People*. Taipei, Taiwan: China Cultural Service, 1953.

Temple, Robert. *The Genius of China: 3000 Years of Science, Discovery and Invention*. New York: Simon & Schuster, 1989.

Teng, Sssu-yu, and John K. Fairbank. *China's Response to the West: A Documentary Survey, 1839–1923*. New York: Atheneum, 1970.

Thayer, H. S. *Newton's Philosophy of Nature*. New York: Hafner, 1953.

Twitchett, Denis, and Michael Loewe, eds. *The Cambridge History of China*, vol. I. Cambridge: Cambridge University Press, 1986.

Waldron, Arthur. *The Great Wall of China: From History to Myth*. Cambridge: Cambridge University Press, 1990.

Walker, Richard Lewis. *The Multi-State System of Ancient China*. Hamdem, Conn.: The Shoestring Press, 1953.

Wang Zhongshu. *Han Civilization*, trans. K.C. Chang. New Haven, Conn.: Yale University Press, 1982.

Watson, Burton. *Records of the Grand Historian of China: Translated From the Shih-chi of Ssu-ma Ch'ien, Vol. II, The Age of Emperor Wo, 140 to Circa 100 B.C.* New York: Columbia University Press, 1961.

_____ , trans. *The Tso Chuan*. New York: Columbia University Press, 1989.

Watson, William. *Cultural Frontiers in Ancient East Asia*. Edinburgh, Scotland: Edinburgh University Press, 1971.

Wheatley, Paul. *The Pivot of the Four Quarters: An Inquiry Into the Origins and Character of the Ancient Chinese City*. Chicago: Aldine Publishing Co., 1971.

Whitehead, Alfred North. *Science and the Modern World*. New York: Macmillan, 1925.

Wilhelm, Richard, and Cary F. Baynes, *The I Ching or Book of Changes*, 3rd ed. Princeton, N.J.: Princeton University Press, 1967.

Wright, Arthur, ed. *Studies in Chinese Thought*. Chicago: The University of Chicago Press, 1953.

Wu, K. C. *The Chinese Heritage*. New York: Crown Publishers, 1982.

Wu, Nelson I. *Chinese and Indian Architecture*. New York: George Barziller, 1963.

Yang, C. K. *Religion in Chinese Society*. Berkeley: University of California Press, 1961.

Yang, Lien-sheng. *Studies in Chinese Institutional History*. Cambridge, Mass.: Harvard University Press, 1961.

Yu Ying-shih. "Han Foreign Relations," in *The Cambridge History of China*, vol. 1. Cambridge: Cambridge University Press, 1986, p. 377.

_____ . "'Oh Soul Come Back!' A Study of Changing Conceptions of the Soul and Afterlife in Pre-Buddhist China," *Harvard Jounal of Asiatic Studies* 47:2 (1987), pp. 363–95.

Index

Administration, 131
Agriculture, 5, 30, 48, 80, 127–129, 144
Ai, Duke, 161
Analects (Confucius), 103–104, 156

Bacon, Francis, 27
Bodde, Derk, 130, 140
Book of Changes (*Yi Jing*), 9, 15, 17, 32, 34, 35–36, 55, 58, 78, 88, 110, 128, 145, 155
Book of History, 10, 42, 48, 88, 111, 126, 134
Book of Lord Shang, 116
Book of Mo, 96–98
Book of Music, 88
Book of Poetry, 10, 42, 49, 70, 88, 134
Book of Rites (*Li Ji*), 60–61, 110, 156
Book of Rituals (*Li*), 88
Book of Zhuang, 100
Buddhism, 10

Calendar, 37–42, 133, 145, 167
Cambridge History of China, 130, 140, 155
Change, 11, 14–16, 25
Chan, Wing-tsit, 89
Ch'en Ch'i-yn, 155
Chen She, 138, 139, 144
China: geography and topography, 3–4, 6–7; climate, 5–7, 103–104; natural vegetation, 6; earliest inhabitants, 3. *See also* Chinese civilization
Chinese civilization: common consciousness, 141–142, 144–145, 154, 166; compared with ancient Greek civilization, 3, 10, 18, 32, 45, 75, 77, 79, 83, 84, 89–90, 101, 110, 113, 151; compared with ancient Indian civilization, 3, 10, 18, 26, 32, 45, 150–151; compared with ancient Roman civilization, 39, 45, 133, 151–152, 165. *See also* Administration, Agriculture, Calendar, Change, Commerce, Domesticated animals, Domesticated

plants, Education, Harmony and unity, Laws, Legalism, Magic, Myth, Philosophy, Public Works, Punishment, Rebellions, Religion, Ritual, Science, Technology, Warfare, Weights and measures, Writing
Chou Wen, 40
Climate, 5–7, 103–104
Commerce, 144
Confucianism. *See Ru Jia*
Confucianists. *See Ru Jia*
Confucius, 10, 71, 75, 83, 87–92, 94–96, 103, 114, 116–117, 119, 126, 139, 142, 153, 155, 158, 160–161. *See also Analects*
Cosmologists. *See Yin/Yang Jia*
Creel, Herrlee, 69

Danao, 37
Dao (the way), 11, 13–14, 25, 105–106
Daoism. *See Dao Jia*
Daoists. *See Dao Jia*
Dao De Jing. See Lao Zi
Dao Jia, 10, 103–109, 142, 144–145, 154
Democritus, 76, 113
Di (Lord on High), 10
Dialecticians. *See Ming Jia*
Doctrine of the Mean, 61, 91, 156–161, 164–165
Domesticated animals, 6–7, 30–31, 48
Domesticated plants, 6–7, 11–13, 31, 104
Dong Zhongshu (Tung Chung-shu), 155
Duyvendak, J. J. L., 128

Education, 144
Er Ya, 42
Explanations of the Inventory of Metals and Minerals According to the Numbers Five and Nine, 82
Fa Jia, 115–119, 125, 154
Fairbank, John K., 162, 165
Five Codes, 126, 141–142, 153

Five Emperors, 9, 30, 31, 38, 45, 46. *See also* Yellow Emperor, Zhuan Xu, Ku, Yao, Shun
Fu Su, 136, 137
Fung Yu-lan, 78, 79, 102, 103, 106
Fuxi, 15, 30, 33, 34

Geography. *See* China: geography and topography
Gong-sun Long, 102–103, 105
Grand Norm (*Hong Fan*), 111
Granet, Marcel, 26, 42, 55
Great Learning, 47, 61, 156–161, 164–165
Great Wall, 132, 134, 136, 137, 144
Greek Civilization. *See* Chinese Civilization: compared to ancient Greek civilization
Guan Zhong, 116
Guan Zi, 116

Han dynasty, 9, 149, 155
Han Feizi, 117, 119, 125, 131, 161
Harmony and unity, 11, 18–19, 25, 84, 132, 142, 155
Hegel, G. W. F., 101
Heraclitus, 75
Historical Memoirs, 95, 113, 130. *See also* Sima Qian
Historical Records, 10, 31. *See also* Sima Qian
Hu Hai, 137–138, 140, 146
Hui, King, 114
Hui Shi, 101, 103

Indian Civilization. *See* Chinese Civilization: compared to ancient Indian civilization

Jia Yi, 139–140
Jie, 48
Jones, William C., 167

Kang Shu, 49
Ku, 38

Lao Zi (Lao Tzu), 75, 103, 105, 107–108
Lao Zi (*Dao De Jing*), 103, 105–107
Laws, 127–128, 131–132

Legalism: and state organization, 115–119, 125–146. *See also Fa Jia*
Legalists. *See Fa Jia*
Lévy-Bruhl, Lucien, 78–79
Li. See Book of Rituals
Li Ji. See Book of Rites
Li Si, 117, 119, 131, 134–138, 140, 144
Liu Bang (Gaodi), 138–139, 155
Liu Yi. See Six Classics
Lu Huiqing, 106

Magic, 35–36, 135–136
Marx, Karl, 97
Maspero, 50
Meeting of East and West (Northrop), 78
Mencius, 91–94, 103–104, 113, 156, 159
Miao, 62
Millet, "King", 21
Ming dynasty, 167
Ming Jia, 94, 99–103, 142, 145, 153–154
Ming Tang (House of the Calendar), 47
Ming Tian, 133
Mohism. *See Mo Jia*
Mohists. *See Mo Jia*
Mo Jia, 93, 94–99, 154
Money, 132
Mongols, 68
Monthly Commands, 110
Mo Zi (Mo Tzu), 75, 94–99, 103, 116, 139, 142
Moore, G. E., 164
Myth, 25–27, 29, 30

Needham, Joseph, 14, 15, 26, 35–36, 79, 82, 99, 101, 109, 112
Newton, Isaac, 77, 83, 99
Northrop, F. S. C., 78
Novum Organum (Bacon), 27

Parmenides, 76
La Pensée Chinoise (Granet), 26
Peru, 32
Philosophy, 87–119. *See also Dao Jia*, *Fa Jia*, *Ming Jia*, *Mo Jia*, *Ru Jia*, and *Yin/Yang Jia*
Pingyuan, Prince, 114
Plato, 18, 76–77, 151
Principia Ethica (Moore), 164
Public works, 132–133, 144